Better Homes and Gardens®

HOLIDAY INSPIRATIONS

Better Homes and Gardens® Books
Des Moines, Iowa

Better Homes and Gardens® Books
An imprint of Meredith® Books

Holiday Inspirations

Contributing Editors: Vicki Ingham, Carrie Holcomb Mills, Joyce Trollope
Contributing Art Director: Marisa Dirks
Contributing Designer: Tim Abramowitz
Copy Chief: Terri Fredrickson
Managers, Book Production: Pam Kvitne, Marjorie J. Schenkelberg
Contributing Proofreaders: Gretchen Kauffman, Margaret Smith
Indexer: Martha Fifield
Contributing Photographer: Peter Krumhardt
Contributing Prop Stylist: Jil Severson
Electronic Production Coordinator: Paula Forest
Editorial and Design Assistants: Judy Bailey, Kaye Chabot, Mary Lee Gavin, Karen Schirm
Test Kitchen Director: Lynn Blanchard

Meredith® Books
Editor in Chief: James D. Blume
Design Director: Matt Strelecki
Managing Editor: Gregory H. Kayko
Executive Food Editor: Jennifer Dorland Darling
Executive Shelter Editor: Denise L. Caringer

Director, Retail Sales and Marketing: Terry Unsworth
Director, Sales, Special Markets: Rita McMullen
Director, Sales, Premiums: Michael A. Peterson
Director, Sales, Retail: Tom Wierzbicki
Director, Book Marketing: Brad Elmitt
Director, Operations: George A. Susral
Director, Production: Douglas M. Johnston

Vice President, General Manager: Jamie L. Martin

Better Homes and Gardens® Magazine
Editor in Chief: Jean LemMon
Executive Food Editor: Nancy Byal
Executive Interior Design Editor: Sandra S. Soria

Meredith Publishing Group
President, Publishing Group: Stephen M. Lacy
Vice President, Finance and Administration: Max Runciman

Meredith Corporation
Chairman and Chief Executive Officer: William T. Kerr

Chairman of the Executive Committee: E. T. Meredith III

All of us at Better Homes and Gardens® Books are dedicated to providing you with the information and ideas you need to enhance your home. We welcome your comments and suggestions. Write to us at: Better Homes and Gardens® Books, Shelter Editorial Department, 1716 Locust St., Des Moines, IA 50309-3023. Visit us online at bhg.com.

Front cover: Festive Package Trims, page 286-287; Rickrack Boxes, page 291;
Quick-and-Easy Swag, page 42; Gilded Ornaments, page 101
Back cover: Teacup Candles, page 55; Snowflake Lantern, page 37
Inside front cover: Candy Cane Vase, page 6; Garden Wreath, page 121; Minestrone, page 209
Inside back cover: Cookie House Front, page 161; Aromatic Bath Oils, page 241; Cards for Kids, page 309

 Our seal assures you that every recipe in *Holiday Inspirations* has been tested in the Better Homes and Gardens® Test Kitchen. This means that each recipe is practical and reliable and meets our high standards of taste appeal. We guarantee your satisfaction with this book for as long as you own it.

table *of* contents

welcome home

page 4 For many of us, the holiday season means coming home and gathering together with those we love. What better way to welcome family and friends than with beautiful and creative decorations. Festive touches such as glowing candles, romantic ribbons, or fragrant flowers can transform all the rooms of your home.

trees and wreaths

page 80 Trees and wreaths are the cornerstone of many holiday settings, so decorate yours to reflect your own personal style. Whether you like sleek and elegant or fresh and from nature, this chapter will give you ideas that please.

gathering together

page 128 Perhaps more than anything else, food plays a central role in many holiday gatherings. Whatever your favorite, a golden-hued turkey or fragrant cup of hot spiced cider, you're sure to find some taste-tempting recipes in this chapter. We also give you ideas, from simple to grand, for decorating your holiday table.

giving from the heart

page 238 A gift from the heart, made with your own hands, can be one of the most cherished. Many of this chapter's ideas use ready-made items—all you have to do is add your own embellishments for a gift your loved one will treasure forever.

kids' stuff

page 296 Kids' energy just seems to skyrocket as the holidays approach. Encourage them to tackle some of this chapter's fun-filled projects—even some they can do with just a little supervision from you.

3

In a Twinkling
Easy-to-use ideas for the holidays

WELCOME

What's your holiday decorating personality?

Are you cozily traditional, happily putting up the same decorations in the same place every year? Or are you experimental, always trying out a new look? Do you like subtle decorations that don't clutter a room? Or do you feel cheated if every room doesn't wear at least a few pieces of holiday finery? Whether you're of the "less is more" school of thought, or the "more is always better" group, you'll find ideas and decorations to inspire you on the following pages. And don't forget to dress up the outside of your house too. Your home is the scene for celebration—let it reflect your personal style.

4

home

5

With just a few ordinary elements, you can create an elegant and welcoming display in the foyer.

dramatic

entrance

In the spirit of "use what you have" decorating, put silver coffee urns, teapots, and sugar bowls to work as vases for flowers and candy canes; fill a silver bowl with red pears for more color. Lay an artificial wreath on the table and nestle a couple of small potted azaleas in the center. Then rest yellow apples around the wreath and add yellow-green bows for a bright accent. To dress up the mirror, buy several yards of red fabric and drape it over the top. For the candy cane crest, bundle canes together with florist's tape. Tie a bow over the tape to hide it, then wire the bundle to the mirror.

Give paperwhite narcissus a ground cover of red cranberries for a merry accent in a foyer, kitchen, or living room. Four to six weeks before you want blooms, plant bulbs on gravel in a shallow bowl. Water as needed, keeping the water level just below the bottom of the bulbs. Cover the gravel with cranberries when you're ready to display the flowers.

In a Twinkling:
Festive Touches

▲ Accent your favorite print with a big bow stitched from fabric. Make the bow from a 37×17-inch strip folded in half lengthwise and stitched into a tube. Turn the tube right side out and stitch the short ends together, then wrap a 4×8-inch strip around the center of the loop for a knot. Make the tails from 17×41-inch strips folded in half lengthwise and stitched. Turn right side out and pin them to the back of the knot.

◀ String large wooden beads, pecans or walnuts, and dried pomegranates on dental floss to make garlands for hanging from bedposts. Use an electric drill with a 1/16-inch bit to pierce the pomegranates and nuts from side to side. With a large tapestry needle, thread them on the dental floss.

◄ Supplement decorations with red and white accessories. Emphasize the Christmas colors in stockings, package wraps, and tree ornaments with simple touches, such as red flowers in white vases, red apples on a white dish, red and white accent pillows, and simple white valances trimmed with red rickrack or ribbon.

▶ Guarantee your guests sweet holiday dreams with a simple swag of fresh cedar tied across the headboard. Their very own Christmas tree also adds festive fragrance. The tree need not be elaborate: Plant a small tree in wet sand in a galvanized metal bucket, then hang miniature ornaments from the branches.

◄ Fluff up a room with homespun holiday pillows. Stitch squares of white or green felt, wool, or cotton; use crewel yarn and a running stitch to make crisscross, snowflake, and 'Noel' designs. Make the dots on the Noel pillow with satin stitches.

Dress your home in new clothes for the season with slipcovers, pillows, a hearth rug, and window scarves.

happy holiday *makeover*

The wardrobe shown here is easy to make from painters' canvas drop cloths, using fabric inks and rubber stamps to supply the holiday motifs.

Dress up your everyday pillows with a button-on overlay or a grommeted tie-on slipcover. Then decorate the mantel, and you're set.

before

after

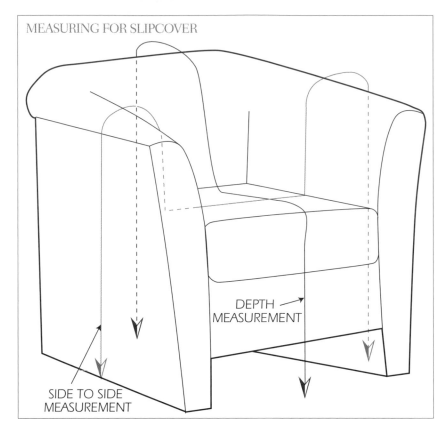

MEASURING FOR SLIPCOVER

DEPTH
MEASUREMENT

SIDE TO SIDE
MEASUREMENT

12

chair slipcover

here's how...

1 To determine the size for the drop cloth, measure the chair as shown in the diagram. Add 24 inches to the side-to-side width measurement. Add 12 inches to the depth measurement. Cut the canvas to these measurements, piecing it if needed. Hem any raw edges.

2 Using a single large stamp, randomly print the same design in different colors to create an overall pattern. (For the slipcover in the photo, the designer used a 2½×5-inch Noel stamp and six colors of fabric ink and printed about 45 images per 3×5-foot section of cloth.)

3 Let the ink dry, then heat-set by pressing for 30 seconds on the right side, using a pressing cloth between the iron and the fabric. Use a dry iron at the cotton setting. Center the drop cloth over the chair. Position the side, front, and back

hems even with the floor. Tuck the excess fabric into the crevice between the seat cushion and the body of the chair, pushing it down as far as possible. The front corners will drape longer, and the back should hang freely.

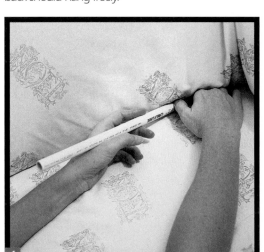
4

Cut two pieces of plastic pipe 4 inches shorter than the side measurements of the seat and one piece 4 inches shorter than the back measurement of the seat. Slide the plastic pipe down into the crevice between the cushion and body of

the chair, pushing it down as far as you can to help hold the slipcover in place.

5 Thread the needle with 1 yard of ribbon. At seat height of one front corner, gather the excess fabric in your hand. Just behind the gathers, push the needle through the fabric from one side to the other. Tie the ribbon over the gathers to hold the billowed fabric in place. Repeat for the other side.

drop cloth tips

Before starting any of these projects, read these general tips.

■ To remove sizing and soften the fabric, wash and dry the drop cloths before cutting them.

■ The fabric may shrink considerably, so buy a drop cloth larger than you need for each project.

■ Cut the drop cloths to the sizes you'll need for each project and iron the fabric before stamping.

■ Let the ink dry completely, then heat-set the designs by pressing with a dry iron. If you're working with large pieces such as a sofa slipcover, it may be easier to have a dry cleaner press the fabric for you.

■ Always wash and dry the stamp before switching from one ink color to another; otherwise, the ink colors will be muddy, and the stamp will become blurry. Use an old toothbrush and warm tap water to clean the stamps.

■ Use fabric markers to touch up any areas that did not stamp well or to fill in gaps in the borders of the swag and floorcloth.

■ Hem cut edges by machine or turn them under and fuse them in place with fusible hemming tape.

■ Use the drop cloth's hemmed edges as the slipcover's hem whenever possible so you'll have fewer edges to stitch.

■ If you accidentally get fabric ink on carpeting or fabric, blot the area with dishwashing liquid and water, using a clean cloth.

■ If you wiggle the stamp or press too hard and leave inked margins around the image, remove the unwanted ink by carefully dabbing the area with dishwashing liquid and water, using a cotton swab.

ottoman slipcover

here's how...

1 Measure the ottoman as shown in the diagram. Add hem allowances and cut the canvas to these measurements. Hem all raw edges.

2 Using a large stamp, print a single row of one design around the hemline. Alternate colors randomly. Let the ink dry, then heat-set as directed in step 3 of the chair slipcover.

3 Center the canvas over the ottoman. Tie the ribbon around the upper portion of the ottoman. If you like, make the bow fluffier by slipping in snippets of coordinating ribbon.

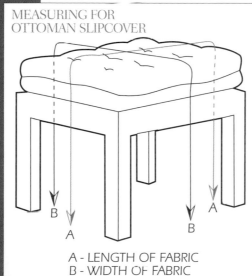

MEASURING FOR OTTOMAN SLIPCOVER

A - LENGTH OF FABRIC
B - WIDTH OF FABRIC

lampshade slipcover

here's how...

1 Measure around the widest part of the shade (usually the bottom). Multiply this measurement by 1½ for the slipcover width. For the depth, measure the lampshade from top to bottom and add 3 inches for the casing, ease, and hem (if needed). Cut out the canvas.

2 Randomly stamp the cloth, alternating colors and designs if you use more than one stamp. Let the ink dry.

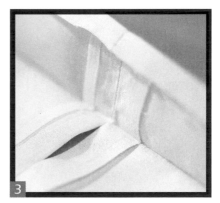

Pin the short ends together, right sides facing. Starting at the top, sew down 1½ inches. Leave a 1-inch opening, then sew the remainder of the seam. At the top, press under ¼ inch, then 1¼ inches to form a casing. Topstitch ¼ inch from top folded edge. Sew around the slipcover 1¼ inches from the top folded edge, catching the lower pressed edge and forming the bottom of the casing. Hem the bottom edge of the slipcover if necessary.

4 Thread ribbon through the casing. Slide the slipcover over the lampshade. Adjust the ribbon to fit the top of the shade and tie the ends in a bow.

13

14

window scarf

here's how...

1 Protect your work surface with kraft paper that extends several inches beyond the long edge of the canvas.

2 To make the bottom stripe, press the stamp pad against the fabric, making a solid rectangle. Repeat, overlapping the rectangles, until the entire hemline is stamped with a solid stripe. Note: Stripes will be uneven and look hand-done. For a more even stripe, see the directions for the floor cloth.

3 Randomly stamp the designs all over the runner, using at least two stamps and all the colors. The front part of the swag (near the hem stripe) should be more heavily stamped; the back part can be more lightly stamped. Let the ink dry; this may take overnight for the stripe. Heat-set the designs.

4 To hang the swag, loosely loop it over the curtain rod several times. Adjust the fabric so it hangs nicely.

mantel cloth

here's how...

1 Stamp two rows of designs along one long hemmed edge, alternating the colors and designs and placing them in a checkerboard fashion.

2 Drape the cloth across the mantel. Pull it up into swags in several spots, using heavy objects on the mantel to hold the cloth in place.

pillows

here's how...

1 For the Button-On Overlay Pillow, pin the two large napkins together, wrong sides facing, and stitch along the hemline, leaving an opening for inserting the pillow form. Slip the pillow inside and stitch the opening closed.

2 For the topper, make a buttonhole in each corner of the cocktail napkin.

3 Center the topper over the pillow and mark the positions for the buttons, then sew one button to each spot.

SHOPPING LIST

2 large napkins
thread to match
pillow or pillow form
For Button-on
  Overlay Pillow:
  coordinating cocktail
  napkin
4 matching buttons
For Grommeted Pillow
  Cover:
  grommet tool and
    16 ½-inch grommets
  ribbon

hearth rug

here's how...

1 If necessary, cut the floor cloth to the desired size. Place kraft paper over your work surface for protection.

2 Run a strip of artist's tape 1 inch from both long edges of the floor cloth. Run a small piece of rigid plastic (such as a credit card) along the tape to seal the edges to the canvas.

SHOPPING LIST

kraft paper (to protect your
  work surface)
pre-primed floor cloth (from
  an art supply store)
ruler
1-inch-wide artist's or
  painter's tape
small piece of rigid plastic,
  such as a credit card

needed. After the ink dries, remove the tape and stamp the short ends in the same manner.

4 After all the borders are dry, create the design stripes in the same way. Measure in 6 inches from the inside edge of the border at each short end. Run a line of tape parallel to the short end. Leave a 1-inch space, then run another line of tape. Repeat to make spaces for six stripes at each end. Stamp the stripes as you did the border stripes.

5 Fill in the center of the floor cloth, if you wish, with stripes or stamped designs; or leave the center blank as shown in the photo on page 11.

Press a stamp pad along the exposed edge, creating a stripe. To make the stripe more even, after it is stamped but while the ink is still wet, drag the stamp pad over the damp ink to eliminate overlap marks or uneven spots. Reink the pad as

For the Grommeted Pillow Cover, use the grommet tool to attach grommets in each corner and along the edges of the napkins, spacing them evenly.

5 Place the napkins with wrong sides facing and holes aligned; lace ribbon through the holes. Insert the pillow and continue lacing; tie the ribbon ends in a bow or knot.

15

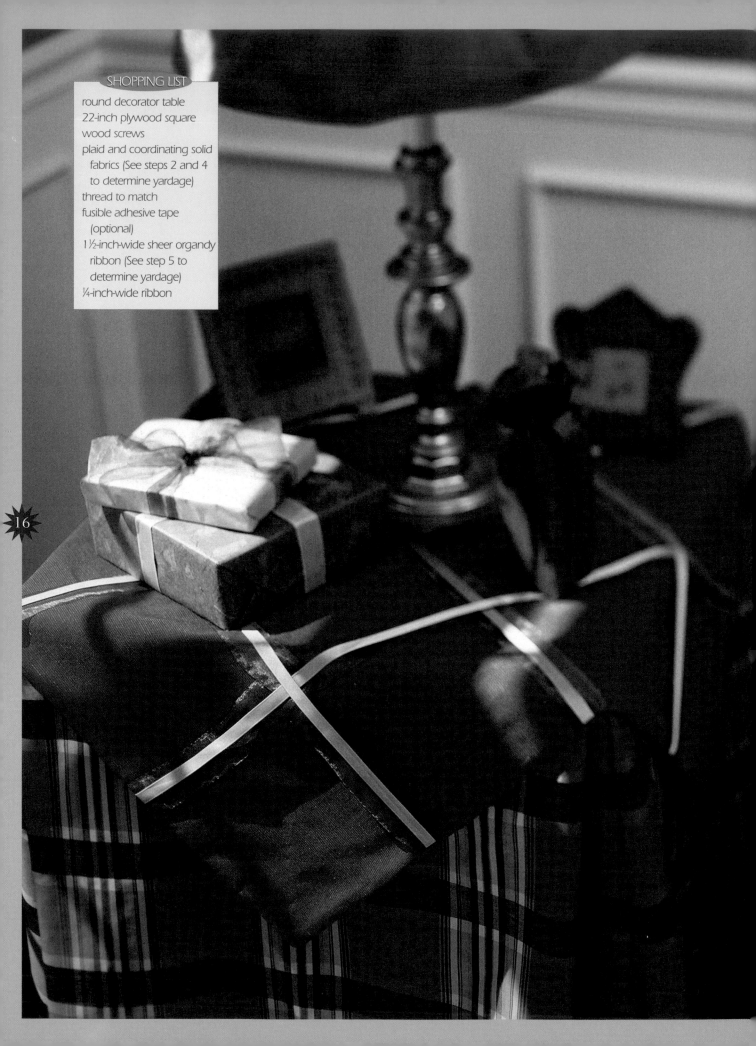

16

I f you have a formal decorating style, choose crisp taffeta and damask for fabric makeovers. Attach a square top to a round decorator table to give yourself more display space.

skirted table

here's how...

Working from the underside of the tabletop, attach the 22-inch plywood square to the top of the round decorator table with wood screws.

2 For the skirt top, cut a 23-inch square of plaid fabric. For the sides, cut four 34-inch-wide panels that are long enough to reach the floor, plus 1 inch for seam allowance and hem. Stitch the panels together and make a 2¾-inch-deep pleat at each corner (see the diagram below right).

3 Stitch the top to the sides, using a ½-inch seam. Stitch or fuse the hem.

4 For the topper, cut two 23-inch squares of solid fabric and stitch them together, right sides facing, leaving an opening for turning. Turn, press, and blindstitch the opening closed.

5 Pin 1½-inch-wide sheer organdy ribbon in a crisscross pattern to the topper, then pin narrow satin ribbon over the sheer ribbon. Fold the ribbon ends to the underside of the topper. Glue the ribbons with fabric glue.

17

Diagram labels: 5 ½ "   2 ¾ "   2 ¾ "

lampshade slipcover

here's how...

Follow the instructions for the stamped lampshade slipcover on page 13. Hem the bottom edge with fusible adhesive tape. Place the slipcover over the lampshade and tie ribbon over the casing.

For an overstuffed look, make the pillow cover one size smaller than the pillow form; for example, for a 12-inch sofa pillow, use a 14-inch pillow form.

18

flanged pillows
here's how...

1 To make the gold herringbone pillow, cut two squares of fabric the size of the pillow form plus 1 inch all around. Place the squares right sides facing and stitch ½ inch from the raw edges, leaving an opening for turning. Make sure the opening is large enough for you to insert the pillow form.

2 Turn the pillowcase right side out and press the edges. Insert the pillow form and blindstitch the opening closed. To make the flange, hand-sew a running stitch ½ inch from the edges, using rust-colored embroidery floss and an embroidery needle.

3 For the floral pillow, cut two squares of fabric the size of the pillow form plus 2 inches all around. With right sides facing, stitch the squares together, using a ½-inch seam allowance and leaving an opening for turning and stuffing.

4 Turn and press; stitch 1½ inches from the edges to create the flange, leaving an opening for stuffing. Fill the pillowcase with polyester fiberfill, then

finish stitching the flange. Turn under the raw edges on the pillow edging and blindstitch the opening closed.

For the plaid pillow, cut two squares of fabric the size of the pillow form plus 3¾ inches all around. Fold under 1⅛ inches on each side and press. Place the two squares with wrong sides facing and mark the stitching line 1¾ inches from the edges. Stitch, leaving an opening for inserting the pillow form. Press to give the flanges a crisp edge. Insert the pillow form or stuff the pillow with polyester fiberfill. Machine-stitch the opening closed.

slipcovered ottoman
here's how...

1 To determine how much fabric you'll need, measure your ottoman as shown in the diagram on page 13. Allow enough additional fabric to cut an 8-inch band for the hem.

2 Cut the fabric to the required size and lay it over the ottoman with the fabric's right side facing you. Use dressmaker's pins to make a pleat at each corner so the slipcover fits the ottoman snugly. Trim the fabric to about 3 inches above the floor.

3 Cut and piece fabric as necessary to make a strip 8 inches wide and long enough to fit all the way around the slipcover's bottom edge. Press the fabric in half lengthwise. Carefully remove the slipcover from the ottoman and pin the hem band to the slipcover, right sides facing and raw edges aligned. Stitch, using a ½-inch seam allowance. Replace the pins holding the pleats with buttons.

NO-SEW OPTION: Instead of hemming the slipcover with a separate band, add 1 inch to the ottoman measurements for a hem. Secure the hem with fusible adhesive tape, following the manufacturer's instructions.

19

A display on a buffet or mantel helps set a holiday mood. It also suggests a feeling of formality or informality, depending on the way you arrange the elements. Symmetrical arrangements create a formal look because they convey stability, order, and classical harmony. To achieve symmetry, draw an imaginary line down the center of your display space and then arrange objects in a mirror-image fashion on each side of the line.

Asymmetry is trickier because things don't match on either side of the center dividing line, but the grouping still should be balanced visually. Asymmetrical groupings feel more dynamic, active, and exciting, but even though they're not as formal as symmetrical arrangements, they can be quite elegant nevertheless.

design *lesson*

symmetry

To produce a symmetrical arrangement like the one on page 20, think in pairs: two tall silver vases, two silver goblets, two crystal candleholders. Arrange flowers and greenery in the vases in a fanlike spray; this is a classic shape that works well with tall, trumpet-shape containers. Insert short pieces of fir in the goblets to make a collar of greenery, and rest a tall sugar pinecone on each. The pinecone supplies a vertical element shorter than the arrangements but taller than the candles.

Place the arrangements on each side of the imaginary center line. To keep the display from being static and boring, give it depth by standing the goblets in front of the arrangements and the candles toward the back. Also overlap elements slightly to lead the eye across the design from the lowest point to the highest and back down again in a fan-shape arc. To tie the vases together visually, rest a low bowl of pears between them and trail sheer ribbon along the buffet.

asymmetry

You can use the same pairs of objects to create an asymmetrical display, too; just add books or boxes to provide different levels, and avoid setting up mirror images. Instead of a fan-shape arc, think of a triangle with sides of unequal length. Raise one flower arrangement on a stack of books to mark the highest point. Place the second arrangement on the sideboard, at the imaginary center line or just to the other side of it.

To anchor the lowest point of the grouping, rest a candlestick on books

21

and couple it with one of the silver goblets. Raising the candlestick gives it greater visual weight, and pairing two smaller objects balances the apparent visual weight of the taller flower arrangement. To supply variety, replace the goblet's sugar pinecone with a pear and place the pinecone in the low bowl with greenery. The bowl, resting at the imaginary center line at the front of the display, helps balance the taller side.

To anchor the display on the right, place the second goblet and the remaining candlestick on that side, toward the back. Your eye should step up from the candle to the cone to the arrangement, then follow the line down to the lowest point and around to the front. Sheer ribbon curling in and out around the base of the arrangement also will help lead the eye in and out across the display.

Here's how to create formal and informal displays for a sideboard or mantel and how to tweak them for seasonal change.

Designed for Change

❧Whether you prefer symmetrical or asymmetrical design, you can build in options for change by starting with a few basic elements and adding seasonal accents.

autumn

Start with a large serving tray and a cachepot or vase filled with florist's foam as the foundation for all three centerpieces. (Look for florist's foam at crafts stores and florist's supply shops. You'll need to replace the foam for each arrangement.) For autumn, spread a tablecloth or runner in neutral or fall colors along the sideboard, then rest the tray on top of it. Fill the cachepot with fresh chrysanthemums, birch twigs, cattails, dried hydrangeas, and fall leaves in a simple, fan-shape arrangement. Mound gourds, winter squash, and miniature pumpkins on the tray, allowing them to spill over onto the sideboard.

For a softer look, tuck pads of reindeer moss around the cachepot and among the gourds at the edge of the tray. Insert stems of flowers into florist's water vials (from a florist's supply shop or crafts store). Slip the vials among the gourds to add some horizontal lines at the base of the display. Bringing the flowers down among the gourds also helps tie the flower arrangement to the base visually.

Stand pillar candles and candlesticks on each side of the display. Use large, sturdy dried leaves as wax catchers for the pillars.

23

christmas

To shift the design toward an elegant holiday look, replace the autumn table runner with one in rich reds and golds. Remove the winter squash and miniature pumpkins, and spray-paint the gourds with a mixture of copper and silver. (For a richer color effect, apply the second color while the first is still wet.)

Save the dried hydrangeas for a winter arrangement, and spray-paint the birch twigs white. Using the painted birch twigs as a starting point, create a new arrangement with fresh caspia, apricot-color roses (to pick up the copper color), and fresh evergreens. Arrange branches of evergreens along the runner as well as on the tray, and rest the painted gourds and pinecones on the greenery. Tuck in the moss as for the autumn design, and thread a garland of small ornaments through the flower arrangement. Keep the pillar candles in place, and add one candlestick on each side for a more formal look.

25

winter

After Christmas, change the arrangement for a more wintry look for New Year's and the weeks following by shifting the color scheme to cool green and snowy white. Replace the Christmas runner with a crisp white crocheted one, and remove the evergreens and spray-painted gourds. Keep the pinecones, moss, caspia, and birch twigs and bring back the dried hydrangeas saved from the autumn arrangement.

Make a new arrangement of caspia, birch twigs, and hydrangeas, adding white carnations to emphasize the winter theme. Mound moss and pinecones on the tray around the cachepot, and add carnations and lengths of ivy, inserting the stem ends in florist's vials to keep the ivy and flowers fresh. Replace the pillar candles with crystal votive candleholders and white tea lights. Leave the candlesticks on each side of the display to maintain the formal look.

No room for lavish decorations?
Choose a focal point and concentrate your efforts there.

Whether you live in an efficiency apartment or a quaint but crowded bungalow, you may find yourself space-challenged for the holidays. That doesn't need to prevent you from creating a festive atmosphere in your already cozy home. The secret is to choose one area, preferably a highly visible one, and focus your decorations in that spot.

bring the holidays in focus

■ If you don't have a fireplace, give your living area a focal point by turning the coffee table or an old trunk into a surface for decorating. A tiny tree, either live or artificial, can provide the center of interest; arrange wrapped packages, votive candles, and a few old toys around it to set a holiday mood.

■ Other surfaces that can be a stage for festive displays include the dining or breakfast table, the top of a tall chest of drawers, or an armoire, sideboard, or sofa table.

■ If the best thing about your apartment is the view, decorate your windows with swags of greenery and lights, hang pretty ornaments from tension rods inserted in the window frames, or arrange candles and greenery on the window sills.

The Mantel

If you have a fireplace, the mantel is a natural place for the eye to rest. Here a wreath hangs in the center of a year-round display of transferware. If you have a painting over the mantel, tuck evergreen branches behind the painting and let their weight hold them in place along the top of the frame.

To soften the mantel, layer it with fabric. A crisp white dresser scarf brings a clean, fresh look to a crowded room. (If you like a weightier look, use a velvet or damask table runner or several yards of fabric draped along the shelf.) For a family Christmas theme, assemble framed photos along the mantel; use a variety of frame sizes and alternate horizontal and vertical formats to keep the eye moving along the mantel. Overlap some of the frames and rest ornaments and evergreens among the photos to create depth. Add a pair of candlesticks for height, and dress them up with bows and greenery.

quick ideas for

small spaces

29

A Side Table

❧ You don't have to host a sit-down dinner to enjoy the company of friends during the holidays. Invite them over for coffee and dessert, and let the food and accoutrements set a festive mood with color: red and white candy, napkins, and cups play on the red-and-white theme of the coffeepot and candles here.

Arrange the items as you would accessories, paying attention to varying heights and shapes, so your presentation is pleasing to look at as well as practical for serving. A pie server is a good way to add height; this one is filled with apples and hydrangeas to continue the red and white theme. (Look for pie servers in the kitchen department of home furnishings stores and in home decorating catalogs.)

The Chandelier

❧ If there's not a free surface to be found, look up for a decorating spot. Chandeliers offer sparkling opportunities for creating a festive mood in the room. Wire sprigs of fresh greenery to the arms of the fixture and tie bows under each light. Hang crystal and teardrop ornaments from the arms, suspending them at different levels to help lead your eye upward to the chandelier.

Lighting options abound. Now you can make as much of a personal statement with lights as you do with ornaments.

lighting up the night

Indoors

 Clear or multicolored, miniature or standard—those used to be about your only choices for holiday lights. Bubble lights were the most adventuresome option you could readily find, and even those eventually fell out of favor. But manufacturers have seen the light. Choose from a variety of bulb covers and color palettes—or mix and match to brighten Christmas trees, mantels, and stairways, or to illuminate the outside of your house.

Bulb Covers—Ornament-style bulb covers snap over miniature bulbs, clipping to tree branches for stability. Scatter a few around the tree for eye-catching results.

A strand or two of snowballs or icicles add an "ahhhh" factor to mantels or stairways. These lights are often oversized, making them overwhelming on a tree, so use them judiciously.

Colors—Which white would you like: clear, frosted, or pearlized? Each gives a different glow. You'll find these whites alone on strands or mixed in with other colors.

If you prefer color, use full strands of a single jewel-toned hue for dramatic effect. Cool teal blues or warm golden yellows are just two of many new colors available. Or choose a multicolor strand. The standard four-color spectrum has a cozily old-fashioned look, or you can opt for more contemporary, vibrant colors that follow a theme—blue, teal, and green, for example. You'll also find strands with a frosty white or clear bulb in the color sequence to accent the colored bulbs.

▲ String a strand of snowball lights around a door, along a mantel, or down a banister for a glittering display reminiscent of a winter's day. Remember, a little goes a long way with big bulbs like this. On a tree, use just a couple of strands in a sweeping overlay—like a scant garland—to supplement your standard lights.

◄ Red, clear, and white lights create a candy-cane look that's charming wherever they're used. Simple combinations of miniature bulbs like this create a sweet scene that blends neatly into the decoration of any tree.

30

lighting standards

■ More color and style options aren't the only improvements in lighting; new strands are designed to be safer, too. In order to receive the Underwriters Laboratories' (UL) seal of approval, all lights produced after January 1, 1997, have to meet these new standards.

■ The insulation around the wires is thicker to reduce the risk of exposing live wires.

■ Wires are tested to ensure they have adequate flex so they'll hold up for installation and storage.

■ Bulbs are now cooler, so less likely to cause burns.

■ Every strand comes with two replacement bulbs.

■ Tips for use, care, inspection, and storage also are included with every strand of lights.

To make sure the bulbs you buy meet the new standards, look for a mark noting UL588-17th edition on the box or on a tag attached to the strand. The new standard applies to lights rated for indoor or outdoor use.

▶

Elegant jewel tones in this renaissance-theme light strand create a deep, rich look. Choose a color scheme that sets the mood you're after, especially for a theme tree.

Outdoors

 Whatever style of outdoor lighting you choose, installing it can be a snap with the new styles of clips and stakes.

Getting a strand of outdoor lights evenly spaced and facing the same direction used to be quite an accomplishment. As much as outdoor lights are a beauty to behold, they can be a beast to install—twisting this way, not turning that way—and you're trying to tame this unwieldy tangle while standing on a ladder on a chilly December day.

A little Yankee ingenuity has come to the rescue. New styles of clips that attach to the gutter or roof shingles make it easier to space bulbs evenly along the roofline and allow you to easily direct the lights (see *page 33*).

Made of a sturdy plastic, the clips snap together and into place with ease. And the clips come in styles suited for standard or miniature lights.

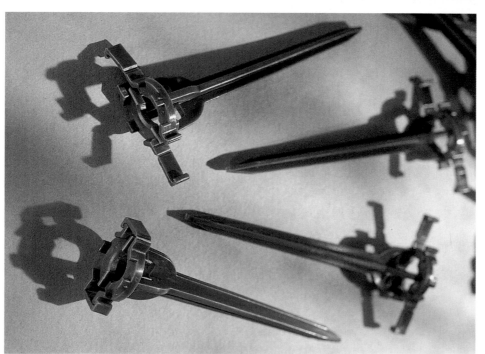

◀ Light the path to your door with a strand of standard or mini lights and these light stakes. Simply push the stakes into the ground, slip in the lights, and close the plastic hinges around both sides of the cord to hold the lights in place. Swish some snow or moss between the lights to cover the exposed cord. (Tip: If the ground is frozen, use an old screwdriver and hammer to create a starter hole.)

before you start

■ Do the math. Measure the distance to cover, and figure out how many lights and clips are needed. Chances are the length of the strands won't match the total length required and you'll need to do some adjusting. For a brighter display, place clips closer together, or run two alternating strands.

■ Test your lights. Plug in each strand ahead of time to be sure each bulb lights up and that the sockets and cords are solid. Replace strands with brittle cords or cracked or loose sockets.

■ Check the connections between strands to be sure they are compatible and the extension cord easily reaches the plug. Check the manufacturer's recommendations for the maximum number of strands to connect to each other. You may need to use a second extension cord.

■ Measure carefully. If you're using special spacing between lights, cut a piece of cardboard or a strip of wood to the exact length. Use it to measure the space between clips.

◀ As icicle lights travel along the outlines of your house, they may need to attach to both gutters and shingles. These universal clips attach firmly to either surface, making installation a breeze.

33

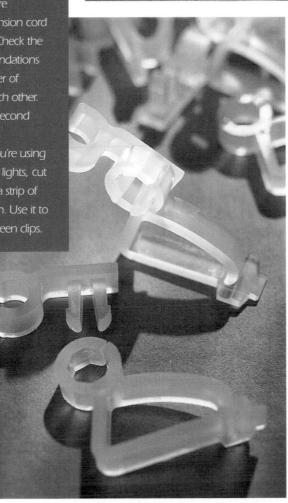

▲ Sometimes simplest is best. For straightforward, straight-line house lighting situations, a good gutter clip may be all that is needed. Choose one like this that fastens firmly to the gutter and snugly secures the cord. Made of thick but flexible plastic, clips like these are designed to withstand years of cold weather and sunlight without becoming brittle.

▲ These two-piece clips firmly attach miniature lights to roof shingles. The adjustable base holder allows you to direct the lights to the angle that best illuminates your house.

Most of your neighbors see only the outside of your house—so what better way to spread your holiday spirit than with outdoor decorations? Let these ideas inspire you.

decorating the
great outdoors

Lights, luminarias, and nearly lifesize wooden cutouts (such as reindeer and angels) are popular, but don't limit yourself to these. Outdoor decorations give you a chance to express your personality. Bears on a porch swing or geese dressed for a party will make passersby smile; vine balls and fresh evergreens blend elegantly into the landscape for a more subtle look.

winter gazing ball

Put your empty birdbath to work for the holidays. Rest a fresh wreath on the rim of the bowl, and place a vine ball in the center. To add some sparkle, thread a strand of battery-operated tiny white lights into the ball through one of the openings. Use green floral wire to attach the light cord to the vines around the ball; otherwise all the lights will fall to the bottom.

welcoming committee

If your porch is protected from the weather, create a holiday vignette with stuffed bears, colorful blankets, skis, sleds, and greenery.

Vine-Ball Accents

❧ Swag a balcony or deck railing with purchased evergreen garland, and accent each swag with a trio of vine balls. Look for the balls in holiday catalogs and garden shops. Use sturdy crafts wire to attach two vine balls to the deck railing, then wire the third ball to the first two.

Snowflake Lantern

SHOPPING LIST:
tissue paper or
    tracing paper
adhesive tape
lantern with glass
    panels
Delta CeramDecor
    paint: silver
paintbrush

❧ Light the way to your front door with a snowflake-painted lantern. Available from chain home furnishings stores, the lantern holds a pillar candle—you add the snowflakes with paint. Stand the lantern in the center of a fresh wreath on a table on your patio or deck, or let it hang from a lantern hook. (The heat from the candle will make the top of the lantern very hot, so use caution when opening the door.)

1 Draw a stick-figure snowflake onto a scrap of tissue paper or tracing paper.

2 Refer to the photograph for placement and tape the snowflake pattern to the inside of the glass.

3 Paint the snowflake on the outside of the glass with silver paint. Reposition the snowflake pattern, and paint a complete or partial snowflake. Continue painting snowflakes on the glass panels until the composition is completed. Allow the paint to dry.

37

Garden Geese

❧ Those rusted-metal geese that adorn your garden year-round are ready to party for the holidays. Perk them up with appropriate party clothes—a child's red-plaid necktie, a Santa cap intended for a teddy bear, a little girl's holiday hair bow, and strands of sparkly plastic Mardi Gras beads dress this foursome.

Give your home a holiday face with outdoor decorations. Whether you opt for a simple wreath on the door or aspire to vignettes that rival Disney's, your decorations extend a merry welcome to passersby and spread a feeling of festivity throughout your neighborhood.

holiday
welcome

In addition to—or instead of—wreaths for the door, consider arrangements of evergreen boughs, berried branches, and pinecones for window boxes and planters. To make the ones shown here, start with plastic hanging baskets and fill them with plastic foam. For a horizontal window, like the one on *page 40,* make the arrangements alike; when you place the pots in the window box, they will blend to make a single long display. For a tall, double-hung window place a few long branches asymmetrically as shown. This provides a more vertical emphasis.

From a garden center:
   four 8-inch-diameter
      plastic hanging baskets
   gravel or rocks
From a crafts store:
   2-inch-thick sheet of
      plastic foam
   hot-glue gun and glue
      sticks
   #19 floral wire
   6-inch-long floral picks
From your yard or a
   florist:
   birch or other long,
      slender twigs
   assorted evergreens, such
      as berried juniper,
      princess pine or
      white pine, noble
      fir, and oregonia or
      boxwood
   rose hips and winterberry
      (or other red-fruited
      branches)

40

here's how...

Place gravel in the bottom of each pot for weight. Cut two pieces of plastic foam to fit each pot, trimming the top piece to fit the rim exactly. Secure the two pieces together with floral picks, then glue the plastic foam into the pot so the top of the foam is even with the rim.

Insert the birch twigs in the back of each pot for height. Next, place the tallest branches of evergreens in front of the twigs. Insert additional evergreens at the sides and front, staggering their heights so they are progressively shorter as you work toward the front of the pot.

3 Insert the winterberry branches and rose hips evenly through each arrangement for bright-red accents, positioning the branches so they repeat the lines of the evergreens.

Attach pinecones to lengths of #19 floral wire and use the wire ends as picks to secure the pinecones to the plastic foam base. After you place the pots in the window box, add greenery at each end so the branches seem to over-flow the window box.

41

here's how...

To make the planter display, follow the same procedure as for the window box arrangements, but position the birch twigs in the center of the pot rather than at the back. This keeps the design from looking flat. Place the tallest evergreens around the birch twigs and work toward the edges of the planter with progressively shorter branches. Fill in the middle of the design with greenery and add the berried branches and pinecones last.

◀ Dress up family photos with holiday corsages. Simply wire together a few sprigs of greenery and berries and bend the wire to form a hook to hang over the frame's edge.

In a Twinkling:
Details

42

▶

A short stick makes a natural form for this quick-and-easy swag. Use floral wire to attach sprigs of greenery, small pinecones, and berries atop new or antique ornaments. Add bows to complete this welcoming Christmas decoration.

For a festive accent at your windows, replace your everyday curtain tiebacks with yards of ribbon. Use three to five different widths of ribbon, and mix satin, grosgrain, and organdy for a rich effect. Attach jingle bells to the ribbon ends by threading the ribbon through the top of the bell and knotting it. To attach pinecones, wrap floral wire around the bottom scales of the pinecone and twist the wire ends to form a loop. Knot the ribbon through the loop.

43

Add a merry touch to every room with holiday light-switch covers. Buy inexpensive plastic covers at the hardware store. Cut holiday gift wrap about an inch larger all around and glue it to the cover with a mixture of equal parts thick white crafts glue and water. Fold the excess paper to the back and glue it in place. From the back, cut an X across the switch opening and glue the tabs to the back of the cover (above left), then coat the front with two or three coats of the glue mixture. Check hardware stores for clear acrylic cover kits (left) for an even easier alternative.

Perk up sofas and chairs with special pillows. Department stores and gift catalogs offer package-shape and novelty pillows for the holidays, but it's easy to make your own.

holiday pillows

SHOPPING LIST:

FOR IVY WREATH:
From a crafts store:
  36 silk ivy leaves
  textile medium
  acrylic paint:
    metallic gold
  paintbrush
  thick white crafts glue
  14 inches of
    1-inch-wide gold
    ribbon

FOR POINSETTIA CORSAGE:
From a crafts store:
  8-inch- or 9-inch-diameter
    silk poinsettia
  4-inch-diameter felt circle
  thick white crafts glue
  1½ yards each of red,
    green, and gold silk
    ribbon for ribbon
    embroidery
  needle and thread
  2 or 3 small safety pins

If you're short on time, buy solid-color throw pillows and glue on a ring of silk ivy for a quick holiday face-lift; or make a corsage from silk poinsettias that you can remove after the holidays.

If you have a little more time, make your own pillows and decorate them with snowy lace or with snowflakes cut from fusible interfacing. The fusible-interfacing snowflakes are simply ironed onto the fabric, then covered with organdy for a frosty look. Because the motif isn't specific to Hanukkah or Christmas, you can leave these pillows out after the holidays for a winter-season decorating accent.

Ivy Wreath

here's how...

1 Clip the plastic stems from the ivy leaves. Mix equal parts textile medium and gold acrylic paint and apply the mixture to the leaves.

2 After the paint dries, glue the ivy leaves to the front of the pillow with thick white crafts glue.

3 Tie the ribbon into a bow and glue it to the wreath.

Poinsettia Corsage

here's how...

1 Remove the poinsettia petals and one or two leaves from the stem. Beginning with the largest petals, glue the center vein of each petal to the felt circle. Glue smaller petals over the large petals to re-create the flower. Glue one or two leaves under the petals.

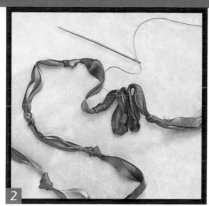

To make the flower center, hold the three ribbons together as one. Beginning 1 inch from one end, knot the ribbons every 1½ inches until you reach the opposite end.

3 Draw a threaded needle through one end of the knotted ribbon strand. Bring the knots together, folding the ribbon as you would a paper fan. Stitch through the V folds between the knots with the needle and thread. Pull the thread tightly and knot it to secure the ribbon pompom.

4 Glue the ribbon pompom to the center of the poinsettia. After the glue dries, use small safety pins to attach the corsage to the pillow.

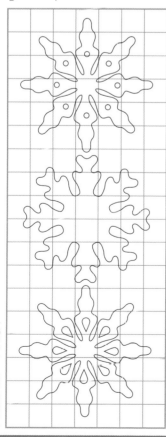

1 SQUARE = 1 INCH

SHOPPING LIST:

⅓ yard of raspberry linen
10x16-inch piece of organdy
scraps of white fusible interfacing for snowflakes
three 2-inch-diameter lace medallions
1½ yards of ¼-inch-diameter cording for piping
½ yard of linen or cotton for the piping
matching thread
purchased or pre-made pillow form

Snowflake Pillow

here's how...

1 Enlarge the snowflake patterns *below* to scale (445 percent on a copier). Trace them onto the interfacing, and cut them out.

Cut two 10x16-inch pieces of linen. Fuse the snowflakes to one piece, following the manufacturer's instructions. Tack the lace medallions to the fabric, too.

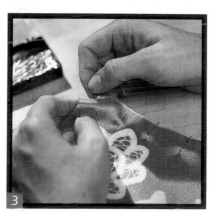

Baste the organdy rectangle over the pillow front.

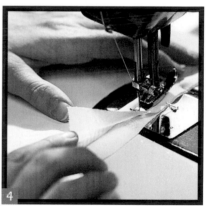

Cut and piece 3-inch-wide bias-cut strips of linen or cotton fabric to measure 1½ yards long. Cover the cording with this strip, then baste the covered cording to the pillow front along the seam line, with raw edges aligned.

5 Sew the pillow front to the pillow back, right sides facing, leaving an opening along one side. Trim the seams, clip the corners, and turn the pillow right side out. Insert the pillow form, and blind-stitch the opening closed.

45

quick pillows *for* hanukkah

It's easy to make these special holiday pillows. Start with purchased pillows and add ribbon with fabric glue.

Menorah Pillow

here's how...

1 To make the menorah's main bar, cut the 2-inch-wide gold ribbon in half. Center and glue the 1½-inch-wide silver ribbon on one 18-inch length of the gold ribbon. To make the candles, center and glue the ⅝-inch-wide silver ribbon on the 1-inch-wide gold ribbon. After the glue dries, center and glue the silver braid over the silver ribbon. Cut this three-ribbon band into eight 6-inch lengths and one 7-inch length.

2 Pin the main bar to the pillow front so the top edge of the ribbon is 9 inches down from the top of the pillow. Turn under the ends at a 45-degree angle, encasing the raw edges. Mark the ribbon's position, and then remove it.

3 Center the 7-inch candle ribbon on the pillow so that the bottom of the candle is even with the bottom of the menorah's main bar. Evenly space the remaining candles on each side of the center candle, leaving ⅝ inch between them. Mark the positions of the candles and then remove them.

4 Fold the remaining wide gold ribbon into a triangle. Position it at the base of the menorah, encasing the raw edges. Mark the position and remove.

5 To make the flames, cut the copper ribbon and gold cord into nine 2-inch pieces. Fold each piece of ribbon and cord in half, and crunch the copper ribbons to give them shape. Pin the copper ribbons onto the pillow at the tops of the candles and pin the gold cords on top of the copper ribbons.

6 Pin the candles, the triangle base, and the menorah's main bar on the marked lines, enclosing or covering all raw edges of ribbons except the tops of the candles (these will be hidden by the buttons). Glue the ribbons to the pillow in this order: copper flame, gold flame, candles, triangular base, menorah's main bar. Use pins to hold the ribbons in place until the glue dries. Let one layer dry before gluing on another.

7 Erase all marking lines. Sew or glue the buttons to the top of the candles, covering the raw edges of the ribbon.

Star of David Pillow

here's how...

Holding the figured ribbon on top of the blue ribbon and working with them as one, pin the ribbons to the pillow front in a triangle that fills the pillow's front. Be sure to center the top point on one edge. Miter the points of the triangle as shown *above*.

2 Make a second triangle opposite to the first, weaving the ribbons through the arms of the first triangle and pinning the ribbon to hold it in place.

3 Use thick white crafts glue to attach the figured ribbon to the blue ribbon, then glue the blue ribbon to the pillow, removing the pins as you go.

If the pillow should become soiled, spot-clean it as recommended for the fabric. Machine-washing isn't recommended.

Add cozy warmth with accent lamps. Place one in a powder room or bedroom, tuck one into a bookshelf, or use a matching pair on a mantel. They make great gifts, too.

shed a little *light*

T o make these lamps, simply adhere paper onto a purchased shade. Look for self-adhesive lampshades at fabric stores, or buy inexpensive fabric-covered shades from a discount store. To adapt the shades for use with candles, look for candle followers at lamp and lighting stores.

SHOPPING LIST:

small lampshade
crafts knife or scissors
old sheet music, pictures,
   or computer-generated
   Christmas carol lyrics
white crafts glue
paintbrush
water-base varnish
fine sandpaper
tack cloth
gold leaf and adhesive size
decorative trims, such as
   cording or tassel fringe

Lyrical Lampshade

here's how...

1 With a crafts knife or scissors, cut out sheet music, pictures, or computer-generated Christmas carol lyrics, using only noncopyrighted images.

2 Lay out the pieces and lightly mark their positions on the lampshade before permanently applying them.

3 Mix a little water with the crafts glue so it will spread easily. Apply the glue-water solution to the back of the sheet music and pictures with a paintbrush. Carefully smooth the pieces onto the lampshade and allow to dry.

4 Apply three coats of the water-base varnish over the lampshade. Let each coat dry, then sand lightly and wipe with the tack cloth before applying the next coat. Apply gold leaf to the top and bottom edges of the shade, using adhesive size and following the manufacturer's instructions. Glue a length of tassel fringe or cording around the bottom inside edge of the shade.

"Joy to the World" Lampshade

here's how...

1 From the green paper, tear four tree shapes, making them about 2½ inches tall. From yellow paper, tear four 1-inch-wide stars. From black paper, tear four rectangles about ½ inch high for tree trunks. From red paper, tear small circles for ornaments. For the worlds, tear four large blue circles and a variety of green shapes for land masses. Tear white paper into ½-inch pieces to cover the background.

2 If you use a self-adhesive lampshade, peel away the paper and adhere the four trees around the upper half of the shade, spacing them evenly. Press a star to the top of each tree and a trunk to the bottom of each tree. Press a blue world below each trunk. (If you use a plain fabric-covered shade, glue the shapes to the shade with a solution of equal parts of glue and water.)

3 Mix equal parts of glue and water in a small bowl and glue paper ornaments to the trees and the land masses to the worlds.

4 Press the ½-inch pieces of white paper onto the shade wherever the adhesive surface is still exposed. (If you use a fabric shade, this step isn't necessary, but you will need to paint the exposed fabric with the glue solution. Otherwise, when the lamp is turned on, you'll see the glue around the shapes.)

5 Paint the entire surface with the glue-water mixture to adhere any loose edges and to seal and varnish the shade.

6 For the wire words, first write "Joy to the World" in cursive on a piece of paper. Bend 19-gauge wire with needle-nose pliers, using the written words as a template.

7 Reinforce joints or intersection points by wrapping them with 24-gauge wire.

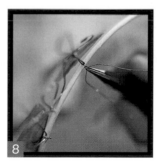

8 Position the four wire words evenly around the shade. Loop the 24-gauge wire around the two or three tallest parts of each word. Poke small holes at the base of the shade and run the wire through the holes. Twist to secure, and then trim any excess wire with the wire cutters.

9 Bend the 19-gauge wire into four small stars. Attach the stars between the wire words in the same manner as directed in Step 8.

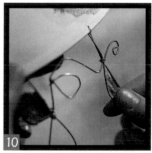

49

10 Dip the remaining bits of fiber paper into the glue solution, and wring them dry between your fingers. Wrap these strips randomly around the letters and stars.

Santa wouldn't dare put sticks and coal in this stocking or the one on the following page. Stitched from velvet and damask, they're easy to make—and sure proof that you've been good.

stockings
with style

Both stockings require only basic sewing skills; but for an even quicker alternative, start with plain purchased stockings and add ribbon streamers or upholstery fringe.

1 SQUARE = 1 INCH

Ribbon-Fringed Stocking

Finished size is approximately 17 inches.

here's how...

1 Enlarge the pattern *at left* by drawing a grid of 1-inch squares and copying the lines, square by square, from the pattern. Or enlarge it 485 percent on a copier—this will require several passes.

2 Fold the velvet in half with right sides facing, and trace the pattern on the wrong side of the fabric.

3 Sew along the drawn line, leaving the top straight edge unstitched. Cut along the top straight edge and then ½ inch beyond the stitched line. Clip the curves and turn the stocking right side out.

4 Cut the organdy ribbons into 8-inch lengths for the fringe. Pin two layers of the organdy ribbons around the top of the stocking, matching one short end of each ribbon to the raw edge of the stocking; baste in place.

5 Cut the gold ribbon into one 8-inch and two 6-inch lengths. (Set the remaining 7 inches of ribbon aside for the hanger.) Thread the 8-inch length through the loop on the large star charm and glue the ribbon end in place to secure the charm. Repeat for the small star charms on the 6-inch lengths. Baste the free ends of the ribbons to the ribbon cuff.

6 Fold the remaining 7 inches of gold ribbon in half for a hanger. Sew the hanger to the top corner of the stocking, matching raw edges.

51

7 Stitch and cut out the lining as directed for the stocking, leaving an opening at the bottom for turning. Do not turn.

8 Slip the stocking into the lining with the right sides facing. Sew around the upper edge of the cuff.

9 Turn the stocking right side out through the opening in the bottom of the lining. Slip-stitch the opening closed. Tuck the lining inside.

10 Trim the ribbon fringe to varying lengths.

SHOPPING LIST

1 yard of red damask fabric

½ yard of fusible fleece

1 ½ yards of ¼-inch
diameter cording for
piping (or use
purchased piping)

¾ yard of dark green
fringe the desired width

4 to 6 yards of 2-inch-wide
red organdy ribbon
for roses

1 ¼ yards of 1-inch-wide
green velvet ribbon
for leaves

matching threads

Damask Stocking

∾ Finished size is approximately 17 inches.

here's how...

1 Enlarge the pattern on *page 50* as directed in Step 1 of the Ribbon-Fringed Stocking.

2 Cut the damask fabric into two ½-yard pieces. From one of the pieces, cut and piece 2-inch-wide bias strips to cover enough cording to outline the stocking. Fold the bias strip over the cording and stitch close to the cording.

3 Cut two 13x20-inch rectangles *each* from the remaining piece of damask and the fleece. Pin a fleece rectangle to the wrong side of each damask rectangle, leaving 2 inches of damask exposed at one short end. This will be the top hemmed edge of the stocking. Trim excess fleece at the bottom edge. Fuse the fleece to the damask.

4 Place the fabric rectangles together, right sides facing, and pin the pattern on top, aligning the top edge of the pattern with the fleece edge at the top. Cut out the stocking front and back, adding a ½-inch seam to the sides and bottom. Set the pieces aside.

Fold the top raw edge of each stocking piece under ½ inch. Fold under again 1½ inches.

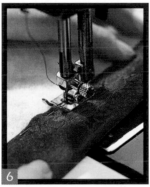

Stitch close to the fold.

Align one end of the piping with the top edge of the stocking front. Pin, then stitch the piping to the stocking front along the seam line. Trim away any excess piping.

With the right sides facing, sew the stocking front to the stocking back along the seam line. Clip the curves, and turn the stocking right side out.

9 Cut a 3x6-inch hanger strip from the damask fabric. Press under ½ inch on the long edges of the strip, and topstitch in place. Fold the strip in half crosswise and tack to the back of the stocking.

Pin, then sew the fringe around the upper edge of the stocking.

For the roses: To make the center of the rose, wrap the organdy ribbon tightly around a pencil 12 times. Do not cut the ribbon.

Slide the ribbon off and hand-tack one end closed.

To make the petals, loosely twist the ribbon tail into loops, bringing the ribbon back to the tacked center at the end of each loop. Tack each petal in place. Continue making petals until the roses are the desired shape and size. Tack securely and trim the end.

14 For leaves: Cut the velvet ribbon into 4-inch lengths. Fold each length in half crosswise, right sides facing. Sew from one corner of the top folded edge diagonally to the center on the other side. Trim excess ribbon and turn the leaf right side out.

15 Tack the leaves and roses to the cuff.

53

Arrange a collar of magnolia leaves on a sconce, holding them in place with a short pillar candle. Add a sprig of pepper berries for color.

Candle lovers take note! Be sure to keep wicks trimmed to prevent the release of soot. If you burn candles often and don't keep the wicks trimmed short, some candles may release enough soot to damage furnishings, fabrics, and ceilings.

In a Twinkling:
Candles

An antique muffin tray makes a rustic base for a bed of votives. Tuck holly and berries around each candle, or use two colors of candles and arrange them in a checkerboard pattern. (An old muffin tin will work, too.)

Give purchased pillar candles a handcrafted designer look by adhering pressed or glycerinized leaves to the surface. Spray the candle with spray adhesive and press the leaves in place. Melt candle wax in an old double boiler and paint the entire candle with two coats of wax, letting the wax cool between coats. After the wax has cooled completely, carefully scrape off the top layer with a paring knife so the surface is uneven, allowing the leaves to show more in some areas than in others.

Make instant seasonal candles by filling flea-market teacups and holiday mugs with wax crystals, available at crafts stores. Insert the wick into the center and trim it to ¼ inch above the wax. As the candle burns, the crystals around the wick will melt, but the outer crystals remain loose, so you can pull out the wick "plug," save the remaining wax crystals, and wash out the cup with hot water.

Dress up purchased pillar candles with assorted natural materials. Use floral tape or a rubber band to hold greenery, twigs, or gilded seedpods around the base, then tie raffia or ribbon over the rubber band.

55

Create your own "antique" candles by applying gold or silver metal leaf to purchased pillar candles. Look for metal leaf and spray adhesive size at crafts stores; spritz the candle surface randomly with the size and let it dry a few minutes until it's tacky. Apply a sheet of metal leaf to the surface and gently rub to adhere it. Wipe off the metal leaf from unsprayed areas for an aged look.

Bring a warm glow to any dark corner with votive candles dropped into unexpected containers. Any clear glass vessel can work; just be sure there's room around the candle so the flame does not burn close to the glass.

Romance your rooms with the cozy glow of candlelight.
Purchased candles are easy to personalize, or craft your own.

illuminating
ideas

Poinsettia and Holly Candles

here's how...

1 Trace the pattern pieces *below* onto the appropriate colors of tissue paper. Cut as many shapes as needed to decorate the candle.

2 Position holly leaves and berries or poinsettia petals and center "berries" on the candle.

3 Brush decoupage medium over the motifs to secure them to the candle. Also brush medium over the entire candle surface. Let the candle dry.

4 Use the green acrylic paint to paint veins on the holly leaves.

SHOPPING LIST:

tissue paper: red, yellow, and green
pillar candles
decoupage medium
paintbrush
green acrylic paint (for holly candle only)

Give purchased pillar candles a handmade touch by gluing on tissue paper in holiday shapes. Choose fragrant candles scented with pine or bayberry so they'll smell as festive as they look.

The milk-carton candles on *page 57* update a 1970s craft with a twist: use a taper candle instead of candle wicking. For fun, add a sprinkling of glitter before pouring the melted wax.

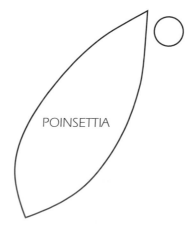

POINSETTIA

HOLLY LEAF AND BERRIES

OPTIONAL VEINS

Milk Carton Candles

here's how...

1 Break the wax into chunks and place it in the can. Pour a few inches of water in the pan, then set the can of wax in the water. Bring the water to simmering and let the wax melt. (To make pouring the wax easier, you may wish to bend the can at the top to form a spout before putting the wax in.)

2 Add stearin to the melted wax. If you're using wax crystals or wax with hardener added, follow the manufacturer's instructions for melting.

3 Partially fill the milk carton with broken ice cubes. Center a taper in the milk carton, then continue filling the carton with ice. Tap the carton on your work surface to settle the ice, then add more ice. Sprinkle glitter over the ice.

Let the wax cool to 170 degrees, then pour it into the carton. As the wax cools and shrinks, add more ice or wax to keep the top of the candle level.

After the wax hardens completely, peel the cardboard carton away from the sides. Trim the top of the taper so it's level with the top of the candle, leaving ½ inch of wick. If the bottom of the candle isn't level, slide it across an old warm skillet to smooth any rough spots.

Caution: Wax is extremely flammable. Never melt wax directly over heat or to a temperature above 220 degrees. Never leave melting wax unattended; if it starts to smoke, remove the pan from the heat immediately. If wax catches fire, smother the flame with a pan lid; don't throw water on the flame. Never leave a burning candle unattended, and never burn candles where the flame might come in contact with flammable surfaces or objects.

let it glow

Soft, sparkling light enhances the holiday mood. Lower the wattage in table lamps, and supplement them with small decorative lamps, picture lights over artwork, and candles. Create a glowing centerpiece for a table by wrapping strings of lights around a grapevine wreath that you've sprayed white. (Use lights on a white cord.) Nest a glass bowl inside the wreath, and lay more lights inside the bowl. Then fill the bowl with clear glass orbs, ornaments, and stars.

If the decoration sits on an end table or in an entry, you can use plug-in lights. Otherwise you'll need to use battery-operated ones.

Mesh Candleholders

To create votive holders similar to those shown here, wrap small jars with bronze screening available from a hardware store.

❧ You can recycle baby food jars or other small glass containers to hold the candles, or use straight-sided votive candleholders. Group the candles with other metallic objects, such as gilded balls and burnished vases, which will reflect the light and create a warm glow. The screening isn't sharp, but the cut edges can be prickly so you may want to wear gloves while working.

SHOPPING LIST

pliers, scissors, compass
small jar
heavy rubber band
votive candle or tea light
From a hardware store:
    bronze screening
    18-gauge brass wire

59

To figure the radius of the circle for the screening, multiply the height of the jar by two, then add the diameter of the bottom plus 2 inches. Divide this measurement in half and set the compass to the resulting figure. Or tie a piece of string to a pencil, cut the string to the length of the radius, and pin the other end to the paper. Draw a circle on a piece of scrap paper. Using the paper circle as a pattern, cut a circle from the screening. Mark the center of the screen circle by folding it in half and then in half again. Open the screen, and center the jar on the circle.

Fold the screening around the jar, and temporarily hold it in place around the jar's neck with a heavy rubber band. Pinch the bottom edges and corners to give the container a boxy shape. Wrap brass wire around the neck, and twist it tightly with pliers. Shape the excess screening as desired to make a flange or collar. Remove the rubber band and insert the votive candle or tea light.

Create holiday drama with seasonal touches that emphasize your home's architecture. And fill the house with festive spirit by dressing up accessories and furnishings you enjoy year-round.

festive
finishing
touches

❧ A staircase makes an instant focal point. All you have to do is add greenery and bright poinsettias to establish a holiday mood.

Fresh garland is usually made by wiring individual branches to a heavy base wire or to twine or rope. A wire base is less flexible, so for closely spaced swags on a staircase, look for garland made on a rope or twine base. For one deep loop, like the swag shown here, a wire base works fine. Before you buy the garland, test the way it droops to make sure you like the effect.

To determine how much garland you need, tie heavy clothesline or twine to the top of the stair rail. Drape the clothesline along the stair in the desired number of swags and wrap it around the newel post. Add a couple of feet to allow for the garland's thickness.

here's how...

Fasten purchased garland to the stair rail with green chenille wire, which won't scratch the woodwork and will blend with the greenery. Look for chenille wires in crafts stores—they're like pipe cleaners, but they come in longer lengths and a variety of colors. After you've wired the garland in place, use floral wire to attach branches of red berries, such as holly, possum haw, winterberry, or yaupon holly, to the greenery. Or, use canella berries, available at crafts stores. Add dried salal leaves for contrasting texture and tone.

Evergreen Cornice

Crown your windows with bow ties of greenery to lift the eye and emphasize a view of the outdoors.

SHOPPING LIST

From a florist, a garden center, or your yard:
  branches of fir or
    hemlock (or
    substitute pine)
  branches of berried
    juniper
  salal
  stems of assorted herbs

From a crafts store:
  spool wire
  canella berries or
    rose hips
  18-inch-long cinnamon
    sticks
  raffia

here's how...

This cornice is easy to make by wiring overlapping boughs together.. Layering herbs, rose hips, and cinnamon sticks over the evergreens creates a classic country-style swag. For a formal look, substitute seeded eucalyptus (available from a florist) and dried roses for the herbs and rose hips, and bind the bow tie with wide satin ribbon.

To hang the swag, tap two small nails into the top of the window frame or into the wall just above it, spacing them an equal distance from the center. Slip the swag's hanging wires over the nails.

1 Cut the fir branches to a little more than half the width of your window frame. Divide the branches into two groups. Lay the stems end to end, overlapping them several inches, and bind the branches together tightly with spool wire.

2 Cut the juniper branches so they're slightly shorter than the fir. Layer them over the fir with stem ends overlapping and wire them in place. In the same way, layer the herbs, berries, salal, and cinnamon sticks, angling the cinnamon sticks as shown in the photo. Wire each layer of materials in place.

3 Tie raffia tightly over the center of the swag, knotting it at the front. To attach hanging wires, place the swag facedown, and wrap wire around a sturdy branch on each side, aligned with the nails in the window frame or wall. Wrap the wires around the nails, adjusting the lengths as necessary.

63

Accent on Accessories

Work holiday magic with decorative details.

SHOPPING LIST

From a fabric store:
  ½ yard of 56-inch-wide
    upholstery fabric
  fusible interfacing
  tassels
  beading needle or
    very fine needle
  thread to match fabric
From a crafts store:
  foil adhesive
  foam brush
  composition leaf in gold,
    silver, or copper
  burnishing tool (optional)
  soft bristle brush
  seed beads
From the grocery store:
  carambolas (star fruit)

❧ Give your rooms a new look for the season with a few simple accessories that go beyond the expected. A quick add-on valance, lampshade trims, a table runner, and pillows will help make spirits bright.

stamped table runner

here's how...

1 Cut a strip of fabric 14×56 inches. Hem the long raw edges with a machine stitch, and press.

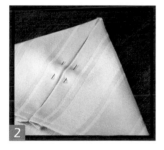

Fold under the fabric at each end to form a point. Press the folded edges, and tack the ends in place; or use fusible interfacing following the manufacturer's instructions.

To stamp the stars, work on a smooth, hard surface and place scrap paper under the fabric. Cut the star fruit in half and blot the cut surface on a paper towel. Using the foam brush, apply foil adhesive to the cut surface.

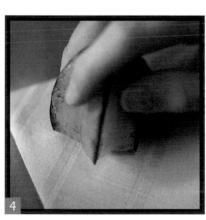

Starting at one end of the runner, press the fruit firmly and gently onto the fabric, making sure each point of the fruit contacts the fabric. Reapply adhesive to the fruit, and repeat the procedure several more times, placing the stars randomly. Work on one small section of the runner at a time so the adhesive doesn't get too dry. When it is tacky to the touch, gently lay a sheet of composition leaf over the adhesive.

Rub the composition leaf firmly and carefully with your fingernail or a burnishing tool. (If you use a burnishing tool, place a piece of heavy plastic, such as a cereal-box liner, between the tool and the leaf to keep from tearing the leaf.) Lift the leaf away from the image, and repeat this procedure to apply composition leaf to the remaining stamped stars. Brush away excess leaf with a soft bristle brush. Repeat to complete the runner. When one star fruit surface starts to wear out, cut a fresh piece of fruit. Using the beading needle and thread, sew a bead at each star point. Stitch a tassel to each end. Because the composition leaf is not washable, you may want to spray the finished runner with spray-on fabric protector; spot-clean any spills.

65

SHOPPING LIST

FOR TEA TOWEL PILLOW:
20×30-inch tea towel
1½ yards each of two
different colors of
⅞-inch-wide ribbon
12 brass grommets,
⅜ inch in diameter
purchased pillow or
pillow form
fusible interfacing

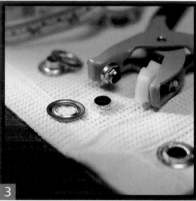

3

Follow the manufacturer's instructions to install the grommets. At each end, work through both layers of fabric.

4 Center the pillow on the wrong side of the towel. Wrap the folded edges over the pillow along the sides, then bring the top and bottom grommeted edges together. If necessary, make a few long handstitches from side to side to keep the folded edges in place before you bring the grommeted edges together.

place mat pillow

here's how...

1 Stack the place mats with wrong sides facing. Mark the placement for the buttons 1½ inches in from the outer edge on all sides, starting in one corner and allowing for six evenly spaced buttons on each long side and four evenly spaced on each short side.

2 Pin the place mats together on the markings and stitch with a few hand or machine stitches. Leave three marked points open along the bottom edge for inserting the pillow form.

3 Use pearl cotton or embroidery floss to sew the buttons over the stitched points. Insert the pillow form. Stitch the last three marked points together and sew the buttons over them.

SHOPPING LIST

FOR PLACE MAT PILLOW:
two place mats about
13½×18 inches
purchased 10×15-inch
pillow or pillow form
From a fabric store or
variety store:
20 shank buttons in
assorted designs
fabric marking pencil
pearl cotton or
embroidery floss

tea towel pillow

here's how...

1 Press under about 3 inches along the two long sides of the towel (the design of the towel may dictate that you turn under a little more or less).

2 On the right side of the towel, about 1⅛ inches from the edge along each short end, mark the placement for six evenly spaced grommets. Reinforce the wrong side of the ends with fusible interfacing.

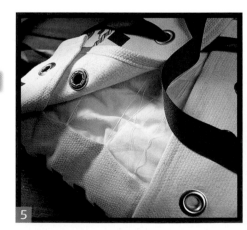

5

Lace ribbon through the grommets as if you were lacing a shoe; tie the ends in a bow. Or, start at opposite ends and lace toward the center as shown on *page 64*.

lampshade necklace

lampshade crown

SHOPPING LIST

From a hardware store:
  6 feet of brass
    beaded or ball chain
  beaded chain connector
  wire cutters, needle-nose
    pliers, round-nose
    pliers
From the jewelry-supply
department of a
crafts store:
  gold head pins
  assorted crystal beads
  7mm gold jump rings
  assorted star charms

here's how...

1 String crystal beads of varying sizes and colors onto the head pins. Wrap the long end of the pin around the round-nose pliers to make a loop. Cut off the excess pin with the wire cutters. Squeeze the loop closed using the needle-nose pliers.

2 To attach the charms and beads to the chain, open the jump rings by separating them at the side—don't pull them apart. Slide a star charm or a string of crystal beads onto each jump ring, then squeeze the jump ring closed over the chain. Connect the ends with the chain connector. Form the chain into a double or triple loop and arrange it as desired on the lampshade.

here's how...

1 Cut a length of ivy garland to fit snugly over the lampshade, either at the top or near the bottom. Pull the leaves off the plastic pegs or stubs, keeping every fourth set of leaves in place.

2 Pull leaves off the holly garland and push them onto every two or three empty stubs on the ivy garland.

3 To make the berry units, slip a bead over an eye pin. Use the round-nose pliers to curl the straight end of the pin into a "pig's tail" to keep the bead from slipping off. Clip off the excess wire. Leave 1½ to 2 inches of wire between the eye and the berry to form a stem; make the stems different lengths. Slip the eyes of one or two pins over the remaining empty plastic stubs on the ivy garland.

SHOPPING LIST

From a crafts store:
  3-inch silver jewelry
    eye pins
  10mm red glass beads
  silk ivy garland
  silk holly garland
From a hardware store:
  wire cutters
  round-nose pliers

room *in the* inn

When the family heads to *your* home for the holidays, set the stage for a happy gathering with festive touches in the guest room. Your attention to details will make their stay a memorable one.

Guest Room Makeover

Give the guest room a holiday face with Christmas bed linens and a few decorations.

dress the bed for the season with a duvet made from red-and-green plaid flannel sheets (for instructions on stitched and no-sew versions, see *page 70*). Add plump pillows in coordinating shams and cases, and toss in a small decorator pillow wrapped with velvet ribbon.

make room for guests' belongings by clearing the dresser top and a drawer or two, and make space

available in the closet, along with hangers for skirts and pants.

provide a bedside reading lamp and a basket of magazines and books. An alarm clock, tissues, a carafe of water, and a drinking glass are also considerate and practical gestures.

if you don't have the luxury of a separate bath for guests, set out an array of scented soaps, bath oils, lotions,

and fluffy towels in the bedroom so your visitors will know they're welcome to indulge themselves.

for late-night snacking, leave a tray of treats in the room. It is also thoughtful to get the coffeemaker set up and ready to go so guests can make a pot if they're first up in the morning.

Holiday Duvet Covers

Start with queen-size flat flannel sheets to make this cover for a double bed comforter or duvet.

SHOPPING LIST

one queen-size plaid
  flannel sheet and one in
  spruce green
For no-sew version:
  65 grommets ½ inch in
    diameter
  grommet tool
  heavy chenille yarn
  two ½-inch-diameter
    wooden beads
For stitched version:
  thread to match fabrics
  heavy-duty snaps
  star-shape novelty
    buttons

here's how...

no-sew version

1 Trim 21 inches from the bottom edge of the green sheet; press under a 3-inch hem on the bottom and side edges of both sheets. Place the sheets with wrong sides facing and the green sheet on top, aligning the bottom and side edges. The plaid sheet will extend beyond the green sheet by 24 inches to make the top flap.

2 At each top corner of the plaid sheet, attach a grommet about 1 inch in from the side and top edges. Fold the flap down over the top edge of the green sheet, overlapping it by about 3 inches. Working through both layers, attach two more grommets in each side of the flap, spacing the grommets about 4¾ to 5 inches apart on center. Continue attaching grommets through both sheets down the sides and across the bottom.

3 To make the flap closure, attach six pairs of grommets across the top edge of the plaid sheet (the bottom of the flap). Space the grommets in each pair about 1 inch apart and space the pairs about 10 to 12 inches apart. Attach six pairs of grommets in the top edge of the green sheet, aligning them with those in the flap edge (plaid sheet).

4 Measure the sides and bottom of the duvet cover. Cut two lengths of chenille yarn to that measurement. Starting at one top corner (with the flap folded down), thread the double strand of yarn through the grommets. Work down the side, across the bottom, and up the other side. At each top corner, thread the yarn ends through a wooden bead and knot the yarn ends.

5 Insert the comforter or duvet. Tie the flap closed by threading a 10-inch length of yarn through the pairs of grommets and making a bow (see the photo *top left*). Trim the yarn ends.

stitched version

1 To make the stitched version, trim 20 inches from the bottom of the green sheet and about 2½ inches from each side of both sheets (otherwise the cover will be too big for the duvet). From the 20-inch green strip, cut a 4¾-inch-wide strip. Press under ½ inch along both long edges; topstitch the strip to the right side of the plaid sheet's top edge to make a decorative border for the flap (see the photo *above right*).

2 Place the sheets (with the green sheet on top) with right sides facing and the bottom and side edges aligned. Fold the flap down over the top edge of the green sheet, overlapping it by 3 inches. Machine-stitch along the sides and bottom edges, using a ½-inch seam allowance. Turn the cover right side out. Attach heavy-duty snaps to the underside of the flap and also to the corresponding top edge of the green sheet. To decorate the flap border, stitch star-shape novelty buttons over the snaps.

Privacy, Please

Turn the den or office into a private retreat for company with an easy-to-install curtain.

❧ When you need the study, family room, or office to do double duty as guest quarters, you can still provide a feeling of privacy for visitors by closing off the sleeping area with folding screens or temporary curtains. A tension rod or shower-curtain rod can be inserted in a cased opening like the one shown here without damaging the woodwork. Slip a simple sleeved curtain over the rod, or cover it with a scrunched tube of fabric and tie fabric panels to the rod with ribbon.

family traditions

W e always have visitors stay in our daughter's room, but she wasn't always happy about having to move out for a couple of days. So we bought a guest book for her room. Now she looks forward to having people stay in her room. From time to time, she reads over this "book of memories."

—*Jeanette Smith*
Onalaska, Wisconsin

Cheerful Touches

❧ Give a holiday lift to your guest bath or a powder room, too. Bring out red and green hand towels and accent them with a perky gold bow. Fill a bowl with fragrant Christmas potpourri, and place a few pinecones on a bed of fresh greenery on the counter.

Explore your family's cultural heritage and add some of those old customs to enrich your own decorations and celebrations.

christmas
traditions

Sinterklaas

Although the saint known as Nicholas was originally a priest and later a bishop in 4th-century Turkey, he came to be the patron saint of a surprising assortment of groups—fishermen, sailors, virgins, children, pawnbrokers, and the country of Russia all claimed him. His church in Demre, Turkey, became a popular destination for pilgrims in the Middle Ages.

Eventually, he became the patron saint of Amsterdam as well.

According to Dutch tradition, Sinterklaas, his servant Piet, and many helpers arrive by boat on December 5 (Sinderklaas Eve). Mounted on a white horse, Sinterklaas rides over the rooftops, listening in to check on children's behavior. Wooden shoes filled with carrots or hay for the horse are left by the fireplace. In the homes of good children, Piet takes the treats and leaves behind a small gift or candy.

Sinterklaas Eve and Sinterklaas Day (December 6) are days of festivity and merriment—including jokes, rhymes, simple gifts in strange wrappings, parties, and general celebration. Traditional foods are spice cookies, hot chocolate, apple fritters, Dutch doughnuts, and Dutch letters.

Because St. Nicholas was known for his good deeds, the Dutch in some areas observe December 5 and 6 as special days for exchanging gifts with family and friends. It's also a time for sharing with the poor.

This hearthside decoration recalls the treats left for Sinterklaas's horse, but replaces the hay with wheat, which is readily available at crafts stores.

hearthside decoration
here's how...

1 Slide several handfuls of blonde and blackbeard wheat into the shoes, trimming the stem ends so the heads extend 6 to 10 inches beyond the shoes. Trim the greens of the carrots on the diagonal so they are 3 to 5 inches long. Tuck several carrots into each shoe. Arrange the shoes as shown here.

2 String the bells on the ribbon so they resemble sleigh bells. Place the fruit, ribbon and bells, and vintage items around, between, and behind the shoes. Be sure to keep the arrangement away from any flames or embers.

Russian Customs

Celebrations in Russia today may occur on one of three different dates, depending on the family's religion and traditions—December 25, January 1, or January 7 (Russian Orthodox). The most common is January 1, which is the New Year's celebration.

Although the Soviets originally banned all celebrations, they later reconsidered and declared New Year's Day a holiday. Many of the old traditions and rituals that could be separated from religious content were revived. These included the Yolka (a decorated fir tree), Ded Moroz (Grandfather Frost), and Snegurochka (his granddaughter). Ded Moroz would bring the tree into the family's home at night and decorate it so when the children awoke on New Year's Day, the tree was a glorious surprise. Today, the family usually decorates the tree beforehand, using fruits, figures made out of fruits, paper or glass ornaments, and painted or carved folk crafts. Traditional Russian symbols such as eggs and matroyska dolls often are used on the tree as well.

The eggs shown here were inspired by the jeweled Fabergé eggs commissioned by the Czar as gifts for special occasions, including Christmas.

fabergé eggs

here's how...

1 Using an awl, make a small hole in the small and large ends of each egg. Slide a skewer through the egg to use as a handle while you work on it. Paint the eggs with one or two coats of acrylic paint in the desired colors.

2 Referring to the photo for guidance, draw simple geometric shapes, such as grids, diamonds, or scallops, onto the eggs. For glitter eggs, draw along the lines with dimensional glitter paint. For foiled eggs, place the adhesive in a squeeze bottle and apply it along the lines. Apply the foil according to the manufacturer's directions.

3 After the glitter or foiling dries, erase any visible pencil lines. Glue the gems and filigree caps in place. Remove the skewer. Glue a necklace finding to each end, making sure the opening of the finding aligns with the hole in the egg. Run wire through the egg. At the large end, loop it around the loop of a tassel and pull the tassel loop up into the egg. At the other end, loop the wire back on itself to create a hanging loop and to hold the wire tightly in place.

73

SHOPPING LIST

awl
wooden skewers
papier-mâché eggs
  (5-inch size)
acrylic paint in the desired
  colors
disposable foam brushes
dimensional glitter paint
dimensional gold foiling
  with a squeeze bottle for
  adhesive, such as Anita's
  Gold Foiling kit
assorted glue-on gems,
  filigree bead caps, and
  other embellishments
necklace finding or end cap
  for end
thick white crafts glue or hot
  glue gun and glue sticks
gold wire or fabric-
  covered wire
small tassels

general numbered tag instructions:

here's how...

Select a set of numerals from an alphabet style book (from art supply and bookstores). Copy the numerals to make numbers 1 through 12, then cut the numbers apart and tape them to another sheet of paper with plenty of space around each number. Photocopy that paper onto the desired color of paper for the numbered tags.

The 12 Days of Christmas

This English counting song, which can help pass the time on long driving trips, has been part of our popular musical tradition for generations. Some people believe that it was written in the 1500s as a coded catechism for teaching the Catholic faith. Religion and politics were inextricably linked in 16th-century Europe, and when Catholics lost control of the English crown after Queen Mary's death, they also lost the freedom to practice their faith openly.

The verses of the song are said to symbolize elements of basic doctrine, although in fact there's nothing in the elements that the Church of England would have argued with. Today, the interpretation can add a spiritual dimension to what otherwise may seem simply whimsical.

The period of Twelve Days (observed by many Protestants as well as Roman Catholics) starts on December 26 and ends January 6, when the Three Wise Men arrived at the manger. Have some fun this year by using the song as the starting point for family activities. To make each day really special, package a small gift in its own themed gift box to leave beside each person's plate at breakfast or dinner.

general box wrapping instructions:

here's how...

Cut pieces of the desired paper ½ to ¾ inch larger than the top and bottom of the box. Place the bottom paper facedown; center the box bottom on it. Fold the long sides up and over the edge to the inside of the box and tape or glue in place. At the ends, fold the paper up, then crease the excess paper at the corners along the diagonal. Unfold the paper and press the diagonal crease in toward the end of the box. Refold the paper to the inside, pressing the fold at the corner of the box; tape or glue in place inside the box.

On the first day of Christmas my true love gave to me a partridge in a pear tree.

The pear tree is said to symbolize the cross; the partridge, Jesus Christ, because a mother partridge risks her own life to save her chicks by luring predators away from the nest.

here's how...

To make this gift box, wrap a small box top and bottom with old sheet music, then layer and wrap rice paper over the sheet music. Glue velvet millinery leaves and a miniature artificial pear to the top. Trim the number label to the desired size and glue in place beneath the leaves.

activities

Partridge may be hard to find in your local supermarket, but pears abound. Buy a couple of each kind and combine them with cheeses (see *pages 130–137* for suggestions), some fresh bread, figs, and other fresh fruit. Serve with wine, sparkling juice, or tea for a European-style lunch or dinner.

and glue the ends together to make loops. Glue the pieces together into a rosette. Cut the number label into a circle with pinking shears to fit just inside the rosette. Add two 1½-inch ribbon streamers and glue to the box top.

activities

Try a new recipe for chicken at one of today's meals. Or try Cornish hens or a game bird.

On the fourth day of Christmas my true love gave to me four calling birds.

The calling birds represent the four Evangelists, Matthew, Mark, Luke, and John, and their Gospel accounts.

here's how...

1 For this box, start with a 6-inch-diameter unfinished circular birch bandbox from a crafts store. Glue flat upholstery braid around the rim of the lid. Coil gold snowflake garland (from a party supply store) into a 5-inch-diameter circle and glue it to the box lid for the wreath.

2 Glue four small artificial birds (from a crafts store) around the wreath, spacing them evenly. Glue small pinecones between each pair of birds, spraying some of the cones silver before gluing them. Weave narrow wire-edge ribbon through the wreath. For the number tag, trim the number label to the desired size and glue it in place.

activities

Telephone at least four friends you've been meaning to contact but just haven't gotten around to calling. (E-mail doesn't count!) If they're not home, leave a message on the answering machine to let them know you're thinking of them.

On the second day of Christmas my true love gave to me two turtle doves.

The doves stand for the Old and New Testaments, but also may represent the doves that were required as an offering when a male child was dedicated in the Temple at the age of 12.

here's how...

1 Glue satin ribbon around the sides of a round box (about 4 inches in diameter); set aside. Trace the box lid onto a color print of doves (from a bird book, a greeting card, or gift paper). Cut out, adding ¼ inch all around. Glue the print to the box lid with matte medium; clip the excess ¼ inch to the edge of the lid, then fold and glue the flaps to the sides of the lid. Glue upholstery trim around the edge of the top to cover the flaps.

2 For the number tag, cut the label into a circle and cover a 1-inch-diameter button form as you would with fabric. Twist narrow ribbon into a rosette slightly larger than the number button and glue to the button back. Clip the ends of a ribbon scrap into a V, then glue to the edge of the lid. Glue the rosette on the ribbon.

activities

Doves represent peace, so during the family dinner make a list of ways to spread peace in your corner of the world. These can range from reducing conflicts between the kids to reaching a quiet solution to a school or work problem.

On the third day of Christmas my true love gave to me three french hens.

Threes usually symbolize the Trinity but also may stand for the theological virtues of faith, hope, and charity.

here's how...

1 Wrap the bottom of a small cardboard box with fabric, using a drop of hot glue to secure the edges inside the box. Sponge-paint the box lid with coordinating acrylic paints.

2 Have a copy shop make a color copy of a clip-art print of hens, using red ink only. Cut out the image and glue it to the top of the lid with matte acrylic medium. Apply a coat of medium to the entire lid.

3 For the number label ribbon, cut four 2-inch lengths of ¼-inch-wide ribbon. Fold

On the fifth day of Christmas my true love gave to me five golden rings.

These are said to represent the first five books of the Old Testament, often referred to as the Pentateuch.

here's how...

Start with a purchased gold box. Slip five gold-color plastic rings (available from crafts stores) onto ¾-inch-wide purple velvet ribbon; then wrap the ribbon around the box, gluing the ends in place. Trim the number label and glue in place.

activities

Give each family member five strips of yellow or gold paper. Have them write the following, one on each strip.

1. their favorite thing that happened this Christmas season
2. their favorite memory of last Christmas
3. their favorite Christmas ever
4. their funniest Christmas memory
5. one thing they hope to accomplish before next Christmas

Staple the strips into circles, joining them into a paper chain. Use the chain to decorate the Christmas tree, a stairway, a window, or a mirror.

On the sixth day of Christmas my true love gave to me six geese a-laying.

Since eggs symbolize new life, the geese stand for the six days of creation described in Genesis.

here's how...

1 Start with a purchased silver box with a lid. From a crafts store or florist's supply shop, buy a miniature vine nest, a beaded egg, and goose feathers. Or make a beaded egg by gluing a strand of amber glass beads around a plastic foam egg.

2 Glue the vine nest to the lid, then glue the beaded egg in the nest. Tuck goose feathers around the egg, then trim the number label to the desired size and glue it in the nest. Glue ribbon around the box, hiding the ends under the nest.

activities

Decorate a dozen or more raw eggs with nontoxic markers or crayons. Write special messages on them, draw faces, or just add squiggles and dots. Place them back in the egg cartons for later use. It will make cooking lots more fun for the next few weeks.

On the seventh day of Christmas my true love gave to me seven swans a-swimming.

Graceful swans symbolize the seven gifts of grace of the Holy Spirit, as listed in the twelfth book of Romans.

here's how...

1 To make a swan container, enlarge the patterns at right on a copier 190 percent and cut them out. On a piece of #120 Bristol Plate cardboard or other lightweight cardboard (from an art supply store), trace two body pieces, two wings, and one bottom piece. Cut out the shapes. (Note: The swan heads and necks must be the exact same size, so cut out both pieces simultaneously.) Trim the tail with scallop-cut and pinking shears and the wings with pinking shears.

2 Using a crafts knife, lightly score the bottom side of the bottom piece along the flaps (the broken lines on the pattern). Turn the piece over and score the center. Fold along the scored lines; set aside. Cut the feathers into the wings and curl them.

3 Glue the wings to the body pieces. Glue black seed beads in place for eyes

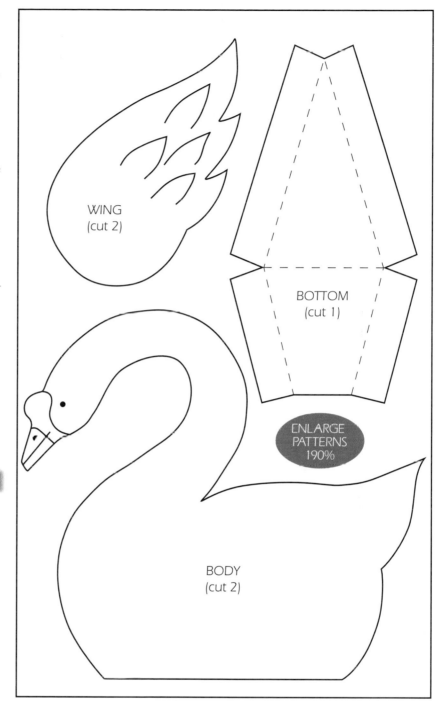

WING (cut 2)

BOTTOM (cut 1)

ENLARGE PATTERNS 190%

BODY (cut 2)

and color the beak with black and orange markers. Glue the bodies together at the head and neck and along the front of the breast. Insert the bottom piece and glue the flaps to the swan pieces. Cut a slit in the beak for the label.

4 Twist several strands of wired berries into a 6-inch garland. Wire the ends to form a wreath. Slip the wreath over the swan's head. Cut the number label into a ¾x6-inch strip; clip the ends and slide into the slit in the beak.

activities

Take the family swimming at an indoor pool at your fitness center, or check into a hotel for the day and use its pool.

across the bridge of the shoe and add ribbon roses as shown.

2 For the number label, cut around the number with scallop-edge scissors and glue it to the side of the shoe. Wrap the gift in tissue paper and slip it into the shoe.

activities

Have family members teach each other new dances. Parents can get out the oldies and do the dances that were hot when they were young; teens can share the newest crazes; and younger ones can show off their new ballet or tumbling moves. End the night with everyone doing the Hokey Pokey, Bunny Hop, or a conga line.

On the eighth day of Christmas my true love gave to me eight maids a-milking.

Milkmaids, as humble servants, are supposed to represent the Beatitudes listed in Matthew.

here's how...

1 Look for a 5-inch diameter aluminum pail (available at crafts stores and florist's supply shops) for the gift container. Wire five small silver balls into a cluster and attach it to one handle of the pail. Make a bow from ribbon scraps and cording, then wire the bow to the pail handle over the ball cluster.

2 Trim the number label to fit a metal-rimmed package label (from a stationery store) and glue it in place. Attach the label to the pail with a short length of silver

bead chain (you can find this at hardware stores). Cut a 13-inch-square of fabric to wrap the gift, and tuck it inside the pail.

activities

Enjoy the end result of all that milking with the season's favorite dairy treats—gourmet hot chocolate or some decadent ice cream.

On the ninth day of Christmas my true love gave to me nine ladies dancing.

The nine ladies symbolize the fruits of the Spirit as listed in Galatians.

here's how...

1 Look for a wire mesh ballet slipper at a crafts store or a florist's supply shop. Spray the shoe with metallic chrome paint and let it dry. Glue a scrap of ribbon

On the tenth day of Christmas my true love gave to me 10 lords a-leaping.

In the Middle Ages, lords could, to some extent, define the law within their own lands. So the 10 lords are the Ten Commandments.

here's how...

1 For a more playful interpretation of this verse, decorate a small oval cardboard box with frog stickers. You'll find all of the supplies at a crafts store.

2 Glue a pink plastic jewel to the center of the box lid; slip small silver beads onto a length of thread with a beading needle to make a chain that fits around the jewel. Cover the sides of the box and lid with ribbon and trim the edge of the lid with silver cord.

activities

Have a family game day. Along with jumping, running, and relay races, include non-traditional sports such as Frisbee tossing, pillow throwing, thumb wrestling, whistling, or finger snapping. Be sure every family member has one category he or she is sure to win. The sillier the categories, the better.

On the eleventh day of Christmas my true love gave to me 11 *pipers piping.*

The pipers are the eleven disciples who remained faithful.

here's how...

For this gift wrap, look through clip-art books for an image of a piper, or use a scrap of toile. To add color, you can have the image enlarged and copied in red onto green paper at a copy center. Cover the box as directed under General Box Wrapping Instructions (page 74) and tie with satin ribbon. Trim the number label to the desired size and glue in place.

activities

Decorate a cake or cookies with piped frosting. To save time and make it easy, use canned frosting and a plain purchased cake or cookies. If you don't have a pastry bag and tips, look for frosting in a tube; it comes in different colors with plastic screw-on tips.

On the twelfth day of Christmas my true love gave to me 12 drummers drumming.

Drummers establish the rhythm for marching. They symbolize the 12 doctrines listed in the Apostles' Creed, an ancient summary of Christian beliefs.

here's how...

1 Start with a frosting can or other round can with a lid. Cut gold foil cardboard to the height and circumference of the can, adding ½ inch at one end for overlap. Glue the cardboard around the can. Trace the lid onto brown paper and cut it out, adding ¼ inch all around. Glue the paper to the lid, then clip the excess to the lid edge; fold it over the sides of the lid and glue.

2 Glue trims around the can and lid edge as desired. Place the lid on the can. Glue metallic gold braid to the drum for the strap and cover the raw ends with gold buttons. Cut two chopsticks or wooden skewers to 5 inches and glue them to the top of the drum. Trim the number label to the desired size; clip the ends in points and glue in place.

activities

Form an instant kitchen band with oatmeal boxes and cooking pans for drums, empty bottles for wind instruments, pan lids for cymbals, jars half-filled with dried beans or unpopped popcorn (for shaking), and glassware for bells or xylophones.

Do you insist on a freshly cut tree each year or prefer an artificial one? Whichever your choice, the following pages contain dozens of decorating ideas for this centerpiece of your home during the holidays. Whether trimmed in gilded pears, ball ornaments you've made yourself, cotton strewn to resemble snow, or nature's own beauty of pinecones and leaves, each tree has a statement to make. You'll also find inspired ideas for dressing up and making your own wreaths for both indoors and outdoors.

TREES *and*

WREATHS

It's the centerpiece of every holiday home, but you don't need to limit yourself to just one. Themed or specialty trees give a lift to every room in your house.

O christmas *tree!*

Tabletop Tree

❧ If you don't have room for a floor-to-ceiling tree, try a short, fat tabletop tree instead. The one shown here has been nailed to a thick slice of wood for a natural base. Grapevines make a freeform garland that wraps randomly through the branches. Blown-glass pinecone ornaments accompany real pinecones dipped in white paint. For instructions on how to turn inexpensive red glass balls into snow-dipped ornaments, see *page 84*. (To create a clothesline for drying the ornaments, tie a length of jute between two sturdy supports, making sure the line is taut.)

keeping your tree fresh

■ When you bring your tree home, cut about ¼ inch off the bottom of the trunk, cutting on the diagonal to expose a larger area to absorb water. Place the trunk in a bucket of water in a garage or basement where it will be protected from freezing temperatures.

■ When you're ready to set up the tree, cut another ¼ inch off the bottom, making a straight cut this time so the tree will be stable in the stand. Check the water reservoir daily—a 6-foot-tall tree can drink up to a gallon of water in the first 24 hours and 2 quarts of water a day thereafter.

SHOPPING LIST

white crafts paint or latex
    interior paint
waxed paper or paper plate
sea sponge
scrap paper
red glass-ball ornaments
jute string

family traditions

F or as long as I can remember, my family has celebrated St. Nicholas Day, December 6. We hang our stockings for that day rather than for Christmas, as was the custom in Germany, the home of my ancestors. My husband and I have continued the tradition with our children and now our grandchild. It's like having a bit of Christmas early, and I sometimes think they enjoy those stocking presents and the early celebration more than the "big day."

— *Marilyn Schmidt*
Kennebunkport, Maine

84

Snow-Dipped Ornaments

here's how...

1 Pour a small amount of white paint onto a piece of waxed paper or a paper plate.

2 Dip a dampened sea sponge into the paint, then pat it on a piece of scrap paper to remove the excess paint. Pat the sponge onto an ornament, being careful not to cover the ball entirely. Tie a length of jute between two supports and hang the ball to dry.

3 For a solid-snow effect, submerge the bottom half of an ornament in the paint, holding the ball at an angle. Let the excess paint drip back into the can. Hang the ornament to dry.

Blanket of Snow

To create a convincing effect of thick snow *(below)*, lay lengths of rolled cotton along the branches. Sprinkle crystal snow over the cotton.

85

The Well-Dressed Tree

Straw hats and kid gloves dress this tree *(above)*. You don't need a whole hat collection to adapt the idea—two or three strategically placed bonnets will do the trick. The same holds true for the gloves. Add ribbon streamers and clusters of dried hydrangeas to evoke a garden-party feeling.

Tea for Two

Almost anything is fair game when it comes to creating a themed tree. If you have a collection of mismatched tea cups and spoons, tie them to the branches with ribbons. You can even glue cups to their saucers with dots of hot glue (the cups can be gently pried from the saucers and the glue popped off after the holidays). Check specialty Christmas shops for ornaments in the shape of cakes and petits fours. For a Victorian accent, weave lengths of lace among the branches.

Hydrangea Bouquets

❧ To suggest the effect of snow, nestle clusters of dried hydrangea on your tree branches. For a garland, swag lengths of gold drapery cording in asymmetrical loops and weave gold-mesh wire-edge ribbon among the branches. Pinch and crimp the ribbon so it traces an interesting, meandering line through the boughs.

Country Inspiration

❧ Add contrasting texture and color to your tree by inserting broad-leaf evergreens among the boughs. In mild-winter areas, collect magnolia, elacagnus, mahonia, or nandina from your yard to soften the look of an artificial tree. On a fresh, less-than-perfect specimen, these branches effectively fill holes and help balance the shape. If you don't have access to broad-leaf evergreens, purchase salal or eucalyptus from a florist or collect branchlets of dried oak leaves or beech leaves and spray them gold, copper, and silver.

To duplicate the oversize red mittens, start with plain red oven mitts. Stitch or glue wide ribbon at the opening to make a cuff. Attach a Santa ornament and a bow.

Collect miniature bottles, such as antique or reproduction medicine bottles or recycled flavoring bottles. Partially fill them with water. Tie narrow ribbon tightly around the neck. Slip floral wire under the ribbon, and wire the bottle to the tree. Insert one or two stems of fresh flowers. Use a small funnel to add water every other day.

In a Twinkling:
Tree Trims

◄ **String together** dried orange slices using raffia and a large-eye tapestry needle. To dry your own oranges, cut slices ¼ inch thick and place them on a baking sheet in an oven set to 200° for 6 to 10 hours; or use a food dehydrator according to the manufacturer's instructions.

▲ Look for old wooden spools of silk buttonhole-twist thread or buy wooden spools at a crafts store and wrap colorful thread around them. Sandwich each spool between sm wooden car wheels and wooden beads from a crafts store, then thre the hanging cord of a purchased tassel through the beads, wheels, and spool.

◄ Check flea markets and antiques shops for chandelier crystals. Thread a wire through the crystal's hanging wire if necessary, and twist it to make a loop. Use ribbon to tie the loop to the tree branch.

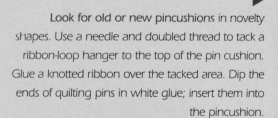

▶

Look for old or new pincushions in novelty shapes. Use a needle and doubled thread to tack a ribbon-loop hanger to the top of the pin cushion. Glue a knotted ribbon over the tacked area. Dip the ends of quilting pins in white glue; insert them into the pincushion.

◄ Show off collectible spoons by tying them with bows and wiring them to the tree. To avoid scratching the spoons, use green cotton-covered florist's wire, available from floral supply shops or crafts stores.

If the job of lighting the Christmas tree makes you reach for the aspirin bottle, here's help. Bob Pranga and Debi Staron, the professional tree-decorating team known as Dr. Christmas, show you how to light your tree efficiently and beautifully—and with many fewer headaches.

lighting
made
easier

ᘓ Creating a magical glow of lights on an artificial tree isn't difficult, but it demands patience; on a fresh tree, it calls for both patience and a trick of the trade described on *page 92*.

Bob Pranga developed his lighting and decorating techniques while he was working as a designer in a Christmas shop in New York City. His talents were so much in demand that he gave up aspirations of becoming an actor and devoted himself fulltime to developing a professional holiday decorating and consulting service. One customer dubbed him Dr. Christmas because of the 24-hour emergency service and house calls he provided, and the name

stuck. After several years, Debi Staron joined him, and they moved the business to California, where they've become known as "tree stylists to the stars." The duo has produced a series of informative videos on buying, lighting, and decorating fresh and artificial trees (for ordering information, call 310/854-0886).

91

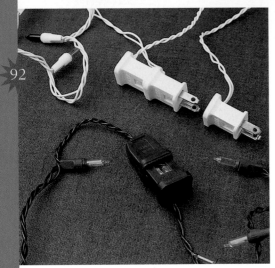

■ *Lighting a fresh tree: We used an artificial tree and lights on a white cord so you can see clearly how the cords weave back and forth in a triangular shape.*

timely tips

■ For safety's sake, never plug more than two extension cords together. Instead, buy them in the lengths you need and make sure they can handle the wattage of the bulbs.

■ Make sure the wattages of all the lights you use are the same; this prevents power surges and prolongs the life of the bulbs.

■ Plug in the lights before you remove them from the box so you can see whether they work before you put them on the tree.

■ Consider using miniature clear (white) lights for your base lighting, then add strands of the new cool-burning large bulbs for color and variety. Or, add sets of novelty lights, such as flicker-flames, flashing lights, bubble lights, or other shapes.

plug it in

Christmas tree lights are either stacked (the white plugs *above*) or end to end, also called string to string (the green plugs *above*). Check the boxes of lights before you buy to make sure they're all compatible. Bob and Debi recommend stacked plugs because you can join more strands than you can with end-to-end type plugs. Be sure to check the box for the manufacturer's recommendations, however. Usually you can string together three 100-light strands or six 50-light strands.

how many lights?

For a fresh tree, plan for three 100-light sets per tree foot.

For an artificial tree, Dr. Christmas recommends using 50-light strands: the 100-light strands are two 50-light strands wired together, and the 50-light strands are easier to work with as you wrap the tree branches. In addition, the 50-light sets are less likely to burn out or have electrical problems. For subdued lighting, use about 12 boxes for a 6-foot tree and about 20 boxes for an 8-foot tree. For moderate lighting, use 20 boxes for a 6-foot tree and 30 boxes for an 8-foot tree. For showcase lighting, use 40 boxes and 80 boxes, respectively.

lighting a fresh tree

Instead of wrapping the lights around the tree in a maypole dance, Bob and Debi suggest that you mentally divide the tree into three triangular sections.

Plug in the first string of lights and nestle the last bulb on the string at the top of the tree next to the trunk. Weave the lights back and forth across the triangle, being careful not to cross the cord over itself. When you reach the end of the first string, plug in the next set and continue weaving the lights back and forth until you reach the bottom, connecting no more than 300 lights end to end. Repeat this procedure for the remaining triangles.

Step back from the tree and look at it with your eyes crossed. Wherever you see dark holes on the tree, rearrange the lights as necessary to fill in. To remove the lights without getting them tangled, simply work in reverse.

lighting an artificial tree

The artificial trees available today come in sections that open like an umbrella. If you use miniature lights, you can wrap them around the branches and leave them on permanently. Just be sure to light each section separately (that is, don't cross a section or point of assembly with a strand of lights).

FOR SUBDUED LIGHTING, begin at the bottom of the tree close to the trunk. Allowing some slack or leader cord in the first strand of lights, separate the cord near the first bulb so it forms a loop. Slip the loop over one of the branchlets or greens near the trunk, and wrap the cord a few times around the green to secure it (see Photo 1). Pull the string of lights taut to the tip of the branch, then work back toward the trunk, wrapping the cord over itself and the branch (see Photo 2). Separate the cord again when you reach the trunk, and slip the cord over a branchlet to secure it. Carry the cord over to the

next branch, wrap it around a green near the trunk, and pull it out to the tip. Wrap the cord over itself and the branch as before. Continue wrapping branches in this manner to the end of the string. Plug in the next set, and keep going to the point where the tree comes apart. Work any extra lights back along the branch rather than crossing the section. When you wrap the top section of the tree, don't wrap the lights around as many branches, so the tree will look evenly lit from top to bottom.

FOR MODERATE LIGHTING, follow the same procedure, but wrap the cord around some of the greens along the branch as you work back toward the trunk (see Photo 3).

FOR SHOWCASE LIGHTING, wrap the cord around every green as you work back along the branch.

outdoor lights

■ If you floodlight evergreens outdoors, use white, blue, or green lamps; red, yellow, amber, and pink lamps will make the trees look a muddy brown.

■ Don't try to hang strings of lights from the eaves with cuphooks—in a strong wind, the wires may swing loose. Instead, use plastic gutter clips that hook onto the gutter and hold the wire tightly in place. Look for packages of gutter clips in crafts stores and hardware stores with the tree lights and supplies.

■ Be sure you have outdoor electrical sockets to plug into when you use outdoor lights.

■ Don't worry about hiding the electrical cords—just keep them organized neatly, and no one will notice them.

93

here's how...

1

Slip the loop over one of the branchlets or greens near the trunk to secure it.

2

Pull the string of lights out to the tip of the branch, then wrap the cord around itself and the branch as you work back toward the trunk.

3

For moderate lighting, wrap the cord around some of the greens along the branch as you work back toward the trunk. For showcase lighting, wrap the cord around every green.

Let your tree reflect your decorating style—elegant, natural, or homespun.

trio of *trees*

Winter White

For a lush, glittering look, choose five or six basic types of ornaments and collect several boxes of each. Here, the wardrobe includes gold, silver, and white balls in different sizes, snowflakes, twiggy silver stars, white pinecones, silver reindeer, and silver pendants. With an array like this, you'll have variety for an interesting tree with enough repetition to create a unified look. Put on the lights first, then distribute each type of ornament evenly, tucking some deep into the tree and hanging others at the branch tips. Add a few specialty ornaments in the same color scheme, and tuck sprigs of holly among the branches for contrasting texture. For the finishing touch, drape a beaded garland around the tree in even swags.

To warm up the silver-and-white combination, add fresh greenery and gilded pears. Use spray paint or metal leaf (from a crafts store) to gild fresh or artificial pears. For a softer gold, brush the gilded pear with brown acrylic paint, quickly wiping off most of the paint to tone down the color but not cover it. (Fresh pears aren't suitable for eating after they've been gilded.)

leafy tree skirt

❧ Cut a circle of the desired diameter from plum-color quilted fabric. Use a real leaf to make a pattern for the fabric leaves, then cut enough leaves from celery-green felt to ring the edge of the skirt. Use fabric glue to secure the leaves, overlapping them as shown and allowing half of the shape to extend beyond the skirt's edge.

97

Naturally Yours

❧ Take your cue from the garden for decorations. Shop crafts stores for small decorative birdhouses and bird nests, twig stars, and pepperberries to hang on the branches. To make a fluffy garland, wire broadleaf evergreens or florist's greenery such as eucalyptus, ruscus, or smilax to jute twine, using paddle wire. Drape the garland on the branches like a feather boa. Topiaries on the mantel reinforce the garden theme.

Fresh & Simple

For a clean, pared-down, yet homespun look, choose just a few types of ornaments with simple shapes. Make sure one group is large enough to provide emphasis, like the handmade burlap stars here. Give large ornaments room to hang by choosing a tree with short needles and sturdy, well-separated branches. Noble fir or spruces are best for this kind of display.

SHOPPING LIST

two 8-inch squares of burlap
   in ivory or tan
6-inch length of jute
matching thread
polyester fiberfill
pinking shears

burlap puffy star

here's how...

1 Draw a star that measures 6 inches from tip to tip. Cut out the pattern and transfer it to one burlap square.

2 With wrong sides facing and the ends of the 6-inch length of jute inserted at the top of the star, stitch the burlap squares together along the pattern outline, leaving an opening for stuffing.

3 Stuff the star lightly with fiberfill and stitch the opening closed. Use pinking shears to trim the fabric to within ¼ inch of the seam lines, being careful not to cut the hanger.

98

ball ornaments

here's how...

1 To make the white, paper-wrapped balls, cut a square of tissue paper about 5 inches larger than a ball's diameter. Center the ball on the paper. Wrap the paper around the ball, twisting both ends like a candy wrapper.

Trim the excess paper just above the twist. Secure the twisted paper with pins.

Wrap jute around the balls as desired, securing it with plain or white-headed pins. Pin a loop hanger at the top.

4 To make the twine-covered balls, spread glue in a 1½-inch circle on a plastic foam ball. Pin the end of the jute twine at the center of the circle, then coil the jute around the center. Continue gluing and coiling until you've covered the ball. To make stripes, alternate between jute and cotton twine. Hold the ends of the twine in place with plain straight pins until the glue is nearly dry, then remove the pins. Attach a loop for hanging at the top.

99

▶ Bright red cranberry balls start with 3-inch-diameter plastic foam balls from a crafts store. Paint them with red acrylic crafts paint, then glue a loop of ribbon to each ball for a hanger. Use a hot-glue gun to attach fresh cranberries to the plastic foam balls. (For a longer-lasting ornament, use red wooden beads instead of cranberries.)

In a Twinkling:
Ornaments

◀ Turn a marble collection into ornaments with mechanic's wire from a hardware store. Use 16-gauge wire for large marbles and 18-gauge for small ones. Wrap a 12-inch length of wire around a large marking pen to make a cradle for the marble. Twist the wire into smaller coils above and below the cradle and bend one end of the wire to make a hook for hanging. Push the marble into the cradle and shape the wire as necessary to hold the marble securely in place.

◀ Jingle all the way with a large sleigh bell ornament dressed up with red canella berries and evergreen sprigs. Wire the berries (available at crafts stores) to the greenery, then wire the bouquet to the hanging loop of the bell. Use narrow ribbon to tie the bell to the tree or to a doorknob.

▼ Holiday ornaments in rich jewel tones become one-of-a-kind originals when touched with gold. To create gilded designs, use a permanent metallic gold marking pen to make swirls, squiggles, or other decorative marks. Sign your work of art with a fine-line marking pen.

▲ Look for miniature pails in crafts stores. Tuck in kumquats and a sprig of red berries for a quick handmade ornament.

No space for a Christmas tree? Make a tabletop tree from a live rosemary plant or from cut greenery and flowers.

wee trees

Rosemary Topiary

This delightfully fragrant alternative to a conifer is the perfect size for a small apartment.

here's how...

1 Prune the rosemary plant into a cone shape.

2 Wrap sheet moss around the container, covering it from top to bottom. Hold the moss in place with a large, heavy-duty rubber band.

3 Cut twigs 2 or 3 inches taller than the container. Slip the twigs under the rubber band, spacing them evenly.

4 Tie raffia tightly around the bottom of the twigs, then slip off the rubber band. Tie the twigs near the top with another piece of raffia.

5 Weave miniature Christmas lights through the rosemary branches.

A Temporary Tree

Bring holiday cheer to a friend with a tree-shape arrangement.

here's how...

1 Stretch a rubber band around the pot. Slip pieces of bark under the rubber band, aligning the bottom of each piece with the bottom of the pot; the top of each piece should extend above the rim as shown. Wrap vines around the container over the rubber band; secure the ends with a twist of floral wire.

2 Tuck sheet moss between the pieces of bark. Fill the pot with floral foam, wedging one full block in the center to extend above the rim by an amount equal to the height of the container.

103

3 Assemble fresh flowers in bunches in water vials. Wire bunches of holly berries to florist's picks and wrap wire around the pinecones.

4 Cover the sides and top of the floral foam with sheet moss. Place a 12-inch-long branch of juniper in the center of the floral foam. Insert additional shorter branches into the sides of the foam to create a cone-shape tree. Let some of the lower branches extend below the sides of the container. Insert the ivy, holly berries, pinecones, and water vials of fresh flowers, spacing them randomly around the tree. Place the materials so they radiate out from the trunk, following the lines of the evergreen branches.

Gather the gifts of the forest to decorate your home. Leaves, pinecones, twigs, and bark bring nature's textures indoors to warm your rooms with elegant simplicity.

decorations *from nature*

 To make the decorations shown on the following pages, collect most of the natural materials from your own yard. Rather than collect moss from the woods, however, buy packages of sheet moss, sphagnum moss, or Spanish moss from crafts stores or floral supply shops. These commercially available products are free of insects and dry enough to accept glue; and, you won't be damaging natural stands that can be slow-growing and difficult to replenish.

moss balls

here's how...

Coat plastic foam balls from a crafts store with thick white crafts glue and press sheet moss or sphagnum moss firmly into the glue. Hold the moss in place with toothpicks until the glue dries. Repeat this procedure to cover the ball entirely with moss. Wrap the ball with fine gold cord as if you were winding a ball of yarn, securing the ends with dressmaker's pins.

From a crafts store:
   miniature basket
   hot-glue gun and glue
     sticks
   floral foam (optional)
   sheet moss
   raffia
   white spray paint
   narrow red satin ribbon
   rubber bands
From your yard:
   holly sprigs
   laurel leaves or
     other broad-leaf
     evergreens, such
     as pittosporum,
     photinia, or bay (also
     available from a florist)
   ¾-inch-thick branch
   large pinecone
   dried leaves and shelf
     fungus
From a florist's shop:
   florist's water vial
   fresh rose

Natural Tree Trims

Highlight your tree with baskets, bouquets, and pendants of nature's materials.

To get the most impact from these ornaments, make 5 to 10 of each and distribute them evenly over the tree. Enhance the theme with other items you may have on hand—oyster shells, moss balls, and pieces of driftwood add interest with a variety of shapes and textures. To unify the various items, use red ribbon to tie the ornaments to the tree. Add clear glass balls to catch the light and lend sparkling textural contrast to the natural materials.

family traditions

When my two sisters and I were in our teens, my family began a tradition of having an indoor picnic on Christmas Eve instead of a big dinner. This was especially fun since we were living in the Midwest and were usually surrounded by snow and ice. We'd get special kosher hot dogs, potato salad, and all the picnic accoutrements; cook the hot dogs in the fireplace; and eat while sitting on a blanket. We'd end a comfortable, casual evening by going to the candlelight service.

— *Ruth A. Baldrige*
Charlotte, North Carolina

rose basket

Attach sprigs of holly to the edges of a miniature basket with hot glue. Or, glue a small piece of floral foam into the basket and insert the holly stems into it. Clip the stem of the rose to about 3 inches. Fill the florist's water vial with water, replace the rubber cap, and insert the rose stem through the hole in the cap. Place the rose in the basket—the weight of the vial should hold it in position. Fill the basket with a pad of sheet moss to hide the vial.

laurel leaf bouquet

Spray fresh laurel leaves (or other broad-leaf evergreen leaves as suggested in the Shopping List on *page 106*) with white spray paint. Bundle several stems together with a rubber band, then wrap narrow red satin ribbon over the rubber band. Tie the ribbon in a knot; cut the ends to the desired length, and knot them to form the hanging loop.

timesaving tip

■ If you don't have much time to decorate, concentrate your efforts in two areas—the one that guests see first and the one where you spend the most time. If you have an entry foyer, create a tabletop display. If the staircase is the first thing guests see when they come in, swag it with garland and decorate the newel post.

pinecone pendant

Use garden loppers to cut a ¾ inch-thick branch into a 4- or 5-inch-long section. Randomly tuck pieces of moss under the scales of a large pinecone and work a piece of raffia under the scales around the bottom of the cone. Knot the raffia to secure it, then tie the raffia ends around the branch and knot the ends to form a 3- or 4-inch-long hanging loop. Use a hot-glue gun to attach dried leaves, shelf fungus, or other embellishments to the pinecone.

Make a few of these for your own home, or craft a whole collection so you'll have some to keep and some to share.

ornaments
on display

Christmas ornaments don't just hang on the tree anymore. Tie them into wreaths and garlands, pile them in bowls, or perch them on candlesticks for a festive display. Use the whimsical wire Christmas tree as a package topper, or make several trees to hang from a café curtain rod in front of a window.

Spicy Stars

here's how...

1 Thin the crafts glue with water to the consistency of cream. Using the paintbrush, cover the stars with the glue.

2 While the glue is still wet, press the stars into pepper berries or star anise.

3 Glue additional pepper berries or star anise to the star shapes where needed.

4 Trim stars with gold cord, if desired.

Spice-Covered Spheres

here's how...

1 Cover the plastic-foam balls with masking tape.

2 Thin the crafts glue with water to the consistency of cream. Using the paintbrush, cover the taped surface with the glue.

3 While the glue is still wet, roll the ball in star anise, cinnamon pieces, whole cloves, and orange and lemon peel.

4 Trim the spheres with ribbon, if desired.

SHOPPING LIST:
glass Christmas
balls
paper towel
gift wrap
From a crafts store:
star paper punch
thick crafts glue
Delta Ceramcoat
Fine Crackle
Finish
acrylic crafts
paints: gold,
silver
paintbrush

Beaded-Wire Tree

here's how...

1 Englarge the pattern *below* 200 to 225 percent on a copier. Transfer the pattern to the scrap of wood using graphite paper and a stylus or ballpoint pen.

2 Hammer nails into the wood, part way, at the points indicated on the pattern.

SHOPPING LIST:
scrap of wood
 (at least 4x5 inches)
graphite paper and a
 stylus (from an art-supply
 store) or ballpoint pen
hammer and nails
 (7 for each ornament)
silver wire: 20- and 24-gauge
wire clippers
assorted glass beads
embroidery floss for
 a hanger

3 Wrap the 20-gauge wire around the nails four times to outline the tree shape.

4 Carefully remove the nails from the wood and the ornament, then wrap the cut wire ends around the tree form to secure it.

5 Wrap the 24-gauge wire around and across the tree shape, randomly adding glass beads. Crimp the wire to hold the beads in place. Wrap the wire ends around the tree form to secure them.

6 To hang the ornament, thread an 8-inch length of embroidery floss through the top of the ornament and knot the ends together.

Nail Placements

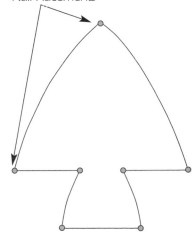

Crackled Christmas Balls

here's how...

1 Wash and dry the Christmas balls.

2 Use the paper punch to punch stars from the gift wrap. Randomly glue the paper stars to the balls.

3 Following the manufacturer's instructions, brush crackle medium over each ball. To let the balls dry, hang them on a folding

wooden clothes-drying rack or a clothesline stretched taut; place newspapers underneath to catch any drips. Use ornament hangers to suspend the balls.

4 After the crackle medium dries, dip the paper towel in the gold and silver paints and dab or swirl them over the ball. If desired, wipe off the excess paint, leaving paint only in the cracks. Let the paint dry.

Hang these ornaments on
your tree—or from a chandelier
or windows—for festive sparkle.

tree jewelry

110

Confetti
Ornaments

here's how...

1 Cut the metallic braid into nine
1-yard lengths. Thread the needle with
one length of braid and knot one end.
Thread 8 to 10 inches with beads.
Remove the needle, knot the other end of
the braid, and push half of the beads
toward each end of the braid. Repeat for
the remaining eight lengths of the braid.

2 Pin together three beaded braids,
keeping half of the beads at each end.
Plait the braids together between the
beaded ends. Knot just above the beads.
Repeat for each group of three braids.

3 Enlarge the patterns on page 113 at
240 percent on a photocopier. Cut out.

4 Cut six 6-inch squares of vinyl. Place
about 1 tablespoon of confetti in the
center of one square. Place the second
square of vinyl on top of the first,
sandwiching the confetti in between.

5 Center a paper pattern under the
vinyl sandwich. Use adhesive tape to hold
the pattern in place.

6 Thread a sewing machine with
metallic sewing thread both on top and
in the bobbin. Place the vinyl sandwich,
paper side down, under the presser foot.
Using the paper pattern as a guide, stitch
¼ inch in from the paper edge through
the vinyl and the paper. Remove the
ornament from the sewing machine. Cut
around the edges of the paper pattern
with pinking shears and carefully tear the
paper away from the stitching.

7 Use a hole punch to make a hole in
the top and bottom of the ornament.
Fold the beaded braid in half. Thread it
through the bottom punched hole and
knot it about 3 inches from the fold.
Thread the folded end through the top
punched hole to serve as the hanger.

20 feet of 22-gauge round
   nickel wire (or use 22-
   gauge copper or
   brass wire)
needle-nose pliers
½-inch diameter dowel
4½x6-inch sheet of
   white cotton linter for
   making paper (from a
   crafts store)
blender
container that is wide and
   deep enough to
   submerge the wire
   ornament
silver glitter fabric paint
   and/or clear spray acrylic
   varnish (optional)
18 inches of 1½-inch-wide
   silver sheer wire ribbon
1 yard of ⅜-inch wide
   silver wire ribbon

Curly Wire Christmas Ball

here's how...

1 To make the hanging loop, begin about 2 inches from one end of the length of wire, and wrap the wire around the dowel. Use the needle-nose pliers to twist the wire to make a loop. Remove the loop from the dowel.

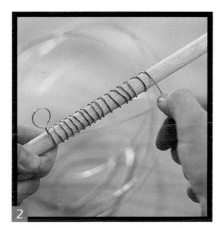

2

Place the loop at the left end of the dowel and just above the dowel. Wrap the wire tightly around the dowel. Remove the coiled wire and stretch the coil into a 1-yard length.

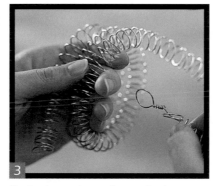

3

Beginning at the end opposite the hanging loop, wrap the coil around your hand as if you were wrapping ribbon to make a bow. Remove the wrapped wire and pull the hanging loop through the middle. Shape the wire until you have a nice ball shape.

4 To frost the wire ball, tear the cotton linter into 1-inch pieces. Place half of the torn linter in your blender and fill the blender with water. Blend on high for about two minutes, using short bursts to keep the blender from overheating, until the mixture is smooth and creamy.

5 Pour the pulp into the container. Clean the blender thoroughly, but don't pour any excess pulp down the drain. Instead, pour it outside in the garden, where it can decompose.

6 Stir the water to bring the paper pulp to the top. Holding the ornament by the loop, dip it into the paper pulp, then hang the ornament over a protected surface to let it dry. For a thicker coat of paper, repeat the dipping and drying.

7 If desired, lightly brush the ornament with fabric glitter paint and spray with clear acrylic varnish.

8 Fold 18 inches of the 1½-inch-wide ribbon in half. From 24 inches of the ⅜-inch-wide ribbon, make a bow. Center the folded ribbon behind the hanging loop and position the bow over the base of the hanging loop. Tie the ribbon and the bow to the base of the hanging loop, using the remaining ⅜-inch-wide ribbon.

ornament patterns

for Confetti Ornaments, page 110

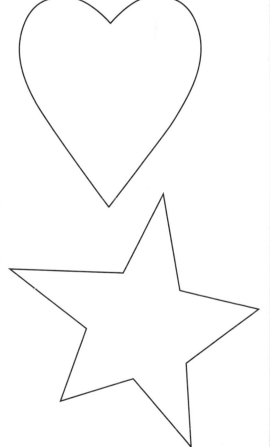

ENLARGE
PATTERNS
240%

Beaded-Wire Ornaments

reindeer

here's how...

1 Cut a 26-inch length of beading wire. Wrap one end around a toothpick to make a tiny loop (this keeps the beads from falling off the wire).

2 String beads onto the wire to within about ¾ inch of the end.

3 Using the photo as a pattern, start with the front antler and bend the beaded wire to outline the deer shape. Twist at the tail and legs to define these parts of the shape. Twist the antlers around each other to hold them in place at the top of the head.

4 Hang with a length of gold cord.

celtic knot

here's how...

1 Cut a 27-inch length of #28 gauge wire. Wrap one end around a toothpick to make a tiny loop for the knot.

2 String red and orange beads onto the wire, changing colors randomly.

SHOPPING LIST

From a crafts store or bead-
  supply shop:
FOR REINDEER:
 #28 gauge silver
  beading wire
 Style 140 gold Rochaille beads
 gold thread or cord

FOR CELTIC KNOT:
 #28 gauge silver
  beading wire
 Style 140 Rochaille beads
  in red and orange
 #34 gauge silver
  beading wire
 gold thread or cord

3 Twist the wire ends together, then fold the loop in half and twist to form one twisted length of beads.

4 Using a small piece of wire, join the ends of the twisted length to form a circle.

5 Using the photo as a pattern, bend and shape the beaded circle to make the knot. Use #34 gauge wire to tie the overlaps together.

6 Hang with a length of gold cord.

Extend a cheerful holiday welcome with a wreath that reflects your own personal style. Outdoor wreaths should be sturdy and weighty looking. Indoors, they can be more delicate.

wreaths to *welcome* the season

114

Making the full traditional style of wreaths shown on these pages is easy if you begin with a purchased grapevine base and glue or wire clusters of leaves to it. For an even faster alternative, use a fresh or artificial fir wreath as a base and insert lemon leaves from the florist or magnolia from your yard for contrasting texture. To make lightweight wreaths to hang indoors, try the holly and ivy wreath or the kumquat ring on *page 117*; both start with a metal ring such as you'd use for macramé.

Citrus Wreath
here's how...

1 Clip the lemon leaves into 8- to 10-inch-long branches. Push the branches into the grapevine wreath, working around the wreath so all the stem ends point in the same direction.

2 Wrap floral wire around the lower scales of each pinecone, twisting the wire ends together to form a tail.

3 To wire the oranges and kumquats, push a piece of floral wire through the fruit near one end. Bring the wire ends together and twist them tightly close to the fruit. Don't clip the wires. Gather the kumquats into bunches of five and twist their wires together.

4 Refer to the photo *above left* for guidance and attach the pinecones, oranges, and kumquat clusters. Twist the wires tightly around the vines on the back of the wreath.

5 Glue the orange slices and cinnamon sticks in place. Cut long orange-peel curls from the remaining oranges and drape them as shown.

Magnolia Wreath

here's how...

1 Wire clusters of magnolia leaves to the grapevine wreath, working counterclockwise and pointing all the stem ends in the same direction. Pack the clusters tightly so the wreath looks very full.

2 Secure the clemantines, pomegranates, and apples on floral wire by pushing a piece of wire through the fruit from side to side. Twist the wire ends together tightly at the base of the fruit, leaving the wires long to form a tail. Refer to the photo for placement and position the fruits on the wreath, nestling them down into the magnolia leaves. Push the wire tail through to the back of the wreath and twist it around the grapevine. Cut off excess wire flush with the back of the wreath.

3 Attach the kumquats and nuts to the wreath with hotmelt adhesive.

4 To make a hanging loop, fold a piece of floral wire in half and wrap it tightly around the vines at the back of the wreath.

115

SHOPPING LIST:

From a crafts store:
  medium-weight
    floral wire
  24-inch-diameter
    grapevine wreath (or
    smaller, if desired)
  hot-glue gun and
    glue sticks
From your yard:
  clusters of fresh
    magnolia leaves
From a grocer:
  fresh fruits such as
    kumquats, clemantines
    (a tangerinelike fruit),
    pomegranates, apples
  mixed in-shell nuts

SHOPPING LIST:

From a crafts store:
lightweight floral wire
green wooden
florist's picks
10-inch diameter
grapevine wreath
hot-glue gun and
glue sticks
plastic purple grapes
artificial limes
From a florist:
branches of fresh bay
or bay laurel

116

Bay Leaves and Limes

here's how...

1
Cut the bay into short sprigs and attach each sprig to a wooden pick with floral wire.

2
Insert the picks into the grapevine wreath, securing them with hotmelt adhesive. Work in one direction until the grapevine is completely covered.

3
Referring to the photo for guidance, glue the plastic grapes and artificial limes to the wreath.

Kumquat Ring

here's how...

1 Cut the branches of leaves into sprigs about 3 to 4 inches long. Lay one sprig along the outside of the brass ring and wire it to the ring, wrapping the wire along the lower inch of the stem. Do not cut the wire.

2 Lay a second sprig over the stem end of the first, covering the wired portion. Wrap the wire down around the stem to secure it to the ring. Continue wiring sprigs in this manner until the brass ring is covered. Hide the stem of the last sprig under the top of the first sprig.

3 Cut a length of wire to fit around the brass ring plus 6 inches. Thread the needle with the wire, then pierce a kumquat with the needle, going through the middle of the fruit from side to side (rather than from blossom end to stem end). Thread the kumquats onto the wire until you have enough to cover the ring. Wrap the wire ends together and cut off the excess.

Attach the kumquat necklace to the leaf-covered brass ring with additional wire, carefully working it between the kumquats.

117

Holly and Ivy

here's how...

1 Wire the fresh ivy vines to the metal ring, arranging them to cover it completely. Let the vines at the bottom hang more loosely for a natural look.

2 To create a focal point, add extra vines around the bottom half of the ring. Allow some of the vines to extend across the opening toward the back of the wreath to give it visual depth.

3 Wire sprigs of holly berries at the bottom to make a bow.

► Screen your view of the outdoors with an indoor forest of skinny Christmas trees. Anchor the trees in wet sand in galvanized buckets, and add watering cans for a garden theme.

In a Twinkling:
Windows

◄ Frame the window from inside with miniature lights. Run a strand of lights along the sill and top of the sash, securing it with small pieces of masking tape. Suspend a lighted tree-topper ornament from the sash (or pop a specialty add-on ornament onto one of the miniature lights—see page 30 for more information). Hide the wires with greenery.

◀ Let it snow—indoors! Dress up a window with a lacy table skirt for a quick valance and hang paper snowflakes from the curtain rod with ribbon.

◀**Arrange red and green** bottles along the top of a window sash where they can catch the light and filter your view with Christmas color.

119

▲ Bring a view into focus with a lightweight wreath of artificial eucalyptus. Wire several stems together in a circle to make the wreath and hang it in front of the window with clear monofilament.

▲ Accent windows with swags of artificial eucalyptus and silk or dried red flowers. Bundle stems of eucalyptus, red twigs, dyed-red baby's breath, and bear grass into a small swag; assemble red yarrow into another smaller bouquet and wire it over the swag's stem ends. Tie a bow over the joining and bend one eucalyptus branch to form a hanger to hook over the curtain rod.

Give a garden-style theme to your outdoor decorations by incorporating hand tools, terra-cotta pots, and watering cans into wreaths, arrangements, and swags.

winter welcome

3

Use florist's wire to attach the trowel to one side of the wreath. Wire the narcissus bulb at an angle above the trowel, and cover the wire with a raffia bow.

Garden Wreath

Give a plain fresh wreath a garden-grown personality by using what you can find in your own tool shed—an old or new trowel, small terra-cotta pots, and a narcissus bulb that's already finished blooming are all you need to create a wreath with character. Use silvery gray and white herbs and berries for a snow-kissed look.

here's how...

1 Cut the artemisia stems into pieces that are slightly shorter than the longest evergreen branches in the wreath. Apply hot glue to the bottom portion of the artemisia stems and insert them into the evergreens. The stems should point in the same direction so the artemisia leads the eye clockwise around the wreath.

2

Glue bunches of Chinese tallow-tree berries (also called popcorn berries) into the wreath in the same way. Add preserved oak leaves and fresh rosemary for contrasting textures.

4

Wire the miniature flowerpots to the opposite half of the wreath. Wedge small green apples into two of the pots. If you use a pot with no hole, you can drill one using a masonry bit at slow speed.

122

Wheelbarrow Arrangement

Fill a wheelbarrow or wooden garden wagon with greenery, pinecones, and pots of fruit for a festive display in your yard or on your porch. Lay long branches of evergreens in the wheelbarrow so they spill over the front edge and extend out from the back. If possible, use several kinds of greenery for a variety of textures and shades of green. Here the homeowner combined western cedar, Douglas fir, red huckleberry, white pine, and variegated privet. Anchor the branches with terra-cotta pots nestled into the greenery, and fill the pots with apples or other fruits. Add large sugar pinecones, bundles of sticks or birch twigs, and an old watering can filled with evergreens for a focal point.

Pinecone Swag

✎ Pinecones and terra-cotta bells make a graceful, country-style swag for your porch or a lamppost.

here's how...

1 Using a ⁹⁄₆₄-inch drill bit, drill a hole in the base of each sugar pinecone. Insert one end of a 4-inch piece of wire into the hole, and secure it with a drop of hot glue. Twist the other end of the wire around itself to make a loop.

2 Cut the rope into 5-foot lengths, one for each cone. Thread one length of rope through the wire loop on each cone.

3 Cut the remaining rope into three pieces of varying lengths. Knot one end of each piece and thread the remaining end through the hole in the bottom of each terra-cotta pot.

4 Gather all the ropes in your hand and adjust them so the cones and pots hang at different lengths. Tie the ropes in a knot.

5 Wire evergreens to the ropes along the length of the swag.

123

Extend a cheerful holiday welcome with a wreath that reflects your personal style. Mix natural materials for a rustic look, or choose apples and plaid ribbon for traditional and country settings. For a touch of whimsy, use vegetables instead of fruit.

wreathed in *splendor*

ᘓ Start with a purchased fresh wreath—or use an artificial one and add sprigs of whatever live greenery is available. Just tuck the cut greens among the wired branches, bending and shaping the branches to hold the material in place. A third option (see *pages 126–127*) is to make your own fresh wreath, using a foam wreath form from a floral supply shop.

nature's wreath

here's how...

1 To make a wreath like the one shown on *page 81*, collect fallen pieces of birch bark or sycamore bark, twigs, cones, and shelf fungus from the woods or your yard. If you can't find shelf fungus, look for "shelf mushrooms" in the dried flower department of a crafts store. Each "mushroom," which is actually a fungus, is glued to a long wooden pick, which you can snip off with pruning shears.

2 Arrange the largest items in the bottom right quadrant of the wreath for a focal point. Use a hot-glue gun to attach the materials. Glue materials of similar size at the 9 o'clock position for visual balance. Add dried pomegranates (available in crafts stores) and dried apple slices around the front and inside edges of the wreath. Wire a red velvet bow to the top right quadrant.

apples and plaids

here's how...

1 To make the bow, cut the ribbon into two 42-inch pieces, two 24-inch pieces, and one 28-inch piece. Fold each of the 42-inch pieces to make three loops of graduated lengths, keeping the bottoms of the loops even. Cut a V-shape notch through all fabric layers at the bottom to eliminate some of the bulk, then wire the base of the loops to a floral pick (see the inset photo on *page 125*). Fold each of the 24-inch lengths to make a 6-inch loop with a 12-inch streamer and wire it to a floral pick. Fold the 28-inch piece in half to make a 2-inch loop with streamers and wire it to a floral pick.

2 Insert the triple loops on each side of the wreath's center top. Shape the loops to resemble a large bow nestled among the greenery. Insert the loops with streamers on each side of the center bow, and add the loop with two streamers at the center (this is the knot).

3 Glue magnolia leaves to the top half of the wreath. Wire the apples among the bow loops. Glue walnuts and pinecones to the front of the wreath as shown on *page 125*.

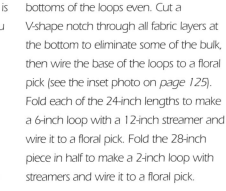

Save on ribbon and achieve the look of a full, fluffy bow with this technique. Fold ribbon to make one, two, or three loops. Notch the ribbon at the bottom of the loops to reduce bulk; wire the loops to wooden floral picks and insert.

SHOPPING LIST

FOR APPLES AND PLAIDS
purchased 24-inch-diameter
   fresh wreath
6-inch wooden floral picks
medium-gauge floral wire
4½ yards of
   2¼-inch-wide
   wire-edge ribbon
15 magnolia leaves (fresh,
   preserved, or silk)
8 pinecones
3 fresh or latex apples
8 to 10 walnuts
hot-glue gun and
   glue sticks

Harvest Home

Hang this wreath for Thanksgiving, then give it a Christmas accent with a big red bow.

The potatoes and onions will last at least a month, and the corn will dry in place. You may need to replace the carrots after about a week. It's easy to make repairs if critters find the vegetables irresistible: Just pull out the nibbled pieces and insert fresh ones on bamboo skewers.

SHOPPING LIST

24-inch wire-reinforced
    wreath form (available
    from a floral supply shop)
pruning shears or utility
    scissors
5- or 6-inch-long woven
    basket with handle
assorted fresh greenery
fresh vegetables: sweet
    corn, potatoes, onions,
    carrots
bamboo skewers or
    wooden floral picks
medium-gauge floral wire
pinecones
mixed nuts

here's how...

1

Use pruning shears or utility scissors to cut off the handle of the basket. Push the handle ends into the front of the wreath form at the top to make a perch for birds.

2

Use floral wire to attach the basket to the front of the wreath form at the bottom.

127

freshness counts

■ Check a wreath for freshness as you would a Christmas tree. Shake it gently to make sure it doesn't drop needles. Bend a branch tip between your fingers to see if the needles are firm but pliable, and give the wreath the sniff test—it should smell strongly fragrant.

■ Wreaths made from freshly cut evergreens should last up to a month (fir will last even longer). Since cool temperatures and high humidity help keep the greenery in good condition, outdoor locations are perfect for displaying wreaths.

3

Cut the stem ends of fresh greenery at an angle to make a point. Starting at the top and working toward the bottom, insert the stem ends into one-half of the foam wreath base, making sure the stem ends all point in the same direction. Repeat to cover the other half.

4

Use bamboo skewers or wooden floral picks to attach the vegetables to the wreath, referring to the photo *opposite* for placement. Fill in around the vegetables with additional greenery and pinecones. Fill the basket with nuts.

GATHERI

From tasty beginnings to sweet endings, you'll find recipes on the following pages to mix and match for parties, family meals, and gift-giving. If you're planning a dinner party, use the buffet menu and planning guide to get started. Or celebrate the season by inviting over a small group of friends for a wine and cheese party. Our tips for decorating the table, roasting a turkey, and serving a crowd will help you create a dazzling setting for conversation, storytelling, and laughter.

NGtogether

130

Poppy Seed Flats
(see recipe, page 137)

There are few ways of entertaining that are simpler or more classic than a wine and cheese party. Just choose and present cheeses with a few accompaniments and open the wine.

cheese, *please*

Whether you're hosting a wine-and-cheese-tasting party for the holidays or serving a French-style after-dinner cheese course any time of year, it's important to choose the cheeses carefully. You'll want variety in terms of each cheese's texture, flavor, and milk source (the animal that contributed the milk to make it). For instance, although Stilton, Roquefort, and Maytag Blue come from different milk sources and have different texture and flavor qualities, they are all blue-veined cheeses—so you'll probably want to serve just one of them.

If you're going to serve a hard, piquant (sharp-tasting) cheese made from sheep's milk, be sure you serve a softer, sweeter—even spreadable—cow's milk cheese to complement it. In making your selections, consider not only the classic, centuries-old European cheeses, such as Italian Parmigiano-Reggiano and Dutch Gouda, but also some of the up-and-coming artisanal cheeses being made regionally in this country—many of which are flavored with herbs, whole black peppercorns, chiles, or wild mushrooms. One such cheese is a full-bodied, aged, dry Monterey Jack from California.

Generally, you'll want to serve between three and five cheeses for a

cheese	origin	milk source	texture	flavor
Manchego	Spain	Sheep	Firm	Mellow
Scamorza	Italy	Cow	Firm	Mildly smoky
Gruyère	Switzerland, France	Cow	Firm	Mild, nutty
Aged cheddar	U.S., England	Cow	Firm, crumbly	Sharp
Parmigiano-Reggiano	Italy	Cow	Hard	Nutty, tangy
Pecorino Romano	Italy	Sheep	Hard	Sharp, piquant
Dry Monterey Jack	California	Cow	Hard	Full-bodied, tangy
Aged Gouda (18 to 24 months)	Holland	Cow	Hard	Nutty, caramel
Stilton	England	Cow	Soft; slightly crumbly	Slightly assertive
Roquefort	France	Sheep	Creamy, rich	Assertive, slightly salty
Maytag Blue	Iowa	Cow	Soft; crumbly	Tangy, peppery
Mascarpone	Italy	Cow	Spreadable	Mild, sweet
Fresh goat cheese	France, U.S.	Goat	Spreadable	Earthy, mild
Brie	France, U.S.	Cow	Creamy	Buttery, slightly tangy
Fresh mozzarella	Italy, U.S.	Cow or buffalo	Soft	Mild, sweet

good sampling. Check your grocery or local gourmet delicatessen to see what is available. For starters, mix and match from the chart above. The cheeses are listed by similar textures, with firm-textured cheeses at the beginning of the list, and the creamy, soft, and spreadable ones at the end.

Fresh mozzarella

Gruyère

Scamorza

Aged Gouda

Mascarpone

Aged cheddar

Dry Monterey Jack

132

wine and cheese

There are several reasons wine and cheese seem to get along so genially. First and foremost, they both rely on living organisms for their very existence—not to mention for their unique flavors. Wines use yeast and cheeses use bacterial cultures. Their

cheese	wine
Manchego	Sherry (fino), Rioja, Spanish sparkling whites (cava)
Scamorza	Pinot Grigio, Orvieto
Gruyère	Riesling, Sauvignon Blanc, Fumé Blanc, Gewürztraminer
Aged cheddar	Syrah (Shiraz), Petite Sirah, Zinfandel
Parmigiano-Reggiano	Chianti Classico, Merlot
Pecorino Romano	Barolo, Gattinara, Barbaresco
Dry Monterey Jack	Dry Riesling, Gewürztraminer, Petite Sirah
Aged Gouda	Pinot Noir, Zinfandel
Stilton	Port, Pinot Noir, good-quality Sauternes
Roquefort	French red Burgundy, Côtes du Rhône, Vouvray
Maytag Blue	Cabernet Sauvignon, Syrah (Shiraz)
Mascarpone	Frascati, Italian Soave
Fresh goat cheese	Beaujolais, dry sparkling wine, Champagne
Brie	Côtes du Rhône, Pouilly-Fuissé, Bordeaux
Fresh mozzarella	Bardolino, Valpolicella

denomination or *terroir*—where they were made—also has tremendous influence on the characteristics of both wine and cheese.

For cheese, a key to flavor may be what the animal whose milk was used to make it grazed on. For wine, the keys may be the soil and the amount of sunshine and rain the grapes got as they were growing. Wine and cheese are also both greatly influenced by centuries—even thousands of years—of techniques, some of which haven't changed much since the first time they were used. Both are aged to varying degrees, ranging from months to years. Aging both wine and cheese contributes to their characters and the complexity of their flavors, texture (cheese), and body (wine).

Perhaps most importantly, though, their compatibility on the palate is a natural: The saltiness of cheese calls for something to sip, and the alcohol in the wine cuts the richness of the cheese on the palate (so you can eat even more cheese!).

Some say a guideline for pairing wines with cheeses is that aged cheeses taste best with old wine, fresher cheeses with younger wines. Since aging intensifies the flavor and complexity of both wine and cheese, you want those qualities of each to be about equal; you don't want your wine to overpower your cheese or vice versa. Another simple guideline to keep in mind is that cheeses and wines from the same regions generally go well together. You don't have to follow those rules exclusively (or even the suggestions made in the box at left), but the chart is a starting place **for** making a good marriage.

fruit and cheese

Good accompaniments for cheeses include breads, crackers, nuts, and of course, fresh and dried fruits. You almost can't go wrong pairing any kind of fruit with any kind of cheese, but consider the combinations listed below.

cheese	fruit
Manchego	Avocado, grapefruit sections, mango
Scamorza	Melon, nectarines
Gruyère	Apples, plums
Aged cheddar	Apples
Parmigiano-Reggiano	Fresh figs, melon
Pecorino Romano	Fresh or dried figs, melon
Dry Monterey Jack	Persimmons, plums
Aged Gouda	Fresh or dried apricots
Stilton	Pears, apples
Roquefort	Prunes, ripe plums
Maytag Blue	Dried cranberries or dried cherries
Mascarpone	Fresh berries, fresh cherries
Fresh goat cheese	Fresh or dried figs, dates, plums
Brie	Red or green grapes
Fresh mozzarella	Orange sections (such as ruby-fleshed blood oranges), peaches

133

staging a wine-and-cheese party

Within the wine-and-cheese genre, there are several ways to go. You might decide to serve only several kinds of sherry, along with an array of Spanish cheeses—or several sparkling wines and Champagne with an assortment of French cheeses. It's nice, too, to offer guests a selection of cheeses (hard, creamy, tangy, mild) to sample, matched with complementary wines (red, white, and sparkling).

You'll want to serve between three and five cheeses, providing a variety of textures, tastes, and origins. Bring them out of the refrigerator one hour before you plan to serve them for maximum flavor—but unwrap them right before serving to prevent them from drying out. Arrange them on a large platter with an assortment of fresh and dried fruits (or arrange those separately). Place a selection of breads and crackers in a linen-lined basket. Be sure to have a variety of sweeter, whole-grain breads and crackers as well as crusty, chewy French-style breads and thin, crisp, lavosh-style crackers.

For a traditional and elegant presentation, you might try arranging the cheeses atop cheese leaves—paper cutouts that look like leaves—which are available where fine cheeses are sold. (Leaves are associated with cheese because many types—such as the Spanish cheese, Cabrales, or Banon, a goat cheese from France—are aged wrapped in various sorts of leaves, which impart their flavor to the rind.) Provide a cheese plane (a kind of slicer that makes thin, melt-in-your-mouth pieces) for harder cheeses and a knife or spreader for each softer cheese. Each cheese needs its own serving utensil to prevent mixing flavors.

You can lay everything out all at once on the buffet or dining room table, or you can follow the guidelines used at formal dinners and bring wines and cheeses on in stages: a dry wine before a sweet one, a white wine before a red, a young wine before an aged wine.

Most people don't have the perfectly appropriate wine glass for each kind of wine, but if you are serving a sparkling wine, be sure to have flutes along with plenty of clean wine glasses for tasting—at least two for each guest, if possible. Be sure to provide your guests with lots of napkins and small dessert or luncheon plates to carry their nibbles as they mingle and make merry.

Roasted Pepper Focaccia

You can substitute roasted peppers that come in a jar. Just be sure to drain them well before cutting into thin strips.

- 3¼ to 3¾ cups bread flour or all-purpose flour
- 1 package active dry yeast
- 2 tablespoons snipped fresh rosemary
- 1 teaspoon salt
- ⅛ teaspoon baking soda
- 1¼ cups warm water (120° to 130°)
- 2 tablespoons olive oil
- ¼ cup finely shredded aged provolone cheese (1 ounce)
- 2 red and/or yellow sweet peppers
- 4 teaspoons olive oil
- ¼ teaspoon freshly ground pepper
- ¼ cup pine nuts
- ½ cup finely shredded aged provolone cheese (2 ounces)

Combine 1¼ cups of the flour, the yeast, rosemary, salt, and baking soda in a large mixing bowl. Add water and the 2 tablespoons oil. Beat with electric

mixer on low to medium speed for 30 seconds, scraping bowl. Beat on high speed 3 minutes. Using a spoon, stir in the ¼ cup cheese and as much remaining flour as you can.

Turn dough out onto a lightly floured surface. Knead in enough remaining flour to make a stiff dough that is smooth and elastic (8 to 10 minutes). Shape dough into a ball. Place in a lightly greased bowl; turn once to grease surface. Cover and let rise in a warm place until double (about 1 hour).

Meanwhile, to roast sweet peppers, quarter the peppers; remove and discard stems, seeds, and membranes. Place pepper quarters, cut sides down, on a baking sheet lined with foil. Bake in a 425° oven for 20 to 25 minutes or until pepper skins are blistered and dark. Remove from oven; reduce oven temperature to 375°. Immediately wrap peppers in the foil. Let stand about 30 minutes to steam so skins peel away easily. Remove and discard skin from peppers. Cut peppers into thin strips.

Grease 2 baking sheets. Punch down dough. Turn out onto a lightly floured surface. Divide in half. Shape each half into a ball and place on a prepared baking sheet. Cover and let rest for 10 minutes. Using your hands, flatten each ball to about 12 inches in diameter. Cover and let rise until nearly double (about 20 minutes). With flour-dusted fingers, press fingers into dough making ½-inch-deep indentations. Repeat to cover dough, spacing indentations 1 to 2 inches apart.

Brush dough with the 4 teaspoons oil. Sprinkle with ground pepper. Top with pepper strips, pine nuts, and the ½ cup cheese. Bake in a 375° oven about 20 minutes or until golden. Transfer to wire racks. Cool completely. Tear or cut into wedges. Makes 16 servings.

Nutrition facts per serving: 161 cal., 6 g total fat (2 g sat. fat), 4 mg chol., 191 mg sodium, 21 g carbo., 1 g fiber, 6 g pro. **Daily values:** 8% vit. A, 26% vit. C, 3% calcium, 9% iron

Manchego

Parmigiano-Reggiano

Pecorino Romano

Maytag Blue

Fresh goat cheese

Roquefort

Brie

Gorgonzola-Onion Tart

Mini Gruyère Puffs

Gorgonzola-Onion Tart

✳

The sweetness of caramelized onions spiked with a little brown sugar is a nice complement to the rich, pungent taste of Gorgonzola, blue, or feta cheese in this appetizer served in wedges.

½ of a 15-ounce package folded refrigerated unbaked piecrust (1 crust)

2 tablespoons butter or margarine

1 tablespoon brown sugar

1 teaspoon vinegar

2 medium onions, quartered lengthwise and thinly sliced (about 1⅓ cups)

4 ounces Gorgonzola, blue, or feta cheese, crumbled (1 cup)

2 eggs

1 teaspoon dried chervil or marjoram, crushed

¼ teaspoon pepper

⅓ cup milk, half-and-half, or light cream

3 tablespoons dry white wine or chicken broth

2 tablespoons snipped fresh parsley

1 beaten egg yolk
Green onions (optional)

Roll piecrust from center to edges on a lightly floured surface forming a circle about 12 inches in diameter. Ease pastry into a 9-inch tart pan with a removable bottom, pressing dough up into fluted sides of tart pan. Trim edges, reserving scraps. Do not prick pastry. Line pastry with a double thickness of foil. Bake in a 450° oven for 8 minutes. Remove foil. Bake 4 minutes more or until crust is dry and set. Reduce oven temperature to 375°.

For filling, melt butter in a medium skillet; stir in brown sugar and vinegar. Add onions. Cook, uncovered, over medium-low heat for 10 to 12 minutes or until onions are tender and light brown, stirring occasionally.

Beat cheese, eggs, chervil or marjoram, and pepper in a mixing bowl with an electric mixer on low speed until combined (cheese will still be lumpy). By hand, stir in onion mixture, milk, wine, and parsley. Ladle filling evenly into baked tart shell.

Bake tart in a 375° oven about 20 minutes or until a knife inserted near center of filling comes out clean and pastry is golden. Cool 15 minutes in pan on a wire rack.

Meanwhile, roll out piecrust scraps to ⅛ inch thickness; cut into decorative shapes with small cutters. Place on ungreased baking sheet. Brush lightly with a mixture of egg yolk and 1 teaspoon *water*. Bake cutouts in 375° oven for 6 to 7 minutes or until golden. Carefully remove sides of tart pan. Decorate top with baked cutouts and add green onion curls, if desired. Cut tart into wedges. Serve while warm. Makes 12 appetizers.

Nutrition facts per appetizer: 163 cal., 11 g total fat (3 g sat. fat), 71 mg chol., 237 mg sodium, 11 g carbo., 0 g fiber, 4 g pro. **Daily values:** 8% vit. A, 2% vit. C, 5% calcium, 2% iron

Poppy Seed Flats

See photo, page 130.

    1¾ cups all-purpose flour
     ¾ cup yellow cornmeal
     2 tablespoons dried minced
         onion
     1 tablespoon sugar
    1½ teaspoons poppy seed
     ½ teaspoon baking soda
     ½ teaspoon salt
     3 tablespoons butter
     ¾ cup milk
     1 egg white
     1 tablespoon poppy seed

Well grease a baking sheet or line with parchment paper; set aside. Stir together flour, cornmeal, onion, sugar, the 1½ teaspoons poppy seed, baking soda, and salt in a medium mixing bowl. Using a pastry blender, cut in butter until mixture resembles coarse crumbs. Make a well in center of flour mixture. Add milk. Using a fork, stir until dough can be gathered into a ball.

Turn dough out onto a lightly floured surface. Knead for 8 to 10 strokes or until dough is almost smooth. Divide into 3 portions. Roll each portion to a 12×9-inch rectangle on a lightly floured surface. Using a fork, prick rectangles well. Using a pastry wheel, cut each into twelve 4½×2-inch rectangles. Place 1 inch apart on baking sheet.

Combine egg white and 1 tablespoon *water*; lightly brush over rectangles. Sprinkle with 1 tablespoon poppy seed.

Bake in a 375° oven for 10 to 12 minutes or until browned and crisp. Transfer to wire racks to cool. Store in an airtight container for up to 3 days. Serve with sliced cheeses, if desired. Makes 36 crackers.

Nutrition facts per cracker: 46 cal., 1 g total fat (1 g sat. fat), 3 mg chol., 65 mg sodium, 7 g carbo., 1 g fiber, 1 g pro. **Daily values:** 1% vit. A, 0% vit. C, 1% calcium, 2% iron

Mini Gruyère Puffs

The French call these little cheese-flavored pastries gougére and they're a classic hors d'oeuvre. Crisp on the outside and soft and custardy on the inside, they're terrific hot out of the oven with chilled white wine or champagne.

     ½ cup water
     ¼ cup butter
     ½ teaspoon dried basil, crushed
     ¼ teaspoon garlic salt
         Dash ground red pepper
     ½ cup all-purpose flour
     2 eggs
     ½ cup shredded Gruyère or Swiss
         cheese (2 ounces)
     2 tablespoons grated Parmesan
         cheese

Combine water and butter in a small saucepan. Add basil, garlic salt, and red pepper. Bring to boiling over medium heat, stirring to melt butter. Add flour all at once, stirring vigorously. Cook and stir until mixture forms a ball that doesn't separate. Remove from heat. Cool 5 minutes.

Grease a baking sheet. Add eggs, one at a time, to saucepan, beating with a spoon after each addition until smooth. Stir in Gruyère cheese. Drop mounds of dough by rounded teaspoons, about 2 inches apart, on a prepared baking sheet. Sprinkle with Parmesan cheese.

Bake in a 450° oven for 10 minutes. Reduce oven temperature to 375° and bake 10 to 12 minutes more or until puffed and golden. Turn off oven. Let puffs remain in oven for 3 minutes. Serve hot. Makes about 20 appetizers.

Nutrition facts per appetizer: 53 cal., 4 g total fat (2 g sat. fat), 31 mg chol., 76 mg sodium, 2 g carbo., 0 g fiber, 2 g pro. **Daily values:** 4% vit. A, 0% vit. C, 3% calcium, 1% iron

137

Prime Rib au Poivre
(see recipe, page 145)

138

Pea Pods and Onions with Dill Butter
(see recipe, page 144)

An elegant sit-down dinner with a multi-course menu is not a gastronomic relic—and here's proof: a soup-to-nuts holiday menu featuring wild mushroom soup, a stunning prime rib roast, and wild rice stuffed into mini squash.

the pleasures *of the* table

table setting tips

As much as we may enjoy the trend toward casual entertaining, a festive occasion such as Christmas or New Year's calls for a more formal (not stuffy!) sit-down dinner.

Once you have your wonderful menu planned, you want a table setting that is equally lovely to complement the great food. A sit-down dinner is a way to serve a group of perhaps 12 guests at the most. If your dining table can't accommodate that many, set up an extra table in the living room. Once you have it covered in pretty linens and set it with sparkling dishes, no one will be the wiser that it's a card table.

The foundation of the table, of course, is the linens. For a formal dinner, consider a lace or crisp white linen tablecloth and napkins. Or, dress the table in a beautiful antique embroidered sheet or quilt topped with a washable coordinating cloth.

As a guideline, use the place setting arrangement sketched below. Of course, complete the table with a lovely centerpiece.

menu *for* twelve

Wild Mushroom Soup

———

Walnut Rolls - Butter

✳

Prime Rib au Poivre

———

Pea Pods and Onions
with Dill Butter

———

Wild Rice-Stuffed Squash

———

Peach-Fig Relish

———

Fennel and Sweet
Pepper Salad

✳

Pumpkin-Pecan Cheesecake

———

Choice of Beverages

140

Walnut Rolls
(see recipe, page 145)

Wild Mushroom Soup

Wild Mushroom Soup

½ cup chicken broth
1 ounce dried porcini or other
    dried wild mushrooms
¼ cup dry Madeira, dry sherry, or
    chicken broth
½ cup butter
¼ cup chopped onion
1 pound fresh button
    mushrooms, sliced
    (about 6 cups)
4 ounces shiitake mushrooms,
    stems removed and
    discarded, and sliced (about
    1½ cups)
⅔ cup all-purpose flour
8 cups chicken broth
½ teaspoon cracked black pepper
1½ cups buttermilk

Bring the ½ cup broth to boiling in a small saucepan; add dried mushrooms and wine to boiling broth. Remove from heat. Let stand, covered, 20 minutes. Drain and discard excess liquid. Coarsely chop mushrooms; set aside.

Melt butter in a 4-quart Dutch oven over medium heat. Add onion; cook and stir for 2 to 3 minutes or until tender. Stir in fresh and dried mushrooms; cook 3 to 4 minutes more or until mushrooms are tender and most of the liquid has evaporated. Stir in the flour.

Add the 8 cups broth and the pepper. Bring to boiling; reduce heat. Simmer, uncovered, 30 minutes more, stirring occasionally.* Stir in buttermilk and heat through, but do not boil. If desired, garnish individual servings with green onion tops. Makes 12 servings.

MAKE-AHEAD TIP: Prepare soup through the *. Cover and refrigerate up to 24 hours. To serve, stir in buttermilk and heat through.

Nutrition facts per serving: 152 cal., 9 g total fat (5 g sat. fat), 22 mg chol., 644 mg sodium, 11 g carbo., 1 g fiber, 6 g pro. **Daily values:** 7% vit. A, 4% vit. C, 4% calcium, 10% iron

MENU TIMETABLE

several days ahead:

■ Have plenty of ice on hand; chill sparkling water, other beverages, and wine, if desired.
■ Iron the tablecloth and napkins.
■ Prepare Walnut Rolls; wrap tightly and freeze.
■ Prepare, cover, and refrigerate the Peach-Fig Relish.
■ Select and set out serving containers to be used.

1 day ahead:

■ Prepare Wild Mushroom Soup through the simmering step. Cover and refrigerate.
■ Prepare rice filling and cook the mini squash for Wild Rice-Stuffed Squash. Cover and refrigerate in separate containers.
■ Prepare dressing for Fennel and Sweet Pepper Salad. Cover and refrigerate.
■ Prepare the Pumpkin-Pecan Cheesecake; cover tightly and refrigerate. Toast pecans for the cheesecake garnish; set aside.
■ Cut butter sticks into pats and place in serving bowl; cover and refrigerate.

4 hours ahead:

■ Set out the plates, flatware, serving pieces, and glassware.
■ Arrange the centerpiece, candles, and other table decorations.
■ Prepare vegetables for the Fennel and Sweet Pepper Salad and place ingredients in large bowls or plastic bags; cover and refrigerate.

3½ hours ahead:

■ Start preparing Prime Rib au Poivre and place in oven (exact time depends on desired doneness of meat). Add squash to oven when meat is 20 to 25 degrees from desired doneness.
■ Remove rolls from freezer to thaw.

1 hour ahead:

■ Prepare the strawberry garnish for the Pumpkin-Pecan Cheesecake; cover and refrigerate.
■ Remove rice filling and squash from the refrigerator and let stand at room temperature for 30 minutes. Then spoon the filling into the squash. Add squash to oven with the beef roast and bake about 25 minutes or until hot.

30 minutes ahead:

■ Remove salad dressing from refrigerator and let the dressing stand at room temperature.
■ Spoon Peach-Fig Relish into a serving dish and add a sprig of mint and some cranberries for the garnish.
■ Stir buttermilk into the Wild Mushroom Soup and heat through.
■ Prepare Pea Pods and Onions with Dill Butter.
■ Start preparations for the coffee and/or tea.

just before serving:

■ Arrange Walnut Rolls in a napkin-lined basket.
■ Pour any chilled beverages.
■ Light the candles.
■ Ladle soup into soup plates or bowls.
■ Shake dressing. Drizzle dressing over salad in bowls. If desired, toss salad lightly to coat with dressing.
■ Place squash on serving platter and add sage leaf and kumquat garnish.
■ Place roast on platter and arrange some of the pea pod mixture around the beef roast; transfer the rest of the vegetables to a serving bowl.
■ Beat the whipping cream. Cut cheesecake into wedges and garnish top of cheesecake with whipped cream and toasted pecans. If desired, trim individual servings with fresh strawberries or other fresh fruit.
■ Pour beverages to go with dessert.

141

Wild Rice-Stuffed Squash

To preserve the pretty presentation of these individual servings of whole stuffed squash, look for small squash varieties such as those suggested. Each squash should weigh only about 6 ounces.

2   14½-ounce cans reduced-
      sodium chicken broth
1   teaspoon dried thyme, crushed
⅔   cup uncooked wild rice, rinsed
3   medium leeks, green parts
      removed, ends trimmed, and
      chopped (1 cup)
⅔   cup uncooked long grain rice
12 small winter squash (such as
      acorn, Sweet Dumpling, or
      Golden Nugget), each about
      3½ to 4 inches in diameter
¼   cup butter or margarine, cut up
½   cup dried cranberries or dried
      currants
½   cup dried apricots, snipped
¼   teaspoon salt
¼   teaspoon pepper
      Fresh sage leaves (optional)
      Fresh kumquats (optional)

Bring chicken broth and thyme to boiling in a large saucepan. Add uncooked wild rice; reduce heat. Cook, covered, for 30 minutes. Add leeks and uncooked long grain rice. Cover and simmer 15 minutes more or until rice is tender. Let stand, covered, 5 minutes. Drain excess liquid, if necessary.

Meanwhile, wash squash; cut off and discard the top one-third from the stem end of each. Scrape out seeds with a spoon. Place squash, cut sides down, in a 15×10×1-inch baking pan. Bake in a 350° oven for 50 minutes or until tender. Remove and set aside.

Stir butter, dried cranberries, dried apricots, salt, and pepper into rice mixture until butter melts.

Mound stuffing into squash. Return to baking pan. Cover with foil. Bake in a 350° oven for 20 to 25 minutes or

until heated through. Garnish with sage leaves and kumquats, if desired. Makes 12 side-dish servings.

MAKE-AHEAD TIP: Prepare rice filling and cook the squash until tender; cover and refrigerate up to 24 hours. To serve, let squash and rice mixture stand at room temperature 30 minutes. Fill and bake as directed until heated through.

Nutrition facts per serving: 205 cal., 5 g total fat (2 g sat. fat), 10 mg chol., 287 mg sodium, 40 g carbo., 5 g fiber, 5 g pro. **Daily values:** 107% vit. A, 38% vit. C, 6% calcium, 14% iron

Peach-Fig Relish

What's a big holiday meal without a great relish like this one—a spiced, aromatic mix of canned and dried fruits.

1   29-ounce can peach slices
1   5½-ounce can peach nectar
¼   teaspoon finely shredded lemon
      peel
2   tablespoons lemon juice
¾   teaspoon ground cardamom
1   12-ounce package dried
      light-colored figs, snipped
      (1½ cups)
2   tablespoons brandy or
      orange juice
      Cranberries (optional)
      Fresh mint sprigs (optional)

Drain peaches, reserving ½ cup syrup. Coarsely chop peaches. Heat peaches, reserved syrup, peach nectar, lemon peel, lemon juice, and cardamom in a medium saucepan until boiling. Boil gently, uncovered, for 5 minutes.

Stir in figs and brandy or orange juice. Cook and stir 2 minutes more or until desired consistency. Remove from heat; cool. Place in a bowl; cover with plastic wrap. Refrigerate at least 2 hours before serving. Garnish with cranberries and fresh mint sprigs, if desired. Makes 4 cups (12 servings).

MAKE-AHEAD TIP: Prepare relish. Cover and refrigerate up to 1 week.

Nutrition facts per serving: 133 cal., 0 g total fat (0 g sat. fat), 0 mg chol., 8 mg sodium, 33 g carbo., 3 g fiber, 1 g pro. **Daily values:** 2% vit. A, 6% vit. C, 3% calcium, 5% iron

Fennel and Sweet Pepper Salad

Many Italians serve slices of crisp, fresh fennel bulbs as a palate-refresher with their big Christmas feast. This holiday salad—made slightly sweet with balsamic vinegar—takes advantage of this anise-flavored vegetable at its seasonal peak. Use white balsamic vinegar if you want the fennel to stay white.

4   large fennel bulbs
4   large red sweet peppers
2   heads Bibb or Boston lettuce,
      torn (10 cups)
2   bunches watercress (2 cups
      leaves)
½   cup olive oil
⅓   cup balsamic vinegar
1   teaspoon fennel seed, crushed
½   teaspoon salt
¼   teaspoon pepper

Discard outer layers of fennel; halve and remove core. Slice fennel crosswise into thin strips (about 4¾ cups). Halve peppers lengthwise; remove seeds. Slice peppers crosswise into thin half-rings.

Combine fennel, sweet peppers, Bibb or Boston lettuce, and watercress in one very large (or two regular-size) salad bowl. Garnish with additional sweet pepper rings, if desired.

For dressing, combine olive oil, balsamic vinegar, fennel seed, salt, and pepper in a screw-top jar. Cover and shake well. Just before serving, drizzle dressing over salad and toss lightly to coat. Makes 12 servings.

Nutrition facts per serving: 108 cal., 9 g total fat (1 g sat. fat), 0 mg chol., 112 mg sodium, 6 g carbo., 10 g fiber, 1 g pro. **Daily values:** 33% vit. A, 94% vit. C, 3% calcium, 3% iron

Fennel and Sweet Pepper Salad

Peach-Fig Relish

143

Wild Rice-Stuffed Squash

Pumpkin-Pecan Cheesecake

remainder aside. Add pumpkin, the 1 egg, milk, cinnamon, ginger, and nutmeg to bowl. Beat on low speed just until combined. Pour pumpkin mixture into prepared springform pan. Top with cream cheese mixture. With a knife or narrow metal spatula, gently swirl through the layers to marble.

Place springform pan in a shallow baking pan. Bake in a 350° oven for 40 to 45 minutes or until center appears set when shaken. Cool on a wire rack for 15 minutes. Loosen crust from sides of pan. Cool 30 minutes more; remove sides of pan. Cool completely. Cover and chill at least 4 hours.

Before serving, beat whipping cream until stiff peaks form. Pipe or spoon into mounds atop cheesecake. Garnish with pecans and fresh strawberries, if desired. Makes 12 to 16 servings.

Nutrition facts per serving: 323 cal., 22 g total fat (13 g sat. fat), 132 mg chol., 195 mg sodium, 26 g carbo., 1 g fiber, 6 g pro. **Daily values:** 102% vit. A, 3% vit. C, 7% calcium, 9% iron

Pumpkin-Pecan Cheesecake

½ cup finely crushed graham crackers
¼ cup finely crushed gingersnaps
2 tablespoons finely chopped pecans
1 tablespoon all-purpose flour
1 tablespoon powdered sugar
2 tablespoons butter or margarine, melted
2 8-ounce packages cream cheese, softened
1 cup granulated sugar
3 eggs
1 15-ounce can pumpkin
1 egg

¼ cup milk
½ teaspoon ground cinnamon
¼ teaspoon ground ginger
¼ teaspoon ground nutmeg
½ cup whipping cream
Toasted pecan halves (optional)
Fresh strawberries (optional)

For crust, stir together graham cracker crumbs, gingersnap crumbs, the 2 tablespoons pecans, flour, powdered sugar, and melted butter in a medium bowl. Press evenly onto the bottom of a 9-inch springform pan; set aside.

Beat cream cheese and granulated sugar in a large mixing bowl with an electric mixer on medium speed until fluffy. Add the 3 eggs all at once; beat on low speed just until combined.

Place 1 cup of the cream cheese mixture in a medium bowl; set

Pea Pods and Onions with Dill Butter

Add a touch of extra color to the meat platter by spooning some vegetables along the side; then place the rest in a separate serving bowl (see photo, page 138).

1 16-ounce package frozen small whole onions*
2 6-ounce packages frozen pea pods
2 cloves garlic, minced, or 1 teaspoon bottled minced garlic
3 tablespoons butter or margarine
1 tablespoon snipped fresh dill or 1 teaspoon dried dillweed
½ teaspoon salt
¼ teaspoon white pepper
Fresh dill sprigs (optional)

Cook onions in a small amount of boiling water in a large saucepan for

2 minutes. Add pea pods and cook 2 to 3 minutes more or just until tender, stirring occasionally. Drain.**

Meanwhile, cook garlic in hot butter in a small saucepan for 30 seconds. Stir in dill, salt, and white pepper. Drizzle over vegetables, tossing to coat. Garnish with fresh dill sprigs, if desired. Makes 10 to 12 servings.

***If desired, substitute** 3½ cups fresh pearl onions for the frozen onions. Cook the fresh onions in a small amount of boiling water in a large saucepan for 8 to 10 minutes. Drain and peel onions. Cook pea pods according to package directions. Drain and combine with onions. Continue with recipe at **.

Nutrition facts per serving: 64 cal., 4 g total fat (2 g sat. fat), 9 mg chol., 144 mg sodium, 7 g carbo., 2 g fiber, 2 g pro. **Daily values:** 3% vit. A, 14% vit. C, 2% calcium, 5% iron

Walnut Rolls

Serve these rolls with either the soup or the salad or both (see photo, page 140).

    3 to 3½ cups all-purpose flour
    1 package active dry yeast
    ¾ cup milk
    ¼ cup sugar
    ⅓ cup butter or margarine
    ¼ teaspoon salt
    ¼ teaspoon ground nutmeg
    1 egg
    ⅓ cup finely chopped walnuts
    1 egg white
    1 tablespoon water
    24 walnut halves

Stir 1 cup of the flour and the yeast together in a large bowl; set aside.

Heat milk, sugar, butter, salt, and nutmeg in a small saucepan until warm (120° to 130°) and butter is almost melted. Add to flour mixture. Add egg. Beat with an electric mixer on low

speed for 30 seconds, scraping bowl constantly. Beat on high speed for 3 minutes. Stir in chopped walnuts and as much remaining flour as you can with a wooden spoon.

Turn dough out onto a lightly floured surface. Knead in enough of the remaining flour to make a moderately stiff dough that is smooth and elastic (6 to 8 minutes total). Shape into a ball. Place in a lightly greased bowl; turn once to grease surface. Cover and let rise in a warm place until double in size (about 1 hour).

Punch down dough. Turn out onto a lightly floured surface. Divide in half. Cover and let rest 10 minutes. Grease baking sheets. Divide each half of dough into 12 pieces. Roll each piece with your hands into a 12-inch-long rope on a lightly floured surface. Tie each rope into a loose knot, leaving two long ends. Tuck top end under roll. Bring bottom end up and tuck into center of roll. Place 2 to 3 inches apart on prepared baking sheets.

Mix egg white with the water. Brush over tops of rolls. Press a walnut half into center of each roll. Cover and let rise in a warm place until almost double (about 30 minutes).

Bake in a 375° oven for 12 to 15 minutes or until rolls are golden. Transfer rolls to wire racks to cool. Makes 24 rolls.

MAKE-AHEAD TIP: Prepare, bake, and cool rolls. Wrap tightly in foil or place in an airtight container. Freeze the rolls up to 2 months.

Nutrition facts per roll: 123 cal., 6 g total fat (2 g sat. fat), 16 mg chol., 55 mg sodium, 14 g carbo., 1 g fiber, 3 g pro. **Daily values:** 3% vit. A, 0% vit. C, 1% calcium, 5% iron

Prime Rib au Poivre

Anything "au poivre" simply means "with pepper"—and plenty of it. This beautiful roast relies on a rainbow of peppercorn varieties for its piquant crust. Black peppercorns—the most intensely flavored—are simply the dried berries of the pepper plant that are picked when they're not quite ripe; white peppercorns are the dried ripe berries from which the skin has been removed; and pungent, slightly sweet pink peppercorns aren't really pepper berries at all, but the dried berries of a type of rose plant (see photo, page 138).

    1 6- to 8-pound beef rib roast
    2 tablespoons Dijon-style mustard
    2 teaspoons bottled minced garlic
      or 4 cloves garlic, minced
    2 tablespoons whole peppercorns
      (black, pink, and/or white),
      coarsely cracked

Have butcher completely loosen bones for easier carving of roast. Trim any excess fat from top of beef, leaving a layer about ¼ inch thick. Combine mustard and garlic in a small bowl; spread over top of beef. Sprinkle peppercorns over mustard mixture.

Place meat, bone side down and mustard side up, in a foil-lined 15½×10½×2-inch roasting pan. Insert a meat thermometer into center of meat, without touching bone. Roast in a 350° oven until thermometer registers 135° for medium rare (2¼ to 2½ hours) and 150° for medium (2¾ to 3 hours)*. Cover meat with foil. Let meat stand 15 minutes before carving. (The meat's temperature will rise 5 to 10 degrees during standing.) Makes 12 servings.

***Add squash to oven** when meat is 20° to 25° from desired doneness (115° for medium rare or 130° for medium).

Nutrition facts per serving: 487 cal., 40 g total fat (17 g sat. fat), 114 mg chol., 145 mg sodium, 1 g carbo., 0 g fiber, 29 g pro. **Daily values:** 0% vit. A, 2% vit. C, 1% calcium, 20% iron

145

Hanukkah brings light to the darkest time of the year and joy to the Jews of the world. Challah, cookies, and a fruit-and-nut tart bring sweetness to the celebration.

hanukkah
nights &
delights

The celebration of Hanukkah, the Festival of Lights, commemorates a victory won by the Jews over the Syrian occupiers more than 2,000 years ago. During the eight nights and days of Hanukkah, Jewish people around the world celebrate with special foods. The most commonly eaten foods in America are potato latkes, crisp-fried and served with applesauce. Some people also eat preserve-filled, sugar-coated little doughnuts called *sufganiyot*.

Other celebratory foods in the Jewish tradition are challah, a soft, rich bread, and rugelach, a flaky rolled cookie filled with raisins or other dried fruit and nuts. Also common are foods prepared with honey (Israel is "the land of milk and honey"). (Note: According to Jewish law, recipes that include dairy products cannot be eaten alongside or following a meat dish.)

To set a festive table for Hanukkah, cover the table with silver lamé fabric, then lay a runner of blue fabric down the center of the table for color, shaping it slightly for dimension. Arrange a variety of clear glass vases on the runner and fill each with one of the following: hazelnuts in the shell, almonds in the shell, silver-wrapped candies, and blue-foil-wrapped candies. Insert glitter-sprayed dried flowers (from a crafts store or florist's supply shop) into the nuts and candies. Stretch Star-of-David garland (from a party-supply store) along the runner and add candleholders in the shape of six-pointed stars.

Challah

148

piece into a 32-inch-long rope. On a greased baking sheet, shape one rope into a triangle; pinch ends together. Form a six-pointed star by weaving the second rope over and under the first triangle, forming a second triangle (as shown below); pinch ends together. Make six 2-inch balls of foil. Place foil in holes that form star points (as shown). Cover; let rise in a warm place until nearly double (about 30 minutes). **Combine egg yolk** and 1 tablespoon water. Brush over loaf. Sprinkle with sesame seed. Bake in a 375° oven about 25 minutes or until bread sounds hollow when tapped, covering with foil after 15 minutes of baking to prevent overbrowning. Remove and cool on a wire rack. Makes 1 loaf (16 servings).

WREATH-SHAPED CHALLAH: Prepare as above, except divide dough into 3 pieces. Cover and let rest 10 minutes. Shape each piece into a 22-inch-long rope. Loosely braid ropes. Place braided dough onto a greased baking sheet. Form braid into a wreath shape; pinch ends together. Cover and let rise; brush with egg yolk and water, sprinkle with sesame seed, and bake as directed.

Nutrition facts per serving: 133 cal., 4 g total fat (1 g sat. fat), 27 mg chol., 109 mg sodium, 20 g carbo., 1 g fiber, 3 g pro. **Daily values:** 2% vit. A, 0% vit. C, 0% calcium, 7% iron

Challah

This most famous of Jewish yeast breads is most often seen in its traditional braided form. Instead of the braid shape, follow the directions for forming Challah (KHAH-luh) into a star shape.

    1 package active dry yeast
    ¾ cup warm water (110°)
    3 to 3½ cups all-purpose flour
    ¼ cup sugar
    1 egg
    1 egg white
    ¼ cup vegetable oil
    ¾ teaspoon salt
      Pinch ground saffron (optional)
    1 egg yolk
    1 tablespoon water
    2 teaspoons sesame seed

Dissolve yeast in the warm water in a large bowl. Let stand until bubbly (about 5 minutes). Stir in 1¼ cups of the flour, the sugar, egg, egg white, oil, salt, and saffron, if desired. Beat with an electric mixer on low speed for 30 seconds, scraping bowl constantly. Beat on high speed for 3 minutes. Stir in as much remaining flour as you can with a wooden spoon.

Turn dough out onto a lightly floured surface. Knead in enough of the remaining flour to make a moderately soft dough that is smooth and elastic (3 to 5 minutes total). Shape into a ball. Place in a lightly greased bowl; turn once to grease surface. Cover; let rise in a warm place until double (1 hour).

Punch down dough. Divide in half. Cover; let rest 10 minutes. Shape each

here's how...

To help retain the shape of the star as the dough rises and bakes, place 2-inch balls of foil in the holes forming the points of the star, as shown.

Dried Fruit Compote with Sweet Biscuits

A shortcake served with simmered dried fruit makes the perfect ending to a meal.

    1   8-ounce package mixed
          dried fruit
    2½ cups apple juice
    ⅛   teaspoon ground nutmeg
    4   teaspoons cornstarch
    ¼   cup packed brown sugar
    1   teaspoon vanilla
    2   cups all-purpose flour
    2   tablespoons granulated sugar
    1   tablespoon baking powder
    ½   teaspoon salt
    ½   cup vegetable shortening
    1   tablespoon granulated sugar

Snip dried fruit into bite-size pieces.
Combine fruit, apple juice, and nutmeg
in a medium saucepan. Bring to boiling;
reduce heat. Cover and simmer
10 minutes or until fruit is softened.
Stir together cornstarch and
2 tablespoons *cold water*. Add to fruit
mixture. Cook and stir until thickened
and bubbly. Cook and stir 2 minutes
more. Stir in brown sugar and vanilla.
Remove from heat; set aside.

For biscuits, stir together flour,
2 tablespoons granulated sugar, baking
powder, and salt in a large mixing bowl.
Cut in shortening until mixture
resembles coarse crumbs. Make well in
center. Add ⅔ cup *water* all at once.
Stir gently with a wooden spoon just
until dough clings together.

Knead dough gently 10 to 12 strokes
on a lightly floured surface. Roll or pat
dough to ½ inch thickness. Cut with a
1½-inch heart-shape cutter to make 18
biscuits. Transfer to ungreased baking
sheet. If desired, using a ½-inch heart-
shaped cutter, make indentation in
center of each biscuit. Brush biscuits
lightly with 1 tablespoon *water* and
sprinkle with remaining sugar.

Bake in a 450° oven for 8 to
10 minutes or until lightly browned.
Serve warm. Makes 6 servings.

Nutrition facts per serving: 498 cal., 18 g total fat
(4 g sat. fat), 0 mg chol., 409 mg sodium,
82 g carbo., 2 g fiber, 5 g pro. **Daily values:**
9% vit. A, 4% vit. C, 16% calcium, 18% iron

Mandel Bread

*This crisp bread, sometimes referred to as
mandelbrot (mandel meaning "almond"
and brot meaning "bread"), is eaten like a
cookie. It's similar to Italian biscotti with
the double-baking preparation technique.*

    ¾   cup sugar
    ¾   cup vegetable oil
    3   eggs
    3   cups all-purpose flour
    1   teaspoon baking powder
    1   cup chopped almonds
    1   cup raisins
    2   teaspoons finely shredded
          lemon peel
    1   teaspoon almond extract

Generously grease a large baking
sheet; set aside. Stir together the sugar,
oil, and eggs in a large mixing bowl until
the sugar dissolves. Combine flour and
baking powder. Stir into egg mixture
along with nuts, raisins, lemon peel,
and almond extract (dough will be
sticky). Form dough into two 12×3-inch
logs on the prepared baking sheet.

Bake in a 350° oven for 30 minutes.
Remove logs from oven and bias-cut
into 1-inch-thick slices. Arrange slices
on baking sheet. Return to the oven
and bake for 10 to 12 minutes more or
until lightly browned. Transfer to wire
racks to cool. Makes 24 to 28 slices.

Nutrition facts per slice: 196 cal., 11 g total fat
(2 g sat. fat), 27 mg chol., 26 mg sodium,
23 g carbo., 1 g fiber, 3 g pro. **Daily values:**
1% vit. A, 1% vit. C, 2% calcium, 5% iron

*Dried Fruit Compote
with Sweet Biscuits*

Rugelach

Rugelach

Rugelach (pronounced roo-ge-LAKH) are usually filled with fruits and nuts, poppy seed paste, or preserves. (Note: According to Jewish dietary law, recipes with dairy products may not be eaten along with or following meals featuring meat.)

  1 cup butter or margarine, softened
  2 tablespoons granulated sugar
  1 8-ounce carton dairy sour cream
  1 egg yolk
  2 cups all-purpose flour
  ⅛ teaspoon salt
  ½ cup finely chopped walnuts or pecans
  ½ cup chopped golden raisins
  ½ cup granulated sugar
  ¼ cup butter or margarine, softened
  1½ teaspoons ground cinnamon
  Powdered sugar

For dough, beat the 1 cup butter in a mixing bowl with an electric mixer for 30 seconds. Add the 2 tablespoons sugar; beat until light and fluffy. Add sour cream and egg yolk. Beat well. Stir in flour and salt with a wooden spoon until combined. Cover and chill 2 hours or until dough is easy to handle.

For filling, combine nuts, raisins, the ½ cup sugar, ¼ cup butter, and the cinnamon; set aside. Divide dough into four portions. Roll one portion of dough to a 10-inch circle. Spread one-fourth of the nut mixture over the circle. Cut dough into 12 wedges. Roll up each wedge, starting at wide end. Repeat. Place 1 inch apart on a foil-lined cookie sheet.

Bake in a 350° oven for 22 to 25 minutes or until edges are lightly browned. Cool on cookie sheet 1 minute. Transfer to wire rack to cool. Sprinkle with powdered sugar. Makes 48 cookies.

Nutrition facts per cookie: 95 cal., 7 g total fat (4 g sat. fat), 19 mg chol., 57 mg sodium, 8 g carbo., 0 g fiber, 1 g pro. **Daily values:** 6% vit. A, 0% vit. C, 0% calcium, 2% iron

---

Hanukkah Cookies

Cut with a Star of David-shape cutter, these sugar cookies are made festive with a drizzle or two of blue almond-flavored icing. (See Note under Rugelach.)

  ⅔ cup vegetable shortening
  ¾ cup granulated sugar
  1½ teaspoons baking powder
  ¼ teaspoon salt
  1 egg
  1 tablespoon milk
  ½ teaspoon vanilla
  2 cups all-purpose flour
  Almond Icing

Beat shortening in a large mixing bowl with an electric mixer for 30 seconds. Add sugar, baking powder, and salt; beat until fluffy. Add egg, milk, and vanilla; beat thoroughly. Beat in as much of the flour as you can with the mixer; stir in any remaining flour with a wooden spoon. Cover and chill dough 1 hour or until it is easy to handle.

Divide dough into three portions. Roll each portion ¼ inch thick on a lightly floured surface. Cut with cookie cutters. Place cookies 1 inch apart on ungreased cookie sheets.

Bake in a 350° oven for 8 to 10 minutes or until edges are lightly browned. Transfer to wire racks to cool. Dip top surface into white Almond Icing. Place on rack set over waxed paper. While icing is moist, drizzle design with blue Almond Icing. Let excess icing drip onto paper. Let cookies stand at room temperature at least 2 hours to allow icing to dry. Makes about 60 (2-inch) cookies.

ALMOND ICING: Stir together 3 cups sifted *powdered sugar*, ⅛ to ¼ teaspoon *almond extract*, and enough *milk* (3 to 4 tablespoons) in a large mixing bowl to make icing of drizzling consistency. Tint one-fourth of the mixture blue with *food coloring*.

Nutrition facts per cookie: 65 cal., 2 g total fat (1 g sat. fat), 4 mg chol., 20 mg sodium, 11 g carbo., 0 g fiber, 1 g pro. **Daily values:** 0% vit. A, 0% vit. C, 0% calcium, 1% iron

Hanukkah Cookies

150

Honey-Pistachio Tart

Honey-Pistachio Tart

Dried fruit-and-nut tarts are a wintertime staple in many culinary traditions. This pistachio-packed tart is rich and dense and infused with the sweet, floral essence of honey. Serve it with full-flavored coffee or hot mint tea.

    ½ cup sugar
    ¼ cup honey
    ¼ cup water
    1½ cups chopped pistachio nuts,
         toasted
    ½ cup mixed dried fruit bits
    ¼ cup orange juice
       Egg Pastry
    1 beaten egg yolk
       Coarse sugar

For filling, stir together sugar, honey, and water in a medium saucepan. Bring to boiling, stirring until sugar is dissolved. Reduce heat to medium-low. Gently simmer, uncovered, 15 minutes or until a light caramel color, stirring occasionally. Stir in pistachios, fruit, and orange juice. Return to boiling; reduce heat. Simmer, uncovered, for 5 minutes or until mixture is slightly thickened, stirring occasionally. Set aside.

Meanwhile, slightly flatten one ball of Egg Pastry into a rectangle. Roll dough into a 16×6-inch rectangle on a lightly floured surface. Wrap around a rolling pin. Unroll onto a 13½×4-inch oblong tart pan with a removable bottom. Ease pastry into pan, pressing it up the fluted sides. Trim pastry even with top edge of pan. Spoon filling evenly into crust.

For top pastry, roll out remaining pastry ball into a 10-inch square. Using a fluted pastry wheel, cut into ½-inch-wide strips. Weave strips diagonally across top of filling for a lattice. Press ends into rim of pan. Brush egg yolk over lattice top and sprinkle with sugar.

Bake in a 375° oven about 35 minutes or until top is golden. (If parts of crust brown more quickly, cover with foil.) Cool in pan on a wire rack. Remove sides from pan. Makes 8 to 12 servings.

EGG PASTRY: Combine 2 cups *all-purpose flour* and ¼ teaspoon *salt* in a large mixing bowl. Cut in ⅔ cup *vegetable shortening* until mixture is the size of small peas. Beat together 1 *egg* and ¼ cup *cold water* in a small bowl. Add egg mixture to flour mixture. Using a fork, toss until dry ingredients are moistened. Divide dough in half. Form each half into a ball.

Nutrition facts per serving: 523 cal., 30 g total fat (6 g sat. fat), 53 mg chol., 84 mg sodium, 57 g carbo., 3 g fiber, 9 g pro. **Daily values:** 7% vit. A, 9% vit. C, 3% calcium, 21% iron

For seven days, from December 26 to January 1, African-Americans celebrate their African heritage and affirm seven important principles of community and family life. As with most holidays, traditional foods play a central role.

kwanzaa

The seven principles of Kwanzaa are unity, self-determination, collective work and responsibility, cooperative economics, purpose, creativity, and faith. The colors of Kwanzaa—green, black, and red—often are visible on the holiday table, along with the symbolic elements (see page 88). Serve these African-inspired foods during your celebration.

African-Creole Turkey Gumbo

For convenience, use 1½ teaspoons Cajun seasoning in place of the crushed red pepper, paprika, thyme, black pepper, and ground red pepper.

    1 pound fresh or frozen medium
         shrimp, peeled and deveined
    3 cups fresh or frozen cut okra,
         thawed (12 ounces)
    2 tablespoons cooking oil
    1 tablespoon sugar
    1 tablespoon vinegar
    ⅔ cup all-purpose flour
    ½ cup cooking oil
    ½ cup chopped onion
    ¼ cup chopped celery

    ¼ cup chopped green
         sweet pepper
    1 clove garlic, minced
    ¼ teaspoon crushed red pepper
    ¼ teaspoon paprika
    ¼ teaspoon dried thyme, crushed
    ¼ teaspoon black pepper
    ⅛ teaspoon ground red pepper
    4 cups reduced-sodium
         chicken broth
    ⅓ cup tomato paste
    1 bay leaf
    6 ounces cooked andouille or
         smoked sausage, halved
         lengthwise and cut into
         ½-inch-thick slices
    1 cup chopped cooked
         turkey or chicken
    4 ounces cooked crabmeat, cut
         into bite-sized pieces
         (optional)
    1 tablespoon creamy
         peanut butter
    ¾ teaspoon filé powder
         (gumbo filé)
    5 cups hot cooked rice
         Bottled hot pepper sauce
         Fresh marjoram sprigs (optional)

Thaw shrimp, if frozen. Rinse shrimp and pat dry; set aside.

Cook okra in the 2 tablespoons oil and sugar in a saucepan about 8 minutes or until almost tender. Remove from heat; stir in vinegar and set aside.

For roux, stir together flour and the

½ cup oil in a heavy 4-quart Dutch oven until smooth. Cook over medium-high heat for 5 minutes, stirring constantly with a long-handled wooden spoon. Reduce heat to medium. Cook and stir constantly 10 to 15 minutes more or until roux is a dark reddish-brown. Stir in onion, celery, green pepper, garlic, crushed red pepper, paprika, thyme, black pepper, and ground red pepper (or Cajun seasoning, if using). Cook and stir over medium heat about 5 minutes or until vegetables are tender.

Gradually stir broth into roux mixture. Stir in tomato paste and bay leaf. Bring mixture to boiling. Add shrimp. Cook 2 minutes or until shrimp turn opaque. Stir in sausage, turkey, crabmeat (if using), cooked okra, peanut butter, and filé powder. Heat through. Discard bay leaf. Season to taste with salt and pepper. Serve over hot cooked rice. Pass hot pepper sauce. Garnish with fresh marjoram sprigs, if desired. Makes 10 servings.

Nutrition facts per serving: 415 cal., 22 g total fat (5 g sat. fat), 77 mg chol., 501 mg sodium, 37 g carbo., 2 g fiber, 18 g pro. **Daily values:** 9% vit. A, 25% vit. C, 5% calcium, 22% iron

152

Corn Sticks (see recipe, page 154)

African-Creole Turkey Gumbo

153

Corn Sticks

If using only one corn stick pan, you may need to refrigerate batter and grease pan between batches (see photo, page 153).

     1 cup all-purpose flour
     1 cup yellow cornmeal
     2 to 4 tablespoons sugar
     1 tablespoon baking powder
     ½ teaspoon salt
     2 beaten eggs
     1 cup milk
     ¼ cup cooking oil or
            shortening, melted

Grease a pan having 6 to 8 corn stick shapes (or twelve 2½-inch muffin cups); set aside.

Stir together the flour, cornmeal, sugar, baking powder, and salt in a medium mixing bowl. Make a well in the center of the dry mixture; set aside.

Combine the eggs, milk, and cooking oil or melted shortening in another bowl. Add egg mixture all at once to dry mixture. Spoon batter into the prepared pans, filling pans ⅔ full.

Bake in a 425° oven for 12 to 15 minutes or until brown. Makes 24 to 26 corn sticks or 12 muffins.

Nutrition facts per corn stick: 74 cal., 3 g total fat (1 g sat. fat), 19 mg chol., 100 mg sodium, 10 g carbo., 0 g fiber, 2 g pro. **Daily values:** 1% vit. A, 0% vit. C, 4% calcium, 3% iron

154

Beef and Groundnut Stew

 1½ pounds boneless beef chuck
            pot roast, cut into 1-inch
            cubes
     1 tablespoon peanut oil
            or cooking oil
     1 large onion, chopped (1 cup)
     2 cups water
     2 large tomatoes, peeled and
            chopped (1½ cups)

     ½ cup finely chopped fresh, mild
            green chili peppers (such as
            Anaheim)
            (see Note, page 83)
     ½ teaspoon salt
     ½ teaspoon crushed red pepper
     ¾ cup peanut butter
     3 cups hot cooked rice
     6 hard-cooked eggs,
            sliced (optional)

Trim fat from meat. In a 4-quart Dutch oven brown half the beef in the hot oil. Remove from pan. Brown remaining beef with the onion, adding more oil if necessary. Drain off fat. Return all beef to pan.

Stir in water, tomatoes, chili peppers, salt, and crushed red pepper. Bring to boiling; reduce heat. Simmer, covered, about 1½ hours or until meat is tender.

Remove about 1 cup of the broth from the meat mixture; stir into peanut butter. Return peanut butter mixture to Dutch oven. Heat through. Serve over hot cooked rice. Garnish with egg slices, if desired. Makes 6 servings.

Nutrition facts per serving: 525 cal., 27 g total fat (7 g sat. fat), 82 mg chol., 395 mg sodium, 35 g carbo., 3 g fiber, 38 g pro. **Daily values:** 5% vit. A, 69% vit. C, 3% calcium, 33% iron

Collard Greens with Coconut Milk

Long a staple of soul food, collard greens taste like a cross between cabbage and kale. The addition of coconut milk adds an exotic hint of intrigue to this Southern favorite.

     1 pound collard greens
     ¾ cup water
     ½ cup chopped onion
     1 cup light coconut milk or
            coconut milk
     ¼ teaspoon salt
     ¼ teaspoon pepper
     1 large tomato, seeded
            and chopped

Wash collard greens well. Remove and discard stems; cut up leaves (should have about 14 cups).

Bring water to boiling in a large pan or Dutch oven. Add collard greens and onion. Return to boiling; reduce heat. Simmer, covered, for 10 minutes. Drain well and return to pan.

Stir in coconut milk, salt, and pepper. Cook, uncovered, over medium-low heat for 10 minutes more or until slightly thickened. Stir in tomatoes; heat through. Serve immediately. Makes 6 to 8 servings.

Nutrition facts per serving: 57 cal., 2 g total fat (1 g sat. fat), 0 mg chol., 117 mg sodium, 9 g carbo., 3 g fiber, 2 g pro. **Daily values:** 25% vit. A, 27% vit. C, 2% calcium, 4% iron

symbolic elements of the kwanzaa table

■ Mkeka: a straw mat represents tradition as the foundation on which everything else rests.

■ Kinara: a seven-branched candleholder symbolizes the ancestors. A candle is lit each day.

■ Mishumaa saba: seven candles represent the principles that are the focus of the celebration.

■ Muhindi: ears of corn stand for the children, or potential for children, and hence posterity.

■ Kikombe cha umoja: the unity cup that is passed from guest to guest filled with a libation to honor the ancestors.

■ Zawadi: small gifts that reward personal achievement.

Pinto Beans and Rice

*Put ham, beans, and rice together and
you have a hearty, spicy starch dish.
If you like, serve smaller portions to
accompany meat.*

1¼ cups dry pinto beans (8 ounces)
1 medium onion, chopped
      (½ cup)
2 cloves garlic, minced
1 bay leaf
½ teaspoon dried thyme, crushed
½ teaspoon pepper
2 small smoked ham hocks (about
      8 ounces each)
8 ounces cooked smoked
      sausage, cut into ¾-inch
      pieces
¼ teaspoon salt
3 cups hot cooked rice

Rinse beans. Combine beans and
3 cups water in a large saucepan. Bring
to boiling; reduce heat. Simmer for
2 minutes. Remove from heat. Cover
and let stand for 1 hour.

Drain beans and return to saucepan.
Add onion, garlic, bay leaf, thyme,
pepper, and 3 cups fresh water. Add
ham hocks. Heat to boiling; reduce
heat. Cover and simmer 1½ to 2 hours
or until beans are tender, adding more
water if necessary and stirring
occasionally.

Remove ham hocks; cool slightly.
Remove meat from ham hocks; chop
meat and set aside. Discard bay leaf.
Cook sausage in a medium skillet over
medium heat about 5 minutes or until
browned, stirring occasionally. Stir
chopped meat, cooked sausage, and salt
into beans. Cover and cook about 5
minutes more or until heated through.
Serve over hot cooked rice. Makes 6
main-dish servings.

Nutrition facts per serving: 413 cal., 14 g total fat
(5 g sat. fat), 38 mg chol., 943 mg sodium,
48 g carbo., 3 g fiber, 23 g pro. **Daily values:**
0% vit. A, 14% vit. C, 5% calcium, 28% iron

Sweet-Potato Biscuits

*Self-rising flour contains baking powder
and salt; however, the extra leavening
added here makes these golden biscuits
tender and very flaky.*

1 cup mashed, cooked
      sweet potato*
¼ cup sugar
1 beaten egg
1 cup milk
3 cups self-rising flour
1 teaspoon baking powder
½ cup shortening

Combine mashed sweet potato, sugar,
and egg. Beat with a fork until smooth.
Stir in milk. Set mixture aside.

Stir together flour and baking powder
in a large mixing bowl. Cut in
shortening until mixture resembles
coarse crumbs. Make a well in the
center of dry mixture. Add sweet-potato
mixture and stir just until combined.

Turn out onto a well-floured surface.
Knead gently for 10 to 12 strokes. Roll
or pat dough to ½-inch thickness. Cut
with a floured 2½-inch biscuit cutter.
Reroll as necessary. Place biscuits
1 inch apart on large baking sheets.

Bake in a 400° oven for 12 to
15 minutes or until biscuits are lightly
browned. Makes 18 to 20 biscuits.

*Note: To make 1 cup mashed
potatoes, peel 2 medium sweet potatoes
(about 1 pound total). Cut into 1½-inch
chunks. Place in a large amount of
boiling water. Simmer about
20 minutes or until very tender. Drain.
Mash with a potato masher or beat with
an electric mixer.

Nutrition facts per biscuit: 165 cal., 6 g total fat
(2 g sat. fat), 13 mg chol., 297 mg sodium,
23 g carbo., 3 g fiber, 3 g pro. **Daily values:**
32% vit. A, 5% vit. C, 9% calcium, 6% iron

155

Sweet-Potato Biscuits

Of all the festivals we celebrate, New Year's Eve is the oldest. Even the ancient civilizations of the Egyptians, Romans, and Druids greeted the new year by wearing masks, making lots of noise, and overindulging in food and drink.

new year's *through* the years

We owe the custom of celebrating New Year's Day on January 1 to Julius Caesar, who, as emperor in the first century B.C., devised the Julian calendar. In almost every country of the world, New Year's Eve is a time for feasting and fun, whether with a small group or a large gathering. Here is a selection of appetizers and beverages to help start your party planning.

Phyllo-Wrapped Brie with Mushrooms

- 1½ cups sliced fresh mushrooms
- 1 tablespoon butter or margarine
- 1 tablespoon snipped fresh parsley
- 1 tablespoon dry sherry
- 1 teaspoon Worcestershire sauce
- ¼ teaspoon dried thyme, crushed
  Dash pepper
- 4 sheets frozen phyllo dough (18×14-inch rectangles), thawed
- 3 tablespoons butter or margarine, melted
- 1 4½-inch round Brie cheese (8 ounces)
  Apple or pear wedges or unsalted crackers

Cook mushrooms in the 1 tablespoon butter in a medium skillet over medium heat until tender, stirring frequently. Stir in parsley, sherry, Worcestershire sauce, thyme, and pepper. Cook, uncovered, about 1 minute or until liquid evaporates. Remove from heat. Set aside to cool.

Lightly brush 1 sheet of phyllo dough with some of the 3 tablespoons melted butter or margarine. Place another sheet of phyllo dough on top of the first sheet and brush with butter. Repeat with 2 more sheets of phyllo, brushing each with butter. Cut an 11-inch circle from the stack. Discard trimmings.

Slice Brie in half horizontally. Place one half in center of phyllo stack. Spoon half the mushroom mixture over cheese. Top with other half of Brie and remaining mushroom mixture.

Wrap phyllo up and over Brie and mushrooms, pleating phyllo as needed to cover. Brush phyllo with remaining butter. Place in a shallow baking pan.

Bake in a 350° oven for 20 to 25 minutes or until golden. Serve at once with apples, pears, or crackers. Makes 6 servings.

Nutrition facts per serving: 242 cal., 19 g total fat (11 g sat. fat), 58 mg chol., 397 mg sodium, 8 g carbo., 0 g fiber, 9 g pro. **Daily values:** 17% vit. A, 5% vit. C, 6% calcium, 7% iron

Italian Chicken Spirals

Italian Chicken Spirals

6 large skinless, boneless chicken
    breast halves (about
    2 pounds total)
6 medium spinach leaves,
    stems removed
6 thin slices prosciutto (about
    2½ ounces total)
½ cup mascarpone cheese or
    cream cheese, softened
1 tablespoon olive oil
¼ teaspoon paprika
    White and/or purple flowering
    kale (optional)
    Basil Mayonnaise

Place a chicken breast half, boned
side up, between 2 pieces of plastic
wrap. Pound chicken lightly to ¼-inch
thickness. Repeat with remaining
chicken breast halves. Set aside.

Place spinach leaves in a colander;
pour boiling water over leaves in the
colander set in sink. Drain spinach on
paper towels.

Place a chicken breast half, smooth
side down, on a cutting board or other
flat surface. Season with salt and
pepper. Arrange a slice of prosciutto on
chicken. Spread a rounded tablespoon
of cheese evenly over prosciutto.
Arrange a spinach leaf on top.

Roll chicken tightly from one long
edge and place, seam side down, in a
greased shallow baking pan. Repeat
with remaining chicken breast halves.
Combine olive oil and paprika; brush
over chicken.

Bake in a 375° oven for 25 to
30 minutes or until chicken is tender
and no longer pink; cool slightly. Cover
and refrigerate several hours.

To serve, trim off ends. Cut each
chicken roll into 6 slices. Arrange slices
on serving plate and garnish with kale,
if desired. Serve with Basil Mayonnaise.
Makes 36 appetizers.

BASIL MAYONNAISE: Place ¾ cup
mayonnaise, ½ cup loosely packed
fresh basil, ½ small shallot, and ½ clove
garlic in a food processor bowl or
blender container. Cover and process or
blend until almost smooth. Cover and
chill up to 4 hours. Serve in a sweet
pepper half and garnish with fresh basil,
if desired.

Nutrition facts per appetizer with mayonnaise:
84 cal., 7 g total fat (2 g sat. fat), 20 mg chol.,
75 mg sodium, 0 g carbo., 0 g fiber, 6 g pro. **Daily
values:** 1% vit. A, 0% vit. C, 0% calcium, 1% iron

Crostini with Olives and Feta Spread

Crostini with Olives and Feta Spread

- 1 loaf baguette-style French bread
- ½ of an 8-ounce jar oil-packed dried tomatoes
- ¼ cup chopped pitted Kalamata or ripe olives
- 1 clove garlic, minced
- 1 3-ounce package cream cheese
- 4 ounces feta or goat cheese, crumbled (1 cup)
- 2 tablespoons milk
  Shredded fresh basil leaves

For crostini, partially freeze bread. Cut forty ¼-inch-thick slices; arrange on baking sheets. Drain tomatoes, reserving oil. Lightly brush one side of each slice with some oil. Bake in a 300° oven 6 minutes. Turn slices over; bake 6 minutes or until golden brown.

Finely chop tomatoes. Stir in olives and garlic. Set aside. Beat cream cheese in a small mixing bowl until softened. Beat in feta and milk until smooth. (If desired, cover both spreads; refrigerate up to 2 days. Bring to room temperature before spreading.)

Spread feta mixture on oiled side of crostini. Top with a small dollop of tomato mixture. Garnish crostini with shredded basil. Makes 40 appetizers.

Nutrition facts per serving: 47 cal., 3 g total fat (2 g sat. fat), 8 mg chol., 124 mg sodium, 4 g carbo., 0 g fiber, 2 g pro. **Daily values:** 2% vit. A, 4% vit. C, 3% calcium, 1% iron

Mango-Kiwi Salsa with Jicama Chips

- 2 ripe mangoes, peeled and finely chopped
- 1 kiwifruit, peeled and finely chopped
- 1 green onion, thinly sliced (2 tablespoons)
- ¼ cup finely chopped red sweet pepper
- 1 teaspoon grated fresh gingerroot
- 1 tablespoon lime juice
- 1 tablespoon snipped fresh cilantro, parsley, or basil
- 1 tablespoon brown sugar
  Dash ground red pepper
- 1 medium jicama

For salsa, combine mango, kiwifruit, green onion, red sweet pepper, gingerroot, lime juice, cilantro, brown sugar, and ground red pepper in a mixing bowl. Toss to coat well. Cover and chill up to 4 hours. Makes about 2 cups salsa.

For jicama chips, peel and halve jicama. Cut jicama into ¼-inch-thick slices with a sharp knife. If desired, cut jicama slices into desired shapes using cookie cutters for the flower shapes shown on *page 93*. Serve with salsa.

Nutrition facts per tablespoon with jicama: 16 cal., 0 g total fat (0 g sat. fat), 0 mg chol., 0 mg sodium, 4 g carbo., 0 g fiber, 0 g pro. **Daily values:** 6% vit. A, 16% vit. C, 0% calcium, 0% iron

Black-Eyed Pea Hummus

In the South, black-eyed peas are eaten on New Year's Day to bring good luck. Here is a nontraditional approach to serving them: ground up in hummus in place of chickpeas.

- 1 15-ounce can black-eyed peas
- ½ cup tahini (sesame seed paste)
- ¼ cup snipped fresh cilantro

- 3 tablespoons lemon juice
- 3 tablespoons milk
- 2 tablespoons olive oil
- ½ teaspoon salt
- ¼ teaspoon ground cumin
- 2 cloves garlic, halved
  Toasted Pita Wedges and/or assorted crackers

Rinse and drain black-eyed peas; reserve a few in the refrigerator, covered, to use for garnish. Combine remaining black-eyed peas, tahini, cilantro, lemon juice, milk, olive oil, salt, cumin, and garlic in a large food processor bowl. Cover and process until mixture is smooth.

Transfer to a serving dish. Serve immediately or cover and chill for up to 24 hours. Before serving, garnish with reserved black-eyed peas. Serve with Toasted Pita Wedges or assorted crackers. Makes 1½ cups spread.

Toasted Pita Wedges: Split 4 small pita bread rounds; cut each half into 6 wedges. Place, cut sides up, on an ungreased baking sheet. Bake in a 375° oven 7 to 9 minutes or until lightly browned. Store in an airtight container.

Nutrition facts per tablespoon (without pita wedges or crackers): 61 cal., 4 g total fat (1 g sat. fat), 0 mg chol., 98 mg sodium, 5 g carbo., 1 g fiber, 2 g pro. **Daily values:** 0% vit. A, 2% vit. C, 1% calcium, 2% iron

Champagne Fruit Punch

Extend a bottle of champagne or sparkling wine by combining it with fruits and juices. Or make a no-alcohol version with pineapple juice.

- 1 16-ounce package frozen whole strawberries or unsweetened peach slices
- ¼ cup sugar
- 2½ cups orange juice
- 2 tablespoons lemon or lime juice
- 1 750-ml bottle champagne or sparkling wine or 4 cups unsweetened pineapple juice

158

Thaw fruit at room temperature but *do not drain*. Place fruit and juice in a food processor bowl or blender container. Add sugar. Cover and process or blend until smooth. To remove strawberry seeds, pour mixture through a fine sieve or a sieve lined with a double thickness of 100-percent-cotton cheesecloth.

Transfer pureed fruit to a 2-quart pitcher. Stir in orange juice and lemon or lime juice. (Punch can be prepared to this point, covered, and refrigerated overnight or until serving time.) Before serving, slowly stir in champagne, sparkling wine, or pineapple juice. Makes about 12 (5-ounce) servings.

Nutrition facts per serving: 94 cal., 0 g total fat (0 g sat. fat), 0 mg chol., 2 mg sodium, 14 g carbo., 1 g fiber, 1 g pro. **Daily values:** 1% vit. A, 67% vit. C, 0% calcium, 2% iron

Make-Believe Champagne

1   33.8-ounce bottle carbonated water, chilled
1   33.8-ounce bottle ginger ale, chilled
1   24-ounce bottle unsweetened white grape juice, chilled
    Party Ice Cubes

Combine chilled carbonated water, ginger ale, and grape juice in a large pitcher. Pour over ice cubes in chilled champagne glasses or wine glasses. Serve immediately. Makes about 20 (4-ounce) servings.

PARTY ICE CUBES: Place small pieces of fruit (berries or tiny citrus wedges), small sprigs of fresh mint, or ½-inch strips of orange peel into the compartments of ice cube trays. Add enough water to fill, then freeze.

Nutrition facts per serving: 37 cal., 0 g total fat (0 g sat. fat), 0 mg chol., 14 mg sodium, 9 g carbo., 0 g fiber, 0 g pro. **Daily values:** 0% vit. A, 0% vit. C, 0% calcium, 1% iron

bubbly tips

No New Year's festivities are complete without a toast of something bubbly at midnight. Champagne is the traditional drink, but there are many other choices among the sparkling wines, as well as a selection of nonalcoholic drinks.

Champagne Safety: It's important to remember that anything bubbly is under pressure. Releasing that pressure, while still enjoying the satisfying pop as the cork comes out, takes a certain amount of skill.

■ The number one rule to safe champagne cork removal is to be sure your wine is well chilled and rested, as jostling before serving can cause nasty accidents.

■ Remove the foil and carefully undo the wires holding the cork in place.

■ Set the bottle down in an upright position and cover with a napkin or towel so the cork can't take off like a rocket. Twist the cork (napkin still in place) back and forth until it pops.

■ Pour gently into chilled tulip-shape glasses (which preserve the fizz) and toast away!

Nonalcoholic Alternatives: For those who are not indulging in champagne, make sure you have a selection of nonalcoholic alternatives. Drinks that come in wine-type bottles tend to make the experience more festive, and some sparkling ciders and fruit spritzers even have a cork. Or try the Make-Believe Champagne recipe, at left.

159

Mango-Kiwi Salsa with Jicama Chips

Create a street full of cookie house fronts. Give them as gifts, creating a house style to match the recipient's home, or choose one style for all the cookies you decorate. Throw a party and invite friends to trim houses to match their own homes.

cookie
boulevard

Prepare either or both of the cookie doughs, depending on how many cookie houses you want to bake and whether you want dark- or light-colored houses. While the dough chills, make pattern(s); follow directions on page 163.

Gingerbread Cookie Dough

One batch of dough is enough to make about 4 house fronts (or 3 house fronts and several details). If you want to make additional cookie houses, prepare separate batches of dough. A double recipe is too much for most large mixing bowls.

½ cup shortening
½ cup sugar
1 teaspoon baking powder
1 teaspoon ground ginger
½ teaspoon baking soda
½ teaspoon ground cinnamon
½ teaspoon ground cloves
½ cup molasses
1 egg
1 tablespoon vinegar
2½ cups all-purpose flour

Beat shortening in a large mixing

bowl with an electric mixer on medium to high speed for 30 seconds. Add sugar, baking powder, ginger, baking soda, cinnamon, and cloves; beat until combined, scraping sides of bowl occasionally. Beat in molasses, egg, and vinegar until combined. Beat in as much of the flour as you can with the mixer. Stir in any remaining flour with a wooden spoon. Cover and chill about 3 hours or until dough is easy to handle. Roll out, cut, and bake as directed.

*Note—To make Gingerbread Cookies instead of house fronts from dough: Prepare dough and roll half at a

time to ⅛-inch thickness on a lightly floured surface. Using a 2½-inch cookie cutter, cut into desired shapes. Place 1 inch apart on a greased cookie sheet. Bake in a 375° oven for 5 to 6 minutes or until edges are lightly browned. Cool on cookie sheet 1 minute. Transfer cookies to a wire rack; cool. If desired, frost cookies. Makes 36 to 48 cookies.

Nutrition facts per cutout cookie: 79 cal., 3 g total fat (1 g sat. fat), 6 mg chol., 30 mg sodium, 12 g carbo., 0 g fiber, 1 g pro. **Daily values:** 0% vit. A, 0% vit. C, 1% calcium, 4% iron

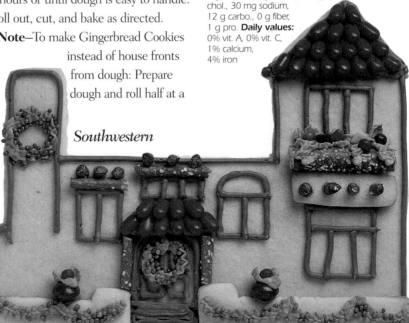

Southwestern

Victorian

Suburban ranch

Tudor

Sugar Cookie Dough

✳

One batch of dough will make about 3 house fronts (or 2 house fronts and several details). If you want to make additional cookie houses, prepare separate batches of cookie dough.

⅓ cup butter, softened
⅓ cup shortening
¾ cup sugar
1 teaspoon baking powder
    Dash salt
1 egg
1 teaspoon vanilla
2 cups all-purpose flour

Beat butter and shortening in a medium mixing bowl with an electric mixer on medium to high speed for 30 seconds. Add sugar, baking powder, and salt; beat until combined, scraping sides of bowl occasionally. Beat in egg

and vanilla until combined. Beat in as much of the flour as you can with the mixer. Stir in any remaining flour with a wooden spoon. If necessary, cover and chill dough about 3 hours or until dough is easy to handle. Roll out, cut, and bake as directed.

*Note—To make Sugar Cookie Cutouts instead of house fronts from dough: Prepare dough and roll half of the dough at a time to ⅛-inch thickness on a lightly floured surface. Using a 2½-inch cookie cutter, cut into desired shapes. Place on ungreased cookie sheet. Bake in a 375° oven for 7 to 8 minutes or until edges are firm and bottoms are very lightly browned. Transfer cookies to a wire rack and let cool. If desired, frost cookies. Makes 36 to 48 cookies.

Nutrition facts per cutout cookie: 74 cal., 4 g total fat, (2 g sat. fat), 10 mg chol., 33 mg sodium, 9 g carbo., 0 g fiber, 1 g pro. **Daily values:** 1% vit. A., 0% vit. C, 1% calcium, 2% iron

Royal Icing

✳

3 tablespoons meringue powder
⅓ cup warm water
1 16-ounce package powdered sugar, sifted (4½ cups)
1 teaspoon vanilla
½ teaspoon cream of tartar
    Paste food coloring

Combine meringue powder, water, powdered sugar, vanilla, and cream of tartar in a small mixing bowl. Beat with an electric mixer on low speed until combined, then on high speed for 7 to 10 minutes or until very stiff. Use the icing immediately.

Divide icing; tint with paste food coloring as desired. When not using icing, keep it covered with plastic wrap to prevent it from drying out. Store in refrigerator. Makes about 3 cups.

162

Georgian

Farmhouse

Cape Cod colonial

cookie house fronts

here's how...

1 Make a sketch of the house you want to duplicate, using a photo. Or use a photocopier to enlarge or shrink a photo to about 6 to 7 inches tall. Simplify small details, but keep those that characterize the house. For example, omit siding and gutter details, but include the style of a door, shutters, and special trim. Alternatively, copy one of the house styles shown here or enlarge the Victorian House pattern *below*.

2 Check supermarkets and bulk candy stores for lots of colorful decorating possibilities—cookies, pretzels, candies, gum, and nuts.

3 Prepare desired dough(s). Cover and chill while preparing patterns.

4 To make patterns, trace house shapes onto graph paper. Make 2 copies for each house. From one pattern, cut out details that you want to add dimension to the house, such as dormers, a roof, or a front porch. If desired, cover pattern pieces with clear self-adhesive shelf paper to make them more durable.

5 Lightly grease the back of a 15×10×1-inch baking pan. Roll some of the dough to ¼-inch thickness on the greased pan. Place some of the pattern pieces 1 inch apart on dough. Cut around piece with a sharp knife, as shown. Remove excess dough (save for

YOU'LL NEED:
several recipes Gingerbread Cookie Dough and/or Sugar Cookie Dough
graph paper
clear self-adhesive shelf paper (optional)
Royal Icing
pastry bags, couplers, and assorted tips (small round, star, zigzag)
waxed paper (optional)
assorted candies, candy-coated gum, peanuts, cookies, and pretzels

rerolling). Leave dough cutouts on the pan and bake in a 375° oven for 10 to 12 minutes or until edges are browned.

6 Place pattern pieces on the warm, baked cookie pieces and trim edges. Cool 3 minutes on pan. Loosen cookie pieces with a spatula. When completely cool, transfer to a wire rack. Repeat with remaining dough and patterns.

7 To decorate, prepare the Royal Icing. Divide and tint icing as desired, using paste food coloring. Fit pastry

bags with couplers and tips. Fill bags with icing, keeping any remaining icing covered with plastic wrap; refrigerate until needed. If desired, place cookie cutouts on waxed paper. Decorate as desired, piping on windows, doors, trim, and other elements as shown. Use icing to attach candies, other cookie cutouts, and edible garnishes. (If icing in bag begins to dry and plugs the decorating tip, just wipe tip with a clean wet cloth.) Use the house front photos on these pages for decorating ideas. Allow decorated cookies to dry about 2 hours.

163

PATTERN FOR VICTORIAN HOUSE

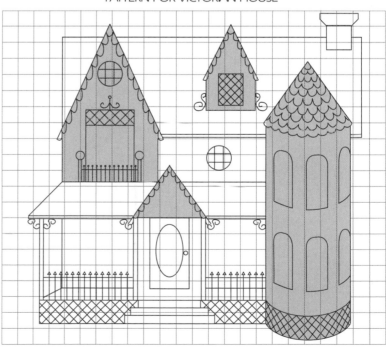

1 SQUARE = ABOUT ⅜ INCH

Orange-Coconut Triangles
(see recipe, page 167)

Nothing says Christmas so sweetly or succinctly as homemade cookies. Here's a selection to suit every taste, from rich chocolate shortbread to airy nut macaroons to bar cookies you can eat with your hands.

small *and* sweet

cookies 101

Everyone loves a homemade cookie, but tastes and preferences aside, some cookies are decidedly better than others. Here are two pointers to make your cookies the best they can be.

There is some truth to the advertising slogan, "butter is better." Anything on the supermarket shelves labeled "margarine" has to be at least 80 percent vegetable oil or fat—which, if used in baking, will provide decent results. You won't, however, get the distinctive rich flavor and desired texture that butter provides. Certain cookie varieties must contain butter, such as shortbread. Avoid ingredients labeled "spread" that come in a tub, or you'll wind up with sodden or rock-hard cookies. If you do decide to use margarine for cookie baking, particularly for rolled cookie dough, keep in mind that the dough will be softer than if you use butter in your preparations. You may need to chill it in the freezer for a few minutes to make it workable.

For all kinds of baking, it's important that your oven temperature is accurate.

To be sure, set your oven at 350° and let it heat for at least 10 minutes. Put an oven thermometer in place and close the door for at least 5 minutes. If the thermometer registers higher than 350°, reduce the oven setting called for in the recipe by the number of degrees your oven is off. If it's lower, increase the temperature. If your oven is off by more than 50°, have your thermostat adjusted by a qualified repair person.

165

Nut Macaroons
(see recipe, page 167)

keep cookies fresh

Though your holiday cookies may look lovely stored in a pretty cookie jar or decorative tin, there are better ways to help them stay fresh.

■ To store cookies for just a few days, cool them completely. Arrange unfrosted cookies in single layers between sheets of waxed paper. If they're frosted, store them in a single layer or place waxed paper between the layers if the frosting is very firm and dry.

■ Avoid mixing soft and crisp cookies in the same container. The moisture from the soft cookies will make the crisp cookies soggy.

■ Store cookies at room temperature for up to three days. If they're frosted with cream cheese or yogurt icing, refrigerate them.

■ To store cookies long-term, let them cool completely, then package them in freezer bags or airtight containers and freeze for up to three months. Before serving, thaw cookies in the container for 15 minutes. If they are to be frosted, glazed, or sprinkled with sugar, wait until they have thawed completely to decorate them, or your decoration may run or smear.

Snowflakes

These rich, lightly spiced sugar cookies might be named for the form they take, but cut into any other shape, they'll still melt in your mouth.

  ½ cup butter
  ⅓ cup shortening
  1 cup granulated sugar
  ⅓ cup dairy sour cream
  1 egg
  1 teaspoon vanilla
  1 teaspoon finely shredded
     lemon peel
  ¾ teaspoon baking powder
  ½ teaspoon ground mace
  ¼ teaspoon baking soda
     Dash salt
  2½ cups all-purpose flour
     Powdered Sugar Icing
     Creamy White Frosting

Beat butter and shortening in a large mixing bowl with an electric mixer on medium to high speed for 30 seconds. Add granulated sugar, sour cream, egg,

vanilla, lemon peel, baking powder, mace, baking soda, and salt. Beat until combined. Beat in as much of the flour as you can with the mixer. Stir in any remaining flour with a wooden spoon. Divide dough in half. Cover and chill for 1 to 2 hours or until easy to handle. **Roll each half of dough** ⅛ to ¼ inch thick on a well floured pastry cloth. Using 2½- to 3-inch snowflake or star-shape cutters dipped in flour, cut out dough. Use a wide spatula to place cutouts 1 inch apart on an ungreased cookie sheet.

Bake in a 375° oven for 7 to 8 minutes or until edges are firm and bottoms are very lightly browned. Transfer to wire racks to cool. When cool, frost with white or tinted Powdered Sugar Icing. Let dry. **Divide Creamy White Frosting** into three or four portions. Leave one white and tint the others the same pale colors used for the icing. Use a small writing tip (1 or 2) on a decorating bag to

here's how...

Decorate Snowflakes with frosting and a candlewicking pattern. (Candlewicking is a kind of embroidery using French knots and simple stitches.) Fit a decorating tube with a small writing tip. Pipe dots in a pattern, making each dot with a swirl action to look like a knot rather than the usual smooth mound.

decorate iced cookies with a pattern of dots and lines to simulate French knots and stitches (see photo, above). Let stand on wire racks until set. Store cookies in layers separated by waxed paper in a shallow, covered container. Makes 48 cookies.

POWDERED SUGAR ICING: Combine 2 cups sifted *powdered sugar* and 2 tablespoons *milk* in a small mixing bowl. Stir in additional *milk*, 1 teaspoon at a time, until of drizzling consistency. Tint icing as desired with liquid or paste *food coloring.*

CREAMY WHITE FROSTING: Beat ½ cup *shortening* with an electric mixer on medium speed for 30 seconds. Slowly add 1 cup sifted *powdered sugar*, beating well. Beat in 1 tablespoon *milk*. Gradually beat in 1¼ cups sifted *powdered sugar* and 1 teaspoon *milk*. Add additional milk, 1 teaspoon at a time, until frosting is of spreading consistency. Tint as desired with liquid or paste *food coloring.*

Nutrition facts per cookie: 127 cal., 6 g total fat (2 g sat. fat), 11 mg chol., 39 mg sodium, 18 g carbo., 0 g fiber, 1 g pro. **Daily values:** 2% vit. A, 0% vit. C, 1% calcium, 2% iron

Snowflakes

Cardamom-Orange Slices

The edges of these cookie slices are coated with light green pistachio nuts.

- ½ cup butter, softened
- ½ cup shortening
- 1 cup packed brown sugar
- 1½ teaspoons ground cardamom
- 1 teaspoon finely shredded orange peel
- ½ teaspoon baking soda
- ¼ teaspoon salt
- 1 egg
- 1 teaspoon vanilla
- 2½ cups all-purpose flour
- ¾ cup very finely chopped pistachio nuts

Beat butter and shortening in a large mixing bowl with an electric mixer on medium to high speed for 30 seconds. Add brown sugar, cardamom, orange peel, baking soda, and salt. Beat until combined. Add egg and vanilla; beat thoroughly. Beat in as much of the flour as you can with the mixer. Stir in any remaining flour with a wooden spoon.

Shape the dough into two 7-inch-long logs. Roll dough logs in chopped pistachio nuts to coat. Wrap the dough logs in waxed paper or plastic wrap. Chill for 4 to 48 hours.

Cut dough into ¼-inch-thick slices. Place 2 inches apart on an ungreased cookie sheet.

Bake in a 375° oven about 8 minutes or until edges are firm. Cool on cookie sheet for 1 minute. Transfer to wire racks to cool. Makes 52 cookies.

Nutrition facts per cookie: 81 cal., 5 g total fat (2 g sat. fat), 9 mg chol., 43 mg sodium, 9 g carbo., 0 g fiber, 1 g pro. **Daily values:** 1% vit. A, 0% vit. C, 0% calcium, 3% iron

Nut Macaroons

Hickory nuts are the fruit of trees that grow wild in American woods and forests. The nuts look like tiny pecans and have a similar, rich flavor. If you can't find hickory nuts, pecans make a fine substitute (see photo, page 165).

- 3 egg whites
- ¼ teaspoon cream of tartar
- 1 cup sugar
- 1 tablespoon all-purpose flour
- 2 cups finely chopped hickory nuts, pecans, or walnuts
- Desired candied fruit pieces, such as red or green cherries or pineapple wedges

Line two cookie sheets with parchment paper; set aside.

Beat egg whites and cream of tartar in a mixing bowl with an electric mixer until soft peaks form (tips bend over). Gradually add sugar, about 1 tablespoon at a time, beating on high speed until stiff peaks form (tips stand straight). Fold in flour and finely chopped nuts.

Drop mixture by rounded teaspoons 2 inches apart onto the cookie sheets.

Bake in a 400° oven for 5 to 7 minutes or until lightly browned. Cool on cookie sheet for 1 to 2 minutes. Press a piece of candied fruit into the top of each cookie. Transfer to wire racks to cool. Makes 36 cookies.

Nutrition facts per cookie: 69 cal., 4 g total fat (0 g sat. fat), 0 mg chol., 5 mg sodium, 8 g carbo., 1 g fiber, 1 g pro. **Daily values:** 0% vit. A, 0% vit. C, 0% calcium, 0% iron

Orange-Coconut Triangles

Cut into triangular pieces or bars—it's up to you (see photo, page 164).

- ½ cup all-purpose flour
- ¼ cup granulated sugar
- ¼ cup butter
- ½ cup finely chopped pecans
- 2 eggs
- ¾ cup granulated sugar
- 2 tablespoons all-purpose flour
- 1½ teaspoons finely shredded orange peel
- 3 tablespoons orange juice
- ¼ teaspoon baking powder
- 1 cup coconut
- Sifted powdered sugar (optional)

For crust, combine the ½ cup flour and the ¼ cup sugar in a medium mixing bowl. Cut in butter with a pastry blender until mixture resembles coarse crumbs. Stir in pecans. Press mixture into an ungreased 8×8×2-inch baking pan. Bake in a 350° oven for 18 to 20 minutes or just until golden.

For filling, combine eggs, the ¾ cup sugar, the 2 tablespoons flour, orange peel, orange juice, and baking powder in another medium mixing bowl. Beat 2 minutes with an electric mixer until combined. Stir in coconut.

Pour coconut mixture over baked crust. Bake 20 minutes more or until edges are lightly browned and center is set. Cool in pan on a wire rack.

Cut into 2½-inch squares, then cut each square in half to make triangles or bars. Sprinkle with powdered sugar, if desired. Makes 18 triangles.

Nutrition facts per triangle: 128 cal., 7 g total fat (3 g sat. fat), 31 mg chol., 41 mg sodium, 16 g carbo., 1 g fiber, 2 g pro. **Daily values:** 4% vit. A, 3% vit. C, 1% calcium, 2% iron

Double Chocolate-Mint Shortbread

The cool taste of mint is a fitting wintertime treat, and chocolate a celebratory food. Make these melt-in-your-mouth shortbread wedges even more festive with a drizzle of melted chocolate and green candy coating.

¾ cup butter
¾ cup sifted powdered sugar
¼ cup unsweetened cocoa powder
¼ teaspoon mint extract
1⅓ cups all-purpose flour
¾ cup miniature semisweet chocolate pieces
Chocolate-flavored candy coating and/or green vanilla-flavored candy coating, melted (optional)*
Hard candies, crushed (optional)

Beat butter in a medium mixing bowl with an electric mixer on medium speed for 30 seconds or until softened. Add powdered sugar, cocoa powder, and mint extract. Beat until smooth. Stir in flour with a wooden spoon until combined. Fold in chocolate pieces. (If necessary, wrap and refrigerate dough a few minutes until easy to handle.)

Lightly grease a cookie sheet. On the prepared cookie sheet, pat the dough into a 9-inch circle. Using your fingers, press to make a scalloped edge. With a fork, prick dough deeply to make 16 wedges.

Bake in a 300° oven about 25 minutes or until edges are firm to the touch and center is set. Let cool for 2 minutes on the cookie sheet. With a long, sharp knife, cut along the fork pricks into wedges. Carefully transfer to a wire rack to cool. Drizzle with melted candy coating and sprinkle with the crushed hard candies before the coating dries, if desired. Makes 16 cookies.

*Tip: If you can't find green candy coating, tint white candy coating with a small amount of green paste food coloring. Dip a toothpick into a little of the paste coloring and stir that amount into the melted coating until the desired shade of green is achieved. (Liquid food coloring may cause the melted candy coating to stiffen.)

Nutrition facts per cookie: 178 cal., 12 g total fat (7 g sat. fat), 25 mg chol., 94 mg sodium, 15 g carbo., 2 g fiber, 1 g pro. **Daily values:** 8% vit. A, 0% vit. C, 1% calcium, 5% iron

Raspberry Cheesecake Bars

What's better than a piece of cheesecake? Why, a piece of cheesecake you can eat with your hands, of course. Try making these bars with apricot preserves for a change of pace.

1¼ cups all-purpose flour
½ cup packed brown sugar
½ cup finely chopped, sliced almonds
½ cup butter-flavored shortening or shortening
2 8-ounce packages cream cheese, softened
⅔ cup granulated sugar
2 eggs
¾ teaspoon almond extract
1 cup seedless raspberry preserves or other preserves or jam
½ cup flaked coconut
½ cup sliced almonds

Combine flour, brown sugar, and the ½ cup finely chopped almonds in a medium mixing bowl. Using a pastry blender, cut in shortening until mixture resembles fine crumbs. Set aside ½ cup crumb mixture for topping.

For crust, press remaining crumb mixture into bottom of an ungreased 13×9×2-inch baking pan. Bake in a 350° oven for 12 to 15 minutes or until the edges are golden brown.

Meanwhile, beat cream cheese, granulated sugar, eggs, and almond extract in another mixing bowl with an electric mixer on low to medium speed until smooth. Spread cream cheese mixture over the hot crust. Return to oven and bake 15 minutes more.

Stir preserves until smooth. Spread over cream cheese mixture. Combine the reserved crumb mixture, the coconut, and sliced almonds in a small mixing bowl. Sprinkle mixture evenly over the preserves.

168

Double Chocolate-Mint Shortbread

Bake about 15 minutes more or until topping is golden brown. Cool in pan on a wire rack. Cover and chill in the refrigerator for at least 3 hours before cutting into bars. Store, covered, in the refrigerator. Makes 32 bars.

Nutrition facts per bar: 180 cal., 11 g total fat (5 g sat. fat), 29 mg chol., 49 mg sodium, 20 g carbo., 1 g fiber, 3 g pro. **Daily values:** 6% vit. A, 0% vit. C, 2% calcium, 5% iron

Oatmeal-Apricot Drops

½ cup butter
½ cup shortening
1 cup granulated sugar
1 cup packed brown sugar
½ teaspoon baking soda
½ teaspoon salt
2 eggs
2 tablespoons apricot nectar or milk
3 cups all-purpose flour
1¾ cups quick-cooking rolled oats
⅔ cup snipped dried apricots
½ cup chopped pecans
Apricot Glaze

Beat butter and shortening in a large mixing bowl with an electric mixer on medium to high speed for 30 seconds or until softened. Add granulated sugar, brown sugar, baking soda, and salt. Beat until combined. Beat in eggs and apricot nectar until combined. Beat in as much of the flour as you can with a mixer. Stir in any remaining flour, the rolled oats, dried apricots, and pecans with a wooden spoon.

Drop dough by rounded teaspoons about 2 inches apart onto ungreased cookie sheets.

Bake in a 375° oven for 8 to 10 minutes or until edges are lightly browned. Cool on wire racks.

To glaze, place cookies on a wire rack over waxed paper. Drizzle Apricot Glaze over cookies. Let glaze dry. Makes 66 cookies.

Holiday Toffee Cakes

APRICOT GLAZE: Stir together 2 cups sifted *powdered sugar* and 2 to 3 tablespoons *apricot nectar or milk* in a small mixing bowl to make a glaze of drizzling consistency.

Nutrition facts per cookie: 101 cal., 4 g total fat (1 g sat. fat), 10 mg chol., 43 mg sodium, 16 g carbo., 1 g fiber, 1 g pro. **Daily values:** 2% vit. A, 0% vit. C, 0% calcium, 3% iron

Holiday Toffee Cakes

These confection-studded little cakes are for those sweet tooths who want to have their cookies and their candy too.

2 1.4-ounce packages chocolate-covered toffee pieces (½ cup)
¾ cup butter
⅓ cup sugar
1 tablespoon milk
2 teaspoons vanilla
2¼ cups all-purpose flour
½ cup semisweet chocolate pieces
2 teaspoons shortening

Finely chop chocolate-covered toffee pieces; set aside. Beat butter in a large mixing bowl with an electric mixer on medium to high speed for 30 seconds. Add sugar; beat until combined. Beat in milk and vanilla. Beat in as much flour as you can with the mixer. Stir in remaining flour and the chopped chocolate-covered toffee pieces with a wooden spoon. If necessary, cover and chill 1 hour or until easy to handle.

Shape dough into 1-inch balls. Place the balls of dough 1 inch apart on ungreased cookie sheets.

Bake in a 325° oven for 15 to 20 minutes or until bottoms are lightly browned. Transfer to wire racks to cool.

Combine chocolate pieces and shortening in a small saucepan over low heat. Heat and stir just until chocolate is melted. Drizzle over cookies on plate. Makes 45 cookies.

Nutrition facts per cookie: 77 cal., 5 g total fat (3 g sat. fat), 10 mg chol., 38 mg sodium, 7 g carbo., 0 g fiber, 1 g pro. **Daily values:** 3% vit. A, 0% vit. C, 0% calcium, 2% iron

Jolly Jingle Santas

Use a bell-shape cookie cutter to make a smiling Santa, complete with a hat and beard.

1½ cups all-purpose flour
1 cup whole wheat flour
1 teaspoon baking soda
½ teaspoon ground cinnamon
¼ teaspoon salt
¼ teaspoon ground allspice
½ cup butter
½ cup packed brown sugar
1 egg
⅓ cup honey
1 teaspoon vanilla
   Creamy Vanilla Frosting

Stir together all-purpose flour, whole wheat flour, baking soda, cinnamon, salt, and allspice in a medium bowl.
Beat butter in a large mixing bowl with an electric mixer on medium to high speed about 30 seconds or until softened. Add brown sugar and beat until fluffy. Beat in egg, honey, and vanilla until combined. Beat in as much of the flour mixture as you can with the mixer. Using a wooden spoon, stir in any remaining flour mixture. Divide dough in half. Wrap in plastic wrap. Chill dough for 2 to 24 hours.
Remove one of the portions at a time from the refrigerator; unwrap. Roll dough ¼ inch thick on a lightly floured surface. Using a 2½- to 3-inch bell-shape cookie cutter, cut dough into bells. Place cookies 2 inches apart on an ungreased cookie sheet.
Bake in a 375° oven for 6 to 7 minutes or until edges are light brown. Transfer cookies to a rack; cool.

170

To decorate, use a decorating bag fitted with a medium star tip and fill it with white frosting; pipe on the brim of the hat about one-third of the way down on the cookie. Using a decorating bag fitted with a small star tip and filled with red frosting, pipe on the hat. Next, pipe on a mustache, beard, and a pom-pom on top of the hat with the white frosting. Using a decorating bag fitted with a small round tip and filled with black frosting, pipe on the eyes and mouth. If desired, miniature semisweet chocolate pieces can be used for the eyes and mouth instead of the black frosting; attach them to the cookie with a dot of icing. Makes 42 cookies.
CREAMY VANILLA FROSTING: Beat ½ cup butter, ½ cup shortening, and 2 teaspoons vanilla in a large mixing bowl with an electric mixer on medium speed for 30 seconds. Slowly add 2 cups sifted powdered sugar, beating well. Add 2 tablespoons milk. Gradually beat in 2½ cups sifted powdered sugar and enough milk (about 1 tablespoon) to make a frosting that's easy to pipe. (For Jolly Jingle Santas, divide frosting, leaving the largest portion white, a smaller portion colored with red food coloring, and the smallest portion colored with black food coloring.)

Nutrition facts per cookie: 145 cal., 7 g total fat (3 g sat. fat), 17 mg chol., 90 mg sodium, 20 g carbo., 0 g fiber, 1 g pro. **Daily values:** 4% vit. A, 0% vit. C, 0% calcium, 2% iron

Chocolate-Topped Peppermint Rounds

1 cup butter
1 cup sugar
1½ teaspoons baking powder
1 egg
¼ teaspoon peppermint extract

2½ cups all-purpose flour
   Small amount of red paste food coloring
66 milk chocolate stars
   Vanilla Icing

Beat butter in a large mixing bowl with an electric mixer on medium to high speed about 30 seconds or until softened. Beat in the sugar and baking powder. Beat in the egg and peppermint extract. Beat in as much of the flour as you can with the mixer. Using a wooden spoon, stir in any remaining flour. Divide dough in half; tint with food coloring. Shape dough into two 9-inch-long rolls, about 1½ inches in diameter. Wrap rolls in plastic wrap. Chill for 2 to 24 hours.
Remove one of the rolls at a time from the refrigerator; unwrap. Using a sharp knife, carefully cut into ¼-inch-thick slices. Place slices 2 inches apart on an ungreased cookie sheet.
Bake in a 375° oven for 8 to 10 minutes or until edges are firm. Place a milk chocolate star in the center of each hot cookie. Cool on cookie sheet for 1 minute. Transfer cookies to a wire rack and cool. Drizzle Vanilla Icing over cooled cookies. Makes 66 cookies.
VANILLA ICING: Stir together 1 cup sifted powdered sugar, 1 teaspoon vanilla, and enough milk (2 to 4 teaspoons) in a small bowl to make an icing that is easy to drizzle. Drizzle from the tip of a spoon. Or, place the icing in a small, self-sealing plastic bag. Using scissors, snip a tiny corner from the bag and pipe icing over cookies.

Nutrition facts per cookie: 79 cal., 4 g total fat (2 g sat. fat), 11 mg chol., 41 mg sodium, 10 g carbo., 0 g fiber, 1 g pro. **Daily values:** 3% vit. A, 0% vit. C, 1% calcium, 1% iron

Lemon and Macadamia Nut Twists
(see recipe, page 172)

Chocolate-Topped Peppermint Rounds

Lemon and Macadamia Nut Twists

These soft, twisted cookies are full of macadamia nuts (see photo, page 171).

- 2½ cups all-purpose flour
- 1 teaspoon baking powder
- ½ teaspoon baking soda
- ¼ teaspoon salt
- ½ cup butter
- 1 cup granulated sugar
- 1 egg
- 1 teaspoon vanilla
- ⅔ cup buttermilk
- ¾ cup ground macadamia nuts or ground almonds
- 2 teaspoons finely shredded lemon peel
- 1 egg white
- 1 tablespoon water
  - Coarse sugar, pearl sugar, and/or colored sugar

172

Stir together the flour, baking powder, baking soda, and salt in a medium bowl. Beat butter in a large mixing bowl with an electric mixer on medium to high speed about 30 seconds or until softened. Add the granulated sugar and beat until fluffy. Beat in the egg and vanilla. Alternately add flour mixture and buttermilk, beating until combined. Stir in the macadamia nuts or almonds and lemon peel. Divide dough in half. Wrap in waxed paper or plastic wrap. Chill for 4 to 24 hours.

Remove one portion of dough at a time from the refrigerator. Unwrap and roll 1 tablespoon of the dough on a lightly floured surface into a 9-inch-long rope. Carefully fold dough in half, overlapping the rope ends to make a loop. Twist ends twice. Place on an ungreased cookie sheet. Repeat with remaining dough, placing twists 2 inches apart. Beat egg white and water together in a bowl. Brush egg white mixture over cookies. Sprinkle with coarse, pearl, or colored sugar.

Bake in a 375° oven for 5 to 6 minutes or until edges are set. Transfer cookies to a wire rack and cool. Makes 45 cookies.

Nutrition facts per cookie: 79 cal., 4 g total fat (2 g sat. fat), 10 mg chol., 61 mg sodium, 10 g carbo., 0 g fiber, 1 g pro. **Daily values:** 2% vit. A, 0% vit. C, 1% calcium, 2% iron

---

Cocoa Sandies

- 1 cup butter
- 1¼ cups sifted powdered sugar
- 2 teaspoons vanilla
- ⅓ cup unsweetened cocoa powder
- ¼ teaspoon salt
- 1⅔ cups all-purpose flour
  - Chocolate Glaze

Beat butter in a large mixing bowl with an electric mixer on medium speed about 30 seconds or until softened. Add powdered sugar and vanilla and beat about 3 minutes or until creamy. Add cocoa powder and salt; mix well. Beat in as much of the flour as you can with the mixer. Using a wooden spoon, stir in any remaining flour. Shape the dough into 1-inch balls or 1½×¾-inch fingers. Place on an ungreased cookie sheet.

Bake in a 325° oven about 20 minutes or until just firm. Transfer cookies to a wire rack and cool.

To glaze cookies, tilt the pan of Chocolate Glaze and dip just the top of each round cookie or half of each finger into the glaze. Place on a waxed-paper-covered rack until the glaze is set. Store cookies in a tightly covered container in a cool place with waxed paper between the layers. Makes 36 cookies.

CHOCOLATE GLAZE: Melt 4 ounces semisweet chocolate, cut up, and 3 tablespoons butter in a small saucepan over low heat, stirring frequently. Remove from heat. Stir in 1½ cups sifted powdered sugar and 3 tablespoons hot water. Stir in additional hot water, if needed, to make an icing that is easy to drizzle.

Nutrition facts per cookie: 121 cal., 7 g total fat (4 g sat. fat), 16 mg chol., 76 mg sodium, 14 g carbo., 0 g fiber, 1 g pro. **Daily values:** 5% vit. A, 0% vit. C, 1% calcium, 3% iron

---

Muddy Fudge Brownies

- ½ cup butter
- 3 ounces unsweetened chocolate
- 1 cup granulated sugar
- 2 eggs
- 1 teaspoon vanilla
- ⅔ cup all-purpose flour
- ¼ teaspoon baking soda
- 1 teaspoon instant coffee crystals
- 1 tablespoon whipping cream
- 1 cup sifted powdered sugar
- 2 tablespoons butter, softened
  - Chocolate Frosting

Melt the ½ cup butter and unsweetened chocolate in a medium saucepan over low heat, stirring constantly. Remove from heat; cool slightly. Stir in granulated sugar. Add eggs, one at a time, beating with a wooden spoon just until combined. Stir in vanilla.

Stir together flour and baking soda in a small bowl. Add flour mixture to chocolate mixture and stir just until combined. Spread batter in a greased 8×8×2-inch baking pan. Bake in a 350° oven for 30 minutes.

Meanwhile, for topping, dissolve the coffee crystals in the whipping cream. Beat together the powdered sugar and 2 tablespoons butter in a small mixing bowl with an electric mixer on medium speed. Add the whipping cream-coffee mixture and beat until creamy. Spread over the warm brownies. Chill about 1 hour or until topping is set. Carefully spread Chocolate Frosting over brownies. Chill until frosting is set. Cut the brownies into triangles or squares. Makes 16 brownies.

CHOCOLATE FROSTING: Combine 1 cup semisweet chocolate pieces and ⅓ cup whipping cream in a small saucepan. Stir over low heat until chocolate is melted and mixture begins to thicken.

Nutrition facts per brownie: 259 cal., 16 g total fat (7 g sat. fat), 54 mg chol., 103 mg sodium, 31 g carbo., 0 g fiber, 3 g pro. **Daily values:** 10% vit. A, 0% vit. C, 1% calcium, 6% iron

---

Cranberry-Pecan Bars

For easier cutting, line the baking pan with foil before adding the crust ingredients. After baking, let the bars cool slightly, then lift the foil lining out of the pan and cut the cookies into bars.

    1 cup all-purpose flour
    2 tablespoons sugar
    ⅓ cup butter
    ½ cup finely chopped pecans
  1¼ cups sugar
    2 tablespoons all-purpose flour
    2 beaten eggs
    2 tablespoons milk
    1 tablespoon finely shredded orange peel
    1 teaspoon vanilla
    1 cup chopped cranberries
    ½ cup shredded coconut
    ½ cup finely chopped pecans

For crust, combine the 1 cup flour and the 2 tablespoons sugar in a medium mixing bowl. Using a pastry blender, cut in the butter until mixture resembles coarse crumbs. Stir in the ½ cup pecans. Press mixture into the bottom of an ungreased 13×9×2-inch baking pan. Bake in a 350° oven for 15 minutes.

Meanwhile, combine the 1¼ cups sugar and the 2 tablespoons flour in a large bowl. Stir in eggs, milk, orange peel, and vanilla. Fold in the cranberries, coconut, and the ½ cup pecans. Spread over baked crust.

Bake in a 350° oven for 30 to 35 minutes more or until top is lightly browned. Cool in pan on a wire rack. While still warm, cut into bars. Cool completely. Makes 36 bars.

Nutrition facts per bar: 89 cal., 4 g total fat (2 g sat. fat), 16 mg chol., 22 mg sodium, 12 g carbo., 0 g fiber, 1 g pro. **Daily values:** 2% vit. A, 1% vit. C, 0% calcium, 2% iron

---

Pistachio-Almond Tarts

To make the tiny tarts, just press balls of cookie dough into muffin cups, then fill, bake, and decorate.

    ½ cup butter
    1 3-ounce package cream cheese
    1 cup all-purpose flour
    1 egg
    ½ cup sugar
    ½ of an 8-ounce can (½ cup) almond paste, crumbled
    ¼ cup coarsely chopped pistachios or almonds
    Chocolate Decorating Frosting
    Pistachios or almonds

For crust, beat butter and cream cheese in a medium mixing bowl with an electric mixer on medium to high speed for 30 seconds. Stir in flour until combined. Cover and chill 1 hour or until the dough is easy to handle.

Form chilled dough into a ball; divide into 24 equal portions. Roll each portion into a ball. Press each ball evenly against the bottom and up the sides of an ungreased 1¾-inch muffin cup. Cover and set aside.

For filling, beat egg, sugar, and almond paste in a small mixing bowl until almost smooth. Stir in coarsely chopped pistachios or almonds. Fill each dough-lined muffin cup with a rounded teaspoon of filling.

Bake in a 325° oven for 25 to 30 minutes or until tops are lightly browned. Cool slightly in pans. Remove tarts from pans and cool completely on wire racks. At serving time, pipe Chocolate Decorating Frosting on top of each tart and top with a pistachio or almond. Makes 24 tarts.

CHOCOLATE DECORATING FROSTING: Beat 3 tablespoons shortening and ½ teaspoon vanilla in a small mixing bowl with an electric mixer on medium speed for 30 seconds. Add ½ cup sifted powdered sugar and 3 tablespoons unsweetened cocoa powder. Beat well. Add 2 teaspoons milk. Gradually beat in ½ cup sifted powdered sugar and enough additional milk to make a frosting of piping consistency.

Nutrition facts per tart: 145 cal., 9 g total fat (4 g sat. fat), 23 mg chol., 53 mg sodium, 15 g carbo., 0 g fiber, 2 g pro. **Daily values:** 5% vit. A, 0% vit. C, 2% calcium, 4% iron

Mix and match red and green plates, placemats, and napkins for a festive table setting. Buy inexpensive holiday-motif salad plates to layer over ordinary dinner plates or chargers (extra-large plates that rest under dinner plates). Tie an ornament to the napkin for a party-favor napkin ring.

In a Twinkling:
Tabletops

◀ Toast the New Year with goblets temporarily embellished with self-adhesive gold stars from a stationer's or office-supply store. Simply peel the stars off when the party is over. Make party favors by dipping fortune cookies in melted chocolate. For each place setting, tie one cookie in a clear cellophane corsage bag (ask your florist to sell you a few bags, or check the candy-making section of a crafts store).

▲ Guide guests to their places with fresh-pear place cards. Decorate a blank card with a pear stamp, write each guest's name, and cut a slit in the top of the pear to hold the card.

▲ Clip a vintage or reproduction ornament to the handle of each coffee or teacup on the table. This unexpected touch will delight guests—especially if they can take the ornament home!

▲ Give each place setting its own cheerful glow with a miniature candle clip. Look for reproduction candle clips, based on Victorian candleholders for trees, in mail order catalogs and Christmas shops. For a napkin ring, thread cranberries onto gold crafts wire and twist the wires together.

▶

String cranberries on fine gold crafts wire to make dainty bobèches for candles. Twist the wire ends together, then wrap the excess wire around a long nail to make fine curls.

*Ham and Salsa with
Zucchini Planks*
(see recipe, page 178)

176

When the inside oven is full of other holiday foods, fire up the grill for your Christmas feast. Don't let the weather stop you—just follow this wintertime grilling advice, then select one of the festive main dishes that fits the season.

winter grilling

grilling 101

Grilling is a great way to cook—it keeps the kitchen less chaotic, and it infuses food with a wonderful, smoky flavor. Although it's easy, there's more to it than simply tossing some shrimp on the "barbie" and watching it cook.

There are two methods of grilling, whether you're using a gas or a charcoal grill. One is called direct grilling. This means the food is placed on the rack directly over the heat. Direct grilling is used for fast-cooking foods such as burgers, boneless chicken, and fish.

Indirect grilling means a covered grill acts as an oven. A disposable drip pan is placed in the center of the charcoal grate and the hot coals are arranged around it. This method is used for slower-cooking foods, such as roasts and bone-in poultry.

For indirect grilling on a gas grill, light the grill according to the manufacturer's directions. Turn the setting to high and let the grill preheat, covered, for 10 to 15 minutes. Reduce the heat on one burner to medium or medium-high, depending on the recipe, and turn the other burner off to set up two heat zones. Place the drip pan directly on the lava rocks, ceramic briquettes, or

flavorizer bars on the burner that's turned off. If your gas grill has a built-in drip pan or grease catcher, you won't need to add one. Otherwise, use a disposable foil pan or make your own with heavy-duty foil. Adjust the gas flow to the burner that's on to maintain the desired temperature. Place food on the grill rack directly over the drip pan. (If food is placed in a roasting pan, a drip pan isn't needed.)

For longer-cooking foods on a charcoal grill, you may need to add

charcoal every 20 to 30 minutes to maintain the heat. Here's a low-tech way to tell the approximate temperature of your coals: Hold your hand over the area where the food will cook for as long as you comfortably can and count while you hold. The number of seconds you can keep your hand over the heat will give you a clue. A 2-second hand count means the coal temperature is *high*, 3 seconds is *medium-high*, 4 seconds is *medium*, and 6 seconds means the coal temperature is *low*.

177

wintertime grilling

For those who live in the Southernmost states, wintertime grilling is really no different from summertime grilling. But if you live in a cold-weather climate, consider these suggestions when grilling outdoors in the winter:

■ Don't grill on a windy day. If you're using a charcoal grill, your coals may not stay lit, and on a gas grill, the flame might blow out.

■ Use the indirect grilling method if you can. It employs a covered grill and is a more hands-off method of grilling so you're not running in and out of the cold to check on dinner.

■ Allow slightly longer cooking times than specified in the recipe. The timings for most grill recipes are based on grilling outdoors on a still, 70° day. A low outdoor temperature may mean your foods need a little longer to cook. Use a meat thermometer to check the doneness of the food. You don't want to undercook the food, but you don't want to leave it out there to get dry and overdone, either.

Ham and Salsa with Zucchini Planks

Check the ham label. If the ham is only partially cooked, increase grilling time as necessary until a meat thermometer inserted into the center of the ham slice reaches 160° (see photo, page 176).

- 1 pink or red grapefruit, peeled, sectioned, seeded, and cut up
- 1 orange, peeled, sectioned, seeded, and cut up
- ⅓ cup canned crushed pineapple, drained
- 2 tablespoons sliced green onion
- 2 tablespoons chopped red sweet pepper
- 1 small fresh jalapeño or habañero pepper, seeded and finely chopped*
- 1 tablespoon honey
- 1 1½- to 2-pound fully cooked center-cut ham slice, cut about 1 inch thick
- 1 pound medium zucchini, ends trimmed and sliced on the bias about ¼ to ½ inch thick
- 1 tablespoon olive oil or cooking oil
- 2 teaspoons sesame seed, toasted (optional)

For salsa, combine grapefruit, orange, pineapple, green onion, sweet pepper, chili pepper, and honey in a small mixing bowl. Cover and chill the mixture up to 2 hours.

Trim fat from ham. Slash edges of ham at 1-inch intervals. Brush zucchini with the oil; set aside. For a charcoal grill, grill ham slice on the rack of an uncovered grill directly over medium-hot coals for 8 minutes. Turn ham slice over and add zucchini to grill rack. Continue grilling about 10 minutes more or until ham is heated through

and zucchini is tender, turning zucchini over once. [For a gas grill, preheat grill. Reduce heat to medium-hot. Place ham and zucchini on grill rack over the heat, cover, and grill as directed at left.]

To serve, cut the ham into serving-size pieces. Spoon the salsa over the ham and serve with the zucchini. Sprinkle with toasted sesame seed, if desired. Makes 6 servings.

*NOTE: Because chili peppers contain very pungent oils, protect your hands when preparing fresh chili peppers. Put gloves or sandwich bags over your hands so your skin doesn't come in contact with the peppers. Don't touch your eyes, and always wash your hands and nails thoroughly in hot, soapy water after handling chili peppers.

Nutrition facts per serving: 221 cal., 8 g total fat (2 g sat. fat), 53 mg chol., 1,624 mg sodium, 14 g carbo., 2 g fiber, 23 g pro. **Daily values:** 6% vit. A, 88% vit. C, 4% calcium, 8% iron

Blue-Cheese-Stuffed Pork Chops

- ½ cup shredded carrot
- ¼ cup chopped pecans
- ¼ cup crumbled blue cheese
- 1 green onion, thinly sliced
- 1 teaspoon Worcestershire sauce
- 4 pork loin or rib chops, cut 1¼ inches thick (about 2¼ pounds total)
- ¼ cup plain yogurt
- 4 teaspoons all-purpose flour
- ¾ cup milk
- ½ teaspoon instant chicken bouillon granules
  Dash pepper
  Chopped pecans (optional)
  Crumbled blue cheese (optional)

Combine carrot, the ¼ cup pecans, the ¼ cup blue cheese, the onion, and Worcestershire sauce in a small mixing bowl; set aside.

Trim fat from chops. Make a pocket in each chop by cutting horizontally into the chop from the fat side almost to the bone. Spoon about ¼ cup of the stuffing into each pocket. If necessary, securely fasten the opening with wooden toothpicks.

For a charcoal grill, arrange medium-hot coals around a drip pan for indirect cooking in a covered grill. Test for medium heat above the pan. Place chops on the grill rack over the drip pan. Cover and grill for 35 to 40 minutes or until juices run clear, turning once. [For a gas grill, preheat grill. Reduce heat to medium. Adjust for indirect cooking (see page 177) and grill as above.]

For sauce, stir together yogurt and flour in a small saucepan. Add milk, bouillon granules, and pepper. Cook and stir until thickened and bubbly. Cook and stir for 1 minute more.

To serve, remove toothpicks from chops and serve sauce over chops. Sprinkle with additional chopped pecans and crumbled blue cheese, if desired. Makes 4 servings.

Nutrition facts per serving: 326 cal., 19 g total fat (6 g sat. fat), 87 mg chol., 334 mg sodium, 8 g carbo., 1 g fiber, 29 g pro. **Daily values:** 44% vit. A, 8% vit. C, 11% calcium, 9% iron

Chutney Roast

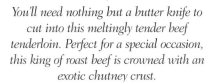

You'll need nothing but a butter knife to cut into this meltingly tender beef tenderloin. Perfect for a special occasion, this king of roast beef is crowned with an exotic chutney crust.

- ⅓ cup unsweetened pineapple juice
- ¼ cup steak sauce or Worcestershire sauce
- 3 tablespoons orange juice
- 2 tablespoons lemon juice

178

1½ teaspoons sugar
½ teaspoon lemon-pepper
   seasoning
1 2½- to 3-pound beef tenderloin
½ cup chutney

For marinade, combine pineapple juice, steak sauce or Worcestershire sauce, orange juice, lemon juice, sugar, and lemon-pepper seasoning in a small mixing bowl. Place meat in a plastic bag set in a shallow dish. Pour marinade over meat in bag. Seal bag and turn meat to coat well. Marinate in the refrigerator for 6 to 12 hours, turning bag occasionally.

Remove meat from bag, reserving marinade. Chill marinade while grilling meat. Insert meat thermometer near the center of the roast.

For a charcoal grill, arrange medium-hot coals for indirect cooking in a covered grill. Test for medium heat where meat will cook. Place meat on a rack in a roasting pan on the grill rack. Cover and grill for 30 minutes or until meat thermometer registers 135°, brushing with reserved marinade halfway through grilling time. Discard any remaining marinade.

Cut up any large pieces of chutney; spoon chutney evenly over the meat. Cover and grill to desired doneness. Allow 35 to 45 minutes total time for 140° (rare) and 45 to 60 minutes total time for 145° (medium-rare). [For a gas grill, preheat grill. Reduce heat to medium. Adjust for indirect cooking (see page 113) and grill on rack in pan as above.] Slice the beef tenderloin to serve. Makes 10 servings.

Nutrition facts per serving: 203 cal., 7 g total fat (3 g sat. fat), 64 mg chol., 212 mg sodium, 11 g carbo., 0 g fiber, 22 g pro. **Daily values:** 0% vit. A, 8% vit. C, 0% calcium, 18% iron

*Double-Glazed
Turkey Breasts*

Double-Glazed
Turkey Breasts

Instead of roasting a turkey in the oven for the holiday meal, try grilling turkey breasts. Go one step further and give your guests a choice of glaze.

⅔ cup orange marmalade
2 tablespoons hoisin sauce
½ teaspoon five-spice powder
½ teaspoon garlic powder
½ cup honey
2 tablespoons Dijon-style mustard
2 tablespoons white wine
   Worcestershire sauce
2 tablespoons butter or
   margarine, melted
2 2- to 2½-pound turkey breast
   halves
1 tablespoon cooking oil
   Orange peel curls

For five-spice glaze, stir together marmalade, hoisin sauce, five-spice powder, and garlic powder in a small mixing bowl; set aside.

For honey-mustard glaze, stir together honey, mustard, Worcestershire sauce, and butter in a

small mixing bowl; set aside. Reserve half of each glaze in separate bowls.

Remove bones from turkey breasts. Brush turkey with oil. Insert a meat thermometer into the center of one of the turkey breasts.

For a charcoal grill, arrange medium-hot coals around a drip pan for indirect cooking in a covered grill. Test for medium heat above pan. Place turkey breasts, side by side, on grill rack over drip pan. Cover; grill for 1½ to 2 hours or until thermometer registers 170°, brushing one breast half with five-spice glaze and the other with honey-mustard glaze several times the last 15 minutes of grilling. If necessary, add extra coals every 20 to 30 minutes to maintain heat. Brush turkey again before serving, if desired. [For a gas grill, preheat grill. Reduce heat to medium. Adjust for indirect cooking (see page 113) and grill as above.] Heat reserved glazes; pass with sliced turkey. Garnish with orange peel curls, if desired. Makes 8 servings.

Nutrition facts per serving: 458 cal., 15 g total fat (5 g sat. fat), 113 mg chol., 327 mg sodium, 38 g carbo., 1 g fiber, 41 g pro. **Daily values:** 2% vit. A, 2% vit. C, 3% calcium, 15% iron

▶ Potato Cutouts: Thinly slice a white potato. Cut several potato slices into shapes using small holiday cookie or hors d'oeuvre cutters. In a small skillet or saucepan cook slices in a small amount of oil until golden brown and crisp. Use the potato cutouts as a garnish for vegetable side dishes or cream soups.

▼ Herb-Topped Rolls: To decorate brown-and-serve dinner rolls, brush the unbaked rolls with a mixture of 1 egg white beaten with a tablespoon of water. While the mixture is still moist, place a small sprig of fresh Italian parsley or other small herb leaves on the rolls. Brush again with the egg-white mixture before baking.

◀ Orange Cups: Remove a very thin slice from the top and bottom of a large navel orange so it will sit flat; slice the orange in half. Use a paring or grapefruit knife and melon baller to remove the flesh from the orange. Orange cups can be used to serve cranberry sauce or chutney. Or, freeze cups and fill with sorbet or other frozen desserts.

In a Twinkling:
Garnishes

180

◀ Festive Appetizer: Spoon guacamole and salsa into several margarita glasses, serving one glassful at a time and keeping the rest refrigerated for replenishing the appetizer table. To prepare, rub the rims of glasses with a lime slice, then dip them into coarse salt. Spoon in guacamole. Fill small bowls (such as votive candleholders) with salsa and press them into the guacamole. (Insert them off-center to allow more room for dipping.) Set on a flat, napkin-lined basket and surround with tortilla chips. Garnish the rim of the glass with a thin lime slice.

◄ Punch Bowl Garnish: To chill punch, freeze a shallow layer of fruit juice in a ring mold. Arrange fruit, such as very thin lime half-slices and fresh cranberries, atop the frozen layer in the mold. Add about 1 inch of fruit juice to hold the fruit in place as it freezes. When frozen, add additional fruit juice to fill the mold and freeze it solid. Unmold and float it in punch.

▲ Stenciled Cookies: Before baking, place sugar cookie dough cutouts on a cookie sheet. Place a very small cookie cutter or stencil on the cookie. Sprinkle inside the stencil with one color of sugar. Add a stencil with a different shape on top, slightly overlapping designs. Sprinkle with a second sugar color.

 181

► Cheese Ball: Spruce up your favorite cheese ball by rolling half of it in a mixture of snipped dried cranberries or cherries. Roll the other half in chopped pistachio nuts. Make sure you roll the ball along a straight edge so there's a definite division where the two ingredients meet.

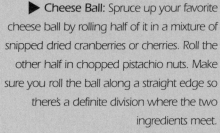

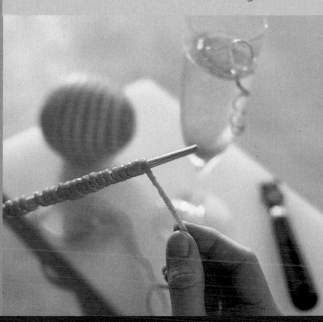

◄ Quick Champagne Cocktail: Add a dash of fruit liqueur to a champagne flute, then carefully pour in champagne. Garnish with a long strip of orange peel (made with a zester) that's been curled tightly around a bamboo skewer. For an alcohol-free version, substitute carbonated water for the champagne and fruit-flavored syrup for the liqueur.

Almond Brunch Loaf

With a bread machine, you can start on a coffee cake or dinner rolls while you're trimming the tree or wrapping presents.

bread-machine *bounty*

Almond Brunch Loaf

Lovely to look at and even better to eat, this orange-almond coffee cake will be the hit of the party. Serve it with fresh-squeezed orange juice and rich, full-bodied coffee.

1½ pound 12 servings	INGREDIENTS	2 pound 16 servings
½ cup	milk	⅔ cup
1 teaspoon	finely shredded orange peel	1¼ teaspoons
¼ cup	orange juice	⅓ cup
1	egg	1
2 tablespoons	butter or margarine, cut up	3 tablespoons
3 cups	bread flour	4 cups
1 tablespoon	sugar	4 teaspoons
¾ teaspoon	salt	1 teaspoon
1½ teaspoons	bread machine yeast or active dry yeast	1¾ teaspoons
⅔ cup	almond cake and pastry filling (not almond paste)	1 cup
3 tablespoons	chopped toasted almonds	⅓ cup
½ teaspoon	finely shredded orange peel	½ teaspoon
1 tablespoon	orange juice	1 tablespoon
2 teaspoons	sugar	2 teaspoons

Select recipe size. Add milk, first measure of orange peel and orange juice, egg, butter, flour, first measure of sugar, salt, and yeast to a bread machine according to the manufacturer's directions. Select the dough cycle. When the dough cycle is complete, remove dough from machine. Punch down. Cover and let rest for 10 minutes.

For filling, combine almond filling, almonds, and remaining ½ teaspoon orange peel; set aside. Lightly grease a baking sheet. Roll the 1½-pound recipe into a 24×8-inch rectangle on a lightly floured surface. (For the 2-pound recipe, roll dough into a 24×12-inch rectangle.) Spread filling over the dough to within ½ inch of the edges.

Fold dough loosely, starting from a short side, making 3-inch-wide folds (see Photo 1). Transfer to prepared baking sheet. On one of the long sides, make eleven cuts for the 1½-pound recipe (15 cuts for the 2-pound recipe) from edge almost to, but not through, the other side, at about ¾-inch intervals.

Flip every other strip of dough over to the opposite side, slightly twisting each strip and exposing the filling (see Photo 2); pull slightly to flatten. Cover and let rise in a warm place until nearly double (about 30 minutes).

Bake in a 350° oven about 30 minutes or until bread sounds hollow when lightly tapped. Cover loosely with foil after 20 minutes of baking to prevent overbrowning. Brush baked bread with the 1 tablespoon orange juice and sprinkle with the 2 teaspoons sugar. Cool on a wire rack.

Nutrition facts per serving (¹/12): 229 cal., 6 g total fat (2 g sat. fat), 24 mg chol., 184 mg sodium, 39 g carbo., 3 g fiber, 6 g pro. **Daily values:** 3% vit. A, 6% vit. C, 2% calcium, 12% iron

here's how...

Make a series of folds in the dough that are 3 inches wide, starting from one of the short sides.

After making cuts along one side almost to the other, pull and flip every other strip of dough to the opposite side. Slightly pull and twist each so the cut side is facing up.

Cheddar Cheese Bows

each half of dough into a 16×12-inch rectangle; cut into sixteen 12×1-inch strips.)

Grease or line baking sheets with foil. Shape each strip into a bow on baking sheet following directions in photo, below. Press dough together at center. Cover; let rise in a warm place until nearly double (20 to 30 minutes). Brush with additional milk and sprinkle lightly with poppy seed. Bake in 375° oven 12 minutes or until golden. Cool on racks.

LOAF: Select basic white bread cycle. If available, select light-crust color setting. Omit brushing with milk and sprinkling with seed. (For 1½-pound loaf, the bread machine pan must have a capacity of 10 cups or more. For the 2-pound loaf, the bread machine pan must have a capacity of 12 cups or more.)

*NOTE: Our Test Kitchen recommends 1 egg for either size.

Nutrition facts per roll (¹/₂₄): 100 cal., 3 g total fat (1 g sat. fat), 16 mg chol., 112 mg sodium, 14 g carbo., 0 g fiber, 4 g pro. **Daily values:** 2% vit. A, 0% vit. C, 4% calcium, 5% iron

here's how...

To shape bows, work on the baking sheet. Form two loops; bring ends to the center and overlap the tails about 1½ inches. Twist the tails together once and press at center against the baking sheet.

184

Cheddar Cheese Bows

Made into a loaf, this mouthwatering cheese bread can be sliced and paired with leftover Christmas ham or roast beef for terrific sandwiches when the cook needs a night off.

1½ pound 24 rolls	INGREDIENTS	2 pound 32 rolls
1 cup	milk	1¼ cups
1	egg*	1
3 cups	bread flour	4 cups
1¼ cups	shredded cheddar, Swiss, or Monterey Jack cheese	1⅔ cups
2 tablespoons	sugar	3 tablespoons
¾ teaspoon	salt	1 teaspoon
1 teaspoon	bread machine yeast or active dry yeast	1¼ teaspoons
	Milk	
	Poppy seed	

Select recipe size. Add milk, egg, flour, cheese, sugar, salt, and yeast to a bread machine according to directions.

ROLLS: Select the dough cycle. When cycle is complete, remove dough from machine. Punch down. Cover; let rest for 10 minutes. Divide dough in half. Roll each half of 1½-pound recipe into a 12-inch square on a lightly floured surface. Cut into twelve 12×1-inch strips. (For the 2-pound recipe, roll

bread machine basics

Although using a bread machine may be a nearly fool-proof way to turn out delicious, fresh bread from your very own kitchen, there are a few things you can do to help assure that your breads are the best they can be.

■ Use bread flour rather than all-purpose flour. Bread flour has more gluten, a type of protein in flour that gives bread dough its elastic consistency. Gluten traps bubbles of carbon dioxide that form when the yeast eats the sugars in the dough. The more gluten in the dough, the higher bread will rise, and the better structural form it will have.

■ If you store flour or grains in the freezer, warm the measured amount to room temperature before using.

■ Store yeast in the refrigerator after opening—and be sure to use it before the expiration date stamped on the package or jar.

Ginger Pumpkin Bread

1½ pound** 16 slices	INGREDIENTS	2 pound** 22 slices
½ cup	milk	⅔ cup
½ cup	canned pumpkin	⅔ cup
1	egg*	1
2 tablespoons	butter or margarine, cut up	3 tablespoons
3 cups	bread flour	4 cups
1 tablespoon	brown sugar	2 tablespoons
¾ teaspoon	salt	1 teaspoon
¼ teaspoon	ground nutmeg	½ teaspoon
1 teaspoon	active dry yeast or bread machine yeast	1¼ teaspoons
½ cup	snipped pitted dates	⅔ cup
2 tablespoons	finely chopped crystallized ginger	3 tablespoons

Select recipe size. Add ingredients to a bread machine according to directions. Select the basic white bread cycle.
***Note:** Our Test Kitchen recommends 1 egg for either size.
****Note:** For 1½-pound loaf, the bread machine pan must have a capacity of 10 cups or more. For the 2-pound loaf, the bread machine pan must have a capacity of 12 cups or more.

Nutrition facts per slice (1/16): 139 cal., 2 g total fat (1 g sat. fat), 18 mg chol., 126 mg sodium, 25 g carbo., 1 g fiber, 4 g pro. **Daily values:** 19% vit. A, 1% vit. C, 1% calcium, 9% iron

Wheat Cloverleaf Rolls

1½ pound 16 rolls	INGREDIENTS	2 pound 24 rolls
¾ cup	buttermilk	1 cup
1	egg(s)	2
¼ cup	butter or margarine, cut up	⅓ cup
1½ cups	bread flour	2 cups
1½ cups	whole wheat flour	2 cups
2 tablespoons	sugar	3 tablespoons
¾ teaspoon	salt	1 teaspoon
1 teaspoon	bread machine yeast or active dry yeast	1¼ teaspoons
1	egg white	1
1 tablespoon	water	1 tablespoon
	Sesame seed	

Select recipe size. Add buttermilk, egg(s), butter, flours, sugar, salt, and yeast to bread machine according to directions.

Rolls: Select the dough cycle. When cycle is complete, remove dough from machine. Punch down. Cover and let rest for 10 minutes. Lightly grease 16 muffin cups (grease 24 cups for 2-pound recipe). Divide dough in half. For the 1½-pound recipe, divide each half into 24 pieces for a total of 48 pieces. (For 2-pound recipe, shape each half into 36 pieces for a total of 72 pieces.) Shape each piece into a ball. **Place 3 balls in each muffin cup.** Stir together egg white and water in a small mixing bowl; brush over rolls. Sprinkle rolls lightly with sesame seed. Cover and let rise in a warm place until nearly double (20 to 25 minutes).
Bake in a 375° oven for 12 to 15 minutes or until golden brown. Serve warm.
Loaf: Select the whole grain or basic white bread cycle. Omit brushing with water and sprinkling with sesame seed. (For 1½-pound loaf, the bread machine pan must have a capacity of 10 cups or more. For the 2-pound loaf, the bread machine pan must have a capacity of 12 cups or more.)

Nutrition facts per roll (1/16): 129 cal., 4 g total fat (2 g sat. fat), 21 mg chol., 149 mg sodium, 20 g carbo., 2 g fiber, 4 g pro. **Daily values:** 3% vit. A, 0% vit. C, 1% calcium, 6% iron

185

Banana-Chocolate Chip Bread

1½ pound** 16 slices	INGREDIENTS	2 pound** 22 slices
½ cup	milk*	½ cup
½ cup	mashed ripe banana	⅔ cup
1	egg(s)	2
2 tablespoons	butter or margarine, cut up*	2 tablespoons
3 cups	bread flour	4 cups
2 tablespoons	brown sugar	3 tablespoons
¾ teaspoon	salt	1 teaspoon
1 teaspoon	active dry yeast or bread machine yeast	1¼ teaspoons
⅓ cup	miniature semisweet chocolate pieces	½ cup

Select recipe size. Add the ingredients to a bread machine according to manufacturer's directions. Select the basic white bread cycle.
***Note:** Our Test Kitchen recommends ½ cup milk and 2 tablespoons butter or margarine for either size loaf.
****Note:** For 1½-pound loaf, the bread machine pan must have a capacity of 10 cups or more. For the 2-pound loaf, the bread machine pan must have a capacity of 12 cups or more.

Nutrition facts per slice (1/16): 145 cal., 3 g total fat (1 g sat. fat), 18 mg chol., 126 mg sodium, 25 g carbo., 1 g fiber, 4 g pro. **Daily values:** 2% vit. A, 1% vit. C, 1% calcium, 8% iron

Easy Christmas Stollen

The traditional shape for this German holiday bread is similar to the coin-purse shape of Parker House rolls. Decorate the top with additional candied fruit, if you like.

1½ pound 12 servings	INGREDIENTS	2 pound 16 servings
1 cup	milk	1¼ cups
2 teaspoons	finely shredded lemon peel	1 tablespoon
1	egg*	1
2 tablespoons	butter or margarine, cut up	3 tablespoons
3 cups	bread flour	4 cups
2 tablespoons	sugar	3 tablespoons
¾ teaspoon	salt	1 teaspoon
½ teaspoon	ground nutmeg	¾ teaspoon
1½ teaspoons	bread machine yeast or active dry yeast	2 teaspoons
½ cup	chopped candied red and/or green cherries and/or candied pineapple	¾ cup
¼ cup	dark raisins	⅓ cup
¼ cup	chopped toasted almonds	⅓ cup
	Powdered Sugar Icing	
	Candied fruit (optional)	

186

Select recipe size. Add milk, lemon peel, egg, butter, flour, sugar, salt, nutmeg, and yeast to a bread machine according to the manufacturer's directions. Select the dough cycle. When the dough cycle is complete, remove dough from machine. Punch down. Cover and let rest for 10 minutes.

Roll dough to a 12-inch square on a lightly floured surface. Sprinkle candied fruit, raisins, and nuts over dough. Fold over one side to center. Fold opposite side over folded side to form 3 layers. Cut dough in half crosswise.

Grease a baking sheet. Roll each portion of the 1½-pound dough into an 8×5½-inch rectangle. (For the 2-pound recipe, roll each portion of the dough into a 9×6-inch rectangle.) Brush top of dough lightly with water. Without stretching, fold a long side over to within 1 inch of opposite side; press edges lightly to seal. Place on baking sheet. Cover and let rise in a warm place until nearly double (45 to 60 minutes).

Bake in a 375° oven for 20 to 25 minutes or until golden and loaf sounds hollow when tapped. Cover loosely with foil the last 10 minutes of baking, if necessary, to prevent overbrowning. Remove from baking sheet and cool on a wire rack. Frost with Powdered Sugar Icing and decorate with candied fruit, if desired. Each recipe makes 2 loaves.

POWDERED SUGAR ICING: Stir together ¾ cup sifted *powdered sugar*, ½ teaspoon *vanilla*, and enough *milk* (about 2 teaspoons) in a small mixing bowl to make an icing of spreading consistency.

*NOTE: Our Test Kitchen recommends 1 egg for either size.

Nutrition facts per serving (1⁄12): 236 cal., 5 g total fat (2 g sat. fat), 25 mg chol., 188 mg sodium, 42 g carbo., 1 g fiber, 6 g pro. **Daily values:** 4% vit. A, 1% vit. C, 4% calcium, 11% iron

Sweet Cardamom Braid

Scandinavian bakers love the warm, spicy-sweet taste of cardamom in all sorts of breads and cookies at this time of year.

1½ pound 12 servings	INGREDIENTS	2 pound 16 servings
½ cup	milk	¾ cup + 1 tablespoon
¼ cup	dairy sour cream	⅓ cup
1	egg*	1
3 tablespoons	butter or margarine, cut up	¼ cup
3 cups	bread flour	4 cups
¼ cup	granulated sugar	⅓ cup
1¼ teaspoons	ground cardamom	1½ teaspoons
¾ teaspoon	salt	1 teaspoon
1½ teaspoons	bread machine yeast or active dry yeast	2 teaspoons
1	egg*	1
1 tablespoon	water	1 tablespoon
	Granulated sugar	
	Powdered Sugar Icing	
2 tablespoons	toasted sliced almonds	2 tablespoons

Select recipe size. Add milk, sour cream, 1 egg, butter, flour, the first sugar, cardamom, salt, and yeast to a bread machine according to the manufacturer's directions. Select the dough cycle. When the dough cycle is complete, remove dough from machine. Punch down. Cover and let rest for 10 minutes. For the 1½-pound recipe, divide dough into thirds; shape each piece into an 18-inch rope. (For the 2-pound recipe, divide dough into 6 equal pieces; shape each piece into a 14-inch rope.)

Grease large baking sheet(s). Place 3 ropes, 1 inch apart on prepared baking sheet. Braid ropes loosely, starting at the center and braiding towards each end. Pinch ends together and tuck under. (For the 2-pound recipe, repeat braiding with remaining 3 ropes, making 2 braids total.) Cover and let rise in a warm place until nearly double (about 45 minutes).

Beat remaining egg and water in a small cup. Brush braid(s) with egg mixture; sprinkle generously with sugar.

Bake in a 375° oven about 25 minutes for large loaf and 20 to 25 minutes for smaller loaves or until bread sounds hollow when tapped. Cover loosely with foil the last 5 minutes of baking, if necessary, to prevent overbrowning. Remove from baking sheet and cool on a wire rack. Drizzle with Powdered Sugar Icing and sprinkle with almonds.

POWDERED SUGAR ICING: Stir together ¾ cup sifted *powdered sugar* and ½ teaspoon *vanilla* in a small bowl. Add enough *milk* (2 to 3 teaspoons) to make drizzling consistency.

***NOTE:** Our Test Kitchen recommends 1 egg for either size.

Nutrition facts per serving (¹/₁₂): 230 cal., 6 g total fat (3 g sat. fat), 46 mg chol., 196 mg sodium, 37 g carbo., 1 g fiber, 6 g pro. **Daily values:** 6% vit. A, 0% vit. C, 3% calcium, 10% iron

Holiday Eggnog Bread

Holiday Eggnog Bread

Here are all the tastes of Christmas—eggnog, nutmeg, and candied fruits and peels—in one beautiful loaf.

1½ pound** 12 slices	INGREDIENTS	2 pound** 16 slices
½ cup	canned or dairy eggnog	¾ cup
¼ cup	water	⅓ cup
1	egg*	1
2 tablespoons	butter or margarine, cut up	3 tablespoons
3 cups	bread flour	4 cups
2 tablespoons	sugar	3 tablespoons
¾ teaspoon	salt	1 teaspoon
¼ teaspoon	ground nutmeg	½ teaspoon
1¼ teaspoons	bread machine yeast or active dry yeast	1½ teaspoons
⅓ cup	mixed candied fruits and peels	½ cup
	Eggnog Glaze	

Select recipe size. Add all of the ingredients except Eggnog Glaze to a bread machine according to the manufacturer's directions. Select the basic white bread cycle. Drizzle cooled loaf with Eggnog Glaze.

EGGNOG GLAZE: Stir together 1 cup sifted *powdered sugar* and enough *canned or dairy eggnog* (1 to 2 tablespoons) in a small mixing bowl to make a glaze of drizzling consistency.

***NOTE:** Our Test Kitchen recommends 1 egg for either size.

****NOTE:** For 1½-pound loaf, the bread machine pan must have a capacity of 10 cups or more. For the 2-pound loaf, the bread machine pan must have a capacity of 12 cups or more.

Nutrition facts per slice (¹/₁₂): 222 cal., 4 g total fat (1 g sat. fat), 23 mg chol., 170 mg sodium, 42 g carbo., 1 g fiber, 5 g pro. **Daily values:** 3% vit. A, 0% vit. C, 0% calcium, 10% iron

Oatmeal Bread

Try toasting slices of the finished bread for a holiday breakfast, spread with butter and jam, and serve with a big pot of hot tea or hot chocolate.

1½ pound 16 slices	INGREDIENTS	2 pound 22 slices
1 cup	quick-cooking rolled oats	1⅓ cups
⅔ cup	milk	¾ cup
⅓ cup	water	½ cup
1 tablespoon	butter or margarine, cut up	2 tablespoons
2½ cups	bread flour	3⅓ cups
3 tablespoons	packed brown sugar	¼ cup
¾ teaspoon	salt	1 teaspoon
1 teaspoon	bread machine yeast or active dry yeast	1¼ teaspoons

Select recipe size. Spread oats in a shallow baking pan. Bake in a 350° oven for 15 to 20 minutes or until light brown, stirring occasionally. Cool.

Add oats and remaining ingredients to a bread machine according to the manufacturer's directions. If available, select whole grain cycle, or select the basic white bread cycle.

Nutrition facts per slice (¹/₁₆): 117 cal., 2 g total fat (1 g sat. fat), 3 mg chol., 115 mg sodium, 22 g carbo., 1 g fiber, 4 g pro. **Daily values:** 1% vit. A, 0% vit. C, 1% calcium, 8% iron

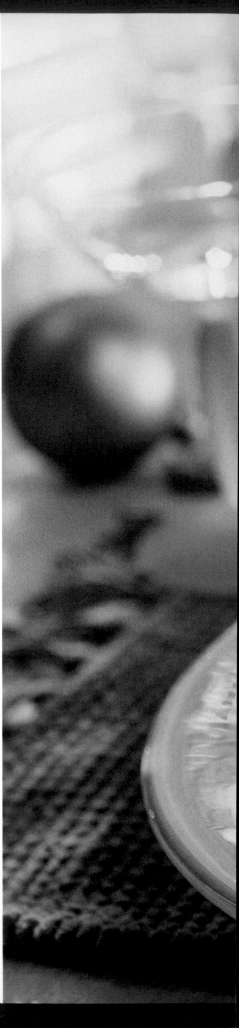

Start Christmas Day with a hearty brunch. Many of these recipes can be made ahead of time, leaving you free to enjoy your family.

morning
glories

On the morning of the brunch, pop the Sausage-Cheese Strata (see *page 191*) and your choice of bread in the oven to warm while you're opening gifts. If you make Caramel-Pecan Rolls (see *page 190*), prepare them the night before, then bake them before placing the strata in the oven.

To serve the brunch, you may wish to keep place settings and dinnerware casual. Or, to enhance the feeling of celebration, bring out your best china, crystal, and silver.

Ginger Fruit Compote

1½ cups water
 1 cup sugar
 3 tablespoons lemon juice
 2 tablespoons snipped crystallized ginger
 8 cups assorted fruit (such as sliced kiwifruit, orange sections, chopped apple, sliced banana, and/or seedless red grapes)

For syrup, combine water, sugar, lemon juice, and crystallized ginger in a medium saucepan. Bring mixture to boiling; reduce heat. Cover and simmer for 5 minutes. Transfer to a bowl. Cool. Cover; chill the mixture up to 24 hours. **Place** fruit in a large serving bowl. Pour syrup over fruit, tossing gently to coat all fruit with syrup. Cover and chill up to 24 hours. Makes 12 servings.

Nutrition facts per serving: 132 cal., 0 g total fat (0 g sat. fat), 0 mg chol., 3 mg sodium, 34 g carbo., 2 g fiber, 1 g pro. **Daily values:** 1% vit. A, 62% vit. C, % calcium, 3% iron

Ginger Fruit Compote

189

Caramel-Pecan Rolls

To make rolls ahead, cover with oiled waxed paper, then plastic wrap. Refrigerate for 2 to 24 hours. Before baking, let the shaped rolls stand, covered, for 20 minutes at room temperature. Remove towel or wrapping. Puncture any surface bubbles with a greased toothpick.
Bake in a 375° oven, uncovered, until golden, allowing 25 to 30 minutes for unchilled rolls and 30 to 35 minutes for chilled rolls. If necessary, cover rolls with foil the last 10 minutes of baking to prevent overbrowning. Cool in pan on a wire rack for 5 minutes. Loosen edges; invert onto a serving platter. Serve warm. Makes 12 rolls.

Nutrition facts per roll: 362 cal., 15 g total fat (7 g sat. fat), 59 mg chol., 155 mg sodium, 51 g carbo., 2 g fiber, 6 g pro. **Daily values:** 12% vit. A, 0% vit. C, 4% calcium, 15% iron

Chocolate-Pistachio-Stuffed French Toast

✳

Caramel-Pecan Rolls

✳

Start with frozen bread dough for wonderfully rich and gooey results in a fraction of the time.

    1¼ cups sifted powdered
         sugar
    ½   cup whipping cream
    ¾   cup pecan pieces
    2   16-ounce loaves frozen sweet
         roll or white bread dough,
         thawed
    3   tablespoons butter, melted
    ½   cup packed brown sugar
    1   tablespoon ground cinnamon
    ¾   cup raisins (optional)

For topping, stir together powdered sugar and whipping cream in a small bowl. Pour into an ungreased 12-inch deep-dish pizza pan or a 13×9×2-inch baking pan. Sprinkle pecans evenly over mixture; set aside.
Roll each thawed loaf into a 12×8-inch rectangle on a lightly floured surface. Brush with melted butter. Stir together brown sugar and cinnamon in a small bowl; sprinkle over both rectangles. Top each with raisins, if desired. Roll up rectangles, jelly-roll style, starting from a long side. Pinch to seal. Cut each log crosswise into 6 slices. Place slices, cut side down, atop pecan mixture in pan. Cover with a towel. Let dough rise in a warm place until nearly double (about 30 minutes).

Make this elegant breakfast dish ahead and freeze until the morning you need it.

    1   1-pound unsliced loaf
         French bread
    2   1- to 1½-ounce milk chocolate
         bars
    ⅓   cup chopped pistachio nuts
    1½ cups graham cracker crumbs
    8   beaten eggs
    2   cups milk
    1   teaspoon ground cinnamon
         Maple syrup or sifted
         powdered sugar

Cut French bread into 12 slices, each approximately 1½ inches thick. Cut a pocket in each slice of bread by starting from the bottom crust and cutting horizontally to, but not through, the top crust. Break candy bars into 12 pieces. Fill each bread pocket with 1 piece of candy and 1 rounded teaspoon of nuts.

Place graham cracker crumbs in a shallow bowl. Beat together eggs, milk, and cinnamon in another shallow bowl. Dip bread into egg mixture, letting bread remain in egg mixture about 15 seconds on each side. Then dip bread into the graham cracker crumbs, turning to lightly coat the other side of the bread. Place coated slice on a greased baking sheet. Repeat dipping remaining stuffed bread into egg mixture and graham cracker crumbs.

Bake in a 450° oven about 6 minutes or until golden brown. Turn slices over and bake for 5 minutes more. Serve warm stuffed toast topped with maple syrup or powdered sugar. (To make ahead, place the baked slices in a freezer container; seal, label, and freeze up to 1 month. To serve, place the frozen stuffed bread slices in a single layer on an ungreased baking sheet. Heat, uncovered, in a 400° oven for 15 minutes or until the slices are hot.) Makes 12 slices.

Nutrition facts per slice: 268 cal., 9 g total fat (3 g sat. fat), 145 mg chol., 355 mg sodium, 34 g carbo., 1 g fiber, 11 g pro. **Daily values:** 9% vit. A, 1% vit. C, 9% calcium, 15% iron

---

Sausage-Cheese Strata

✳

- 10 cups French bread cubes (½- to ¾-inch cubes)
- 12 ounces cooked smoked sausage links, cut into ¾-inch pieces
- 1 4-ounce can sliced mushrooms, drained
- 1 cup chopped green sweet pepper
- 6 ounces shredded sharp cheddar cheese (1½ cups)
- 4 ounces shredded Monterey Jack cheese (1 cup)
- 7 beaten eggs

- 3½ cups milk
- 2 tablespoons snipped chives
- 1 tablespoon snipped fresh oregano or 1 teaspoon dried oregano, crushed
- ½ teaspoon salt
- ¼ teaspoon pepper

Divide half of the bread cubes between 2 greased 2-quart rectangular baking dishes. Top with sausage, mushrooms, and sweet pepper. Sprinkle with cheeses. Place remaining bread cubes on top.

Combine eggs, milk, chives, oregano, salt, and pepper in a large mixing bowl. Pour half of the mixture over bread mixture in each baking dish. Cover and refrigerate for 2 to 24 hours.

Bake in a 325° oven, uncovered, for 40 to 45 minutes or until a knife inserted near centers comes out clean. Let stand 10 minutes before serving. Makes 12 servings.

Nutrition facts per serving: 378 cal., 22 g total fat (10 g sat. fat), 172 mg chol., 966 mg sodium, 23 g carbo., 0 g fiber, 21 g pro. **Daily values:** 17% vit. A, 12% vit. C, 25% calcium, 12% iron

191

Sausage-Cheese Strata;
Breakfast Buttered Potatoes
(see recipe, page 192)

Apricot Breakfast Biscuits

These sweet biscuits are light and tender, perfect for brunch or breakfast.

- 2 cups all-purpose flour
- 1 tablespoon baking powder
- ¼ teaspoon salt
- ⅓ cup butter
- ⅓ cup apricot preserves
- ½ cup milk
  Milk
- 2 teaspoons sugar
- ⅛ teaspoon ground cinnamon

Stir together flour, baking powder, and salt in a medium mixing bowl. Using a pastry blender, cut in butter until mixture resembles coarse crumbs. Make a well in the center.

Snip any large pieces of preserves. Combine ½ cup milk and the preserves in a small bowl. Add all at once to dry ingredients. Stir just until dough clings together. Turn out onto a lightly floured surface. Quickly knead by gently folding and pressing dough 10 to 12 strokes or until nearly smooth.

Lightly roll or pat until ½ inch thick. Cut with a floured 2½-inch biscuit cutter, dipping cutter into flour between cuts. Place biscuits 1 inch apart on an ungreased baking sheet. Brush tops with milk. Combine sugar and cinnamon in a small bowl. Sprinkle over biscuits.

Bake in a 450° oven for 7 to 10 minutes or until golden brown. Serve warm. (To make ahead, cool completely and place biscuits in freezer containers or bags. To reheat for serving, wrap frozen biscuits in foil;

heat in a 325° oven about 20 minutes or until hot.) Makes 10 biscuits.

Nutrition facts per biscuit: 177 cal., 7 g total fat (4 g sat. fat), 17 mg chol., 233 mg sodium, 27 g carbo., 1 g fiber, 3 g pro. **Daily values:** 6% vit. A, 0% vit. C, 10% calcium, 9% iron

Country Scones

- ½ cup dried currants
- 2 cups all-purpose flour
- 3 tablespoons brown sugar
- 2 teaspoons baking powder
- ½ teaspoon baking soda
- ½ teaspoon salt
- ⅓ cup butter
- 1 8-ounce carton dairy sour cream
- 1 beaten egg yolk
- 1 slightly beaten egg white
- 1 tablespoon water
- 1 tablespoon coarse sugar

Place currants in a bowl and pour enough hot water over currants to cover. Let stand 5 minutes; drain well.

Stir together flour, brown sugar, baking powder, baking soda, and salt in a large mixing bowl. Using a pastry blender, cut in butter until mixture resembles coarse crumbs. Add drained currants; toss until mixed. Make a well in the center.

Combine sour cream and egg yolk in a small bowl. Add all at once to dry ingredients. Using a fork, stir just until moistened. Turn out onto a lightly floured surface. Quickly knead by gently folding and pressing dough 10 to 12 strokes or until nearly smooth.

Divide dough in half. Lightly roll or pat each half into a 6-inch circle about ½ inch thick. Cut each circle into 6 wedges. Brush tops with a mixture of egg white and 1 tablespoon water. Sprinkle with coarse sugar. Place 1 inch apart on an ungreased baking sheet.

Bake in a 425° oven for 12 to 15 minutes or until lightly browned. Cool on a wire rack for 10 minutes and serve warm. (To make ahead, cool completely and place scones in freezer containers or bags. To reheat for serving, wrap frozen scones in foil and heat in a 325° oven for 25 to 30 minutes or until heated through.) Makes 12 scones.

Nutrition facts per scone: 193 cal., 10 g total fat (6 g sat. fat), 40 mg chol., 270 mg sodium, 24 g carbo., 1 g fiber, 3 g pro. **Daily values:** 11% vit. A, 0% vit. C, 7% calcium, 8% iron

Breakfast Buttered Potatoes

Serve these herbed potatoes with the Sausage-Cheese Strata on page 191.

- 12 small red potatoes (about 3 pounds)
- ¼ cup butter or margarine
- 1 tablespoon snipped fresh rosemary or 1 teaspoon dried rosemary, crushed (optional)
- ½ teaspoon salt
- ¼ teaspoon pepper

Scrub potatoes thoroughly with a stiff brush. Cut potatoes into quarters. Cook potatoes in a 4-quart Dutch oven in a small amount of boiling, lightly salted water for 15 to 20 minutes or until tender; drain.

Meanwhile, heat butter or margarine in a small skillet over low heat until melted. Stir in the rosemary, if using, salt, and pepper. If using rosemary, cook and stir over low heat for 2 minutes. Gently toss cooked potatoes in a bowl with the butter mixture until potatoes are coated. Makes 12 servings.

Nutrition facts per serving: 143 cal., 4 g total fat (2 g sat. fat), 10 mg chol., 136 mg sodium, 25 g carbo., 1 g fiber, 3 g pro. **Daily values:** 3% vit. A, 24% vit. C, 1% calcium, 12% iron

Apricot Breakfast Biscuits

Country Scones

194

Hot Buttered Cider

Strudel Sticks

Strudel Sticks

2 3-ounce packages cream
   cheese, softened
⅓ cup granulated sugar
2 teaspoons finely shredded
   lemon peel
1 17¼-ounce package
   (2 sheets) frozen puff
   pastry, thawed
2 to 3 tablespoons chopped,
   sliced almonds
1 tablespoon coarse sugar

For filling, combine cream cheese,
granulated sugar, and lemon peel in a
small mixing bowl; set aside.
Unfold puff pastry sheets on a lightly
floured surface. Cut each sheet into six
5×3-inch rectangles. Spread about
1 tablespoon cheese filling over each
rectangle to ½ inch from edges. Roll up
jelly-roll style, starting from one long
side. Moisten edge of dough and pinch
edges to seal. Place pastry sticks, seam
sides down, on a lightly greased baking
sheet. Make 3 or 4 diagonal cuts in top
of each pastry. Lightly brush with water.
Sprinkle with almonds and sugar.
Bake in a 350° oven for 30 to
35 minutes or until golden brown.
Serve warm or cool. (To make ahead,
cool completely and place in freezer
containers or bags. To reheat for
serving, wrap in foil and heat in a
325° oven for 15 to 20 minutes or until
heated through.) Makes 12 pastries.

Nutrition facts per pastry: 262 cal., 18 g total fat
(3 g sat. fat), 16 mg chol., 196 mg sodium,
22 g carbo., 0 g fiber, 3 g pro. **Daily values:**
6% vit. A, 0% vit. C, 1% calcium, 1% iron

Hot Buttered Cider

*To make a hot buttered rum drink to
enjoy later in the day, add ½ cup rum to
this recipe.*

8 cups apple cider or apple juice
2 tablespoons brown sugar
4 inches stick cinnamon
1 teaspoon whole allspice
1 teaspoon whole cloves
   Peel from 1 lemon, cut into
   strips
2 tablespoons butter
   Cinnamon sticks (optional)

Combine cider and brown sugar in a
large saucepan. For a spice bag, tie
cinnamon, allspice, cloves, and lemon
peel in a 6 inch square of 100% cotton
cheesecloth. Add spice bag to cider
mixture. Bring to boiling over medium-
high heat; reduce heat. Cover and
simmer for 15 minutes. Remove and
discard spice bag.
Top each serving with ½ teaspoon
butter and serve with a cinnamon stick
stirrer, if desired. (To make ahead, after
discarding spice bag, chill cider and
reheat to serve. Or, keep prepared cider
warm in a crockery cooker on low-heat
setting.) Makes 10 to 12 servings.

Nutrition facts per serving: 128 cal., 2 g total fat
(1 g sat. fat), 6 mg chol., 30 mg sodium,
30 g carbo., 0 g fiber, 0 g pro. **Daily values:**
2% vit. A, 3% vit. C, 1% calcium, 6% iron

195

Sugar-and-Spice Almonds
(see recipe, page 199)

Tropical Fruit-Black Bean Salsa

196

Corn Bread Rounds
with Jalapeño Jelly

Turkey and Vegetable
Tortilla Rolls
(see recipe, page 198)

'Tis the season for parties! Make it easy on yourself. Choose from the make-ahead appetizer recipes that follow, and keep your last-minute preparations to a minimum.

party*perfect*

 If you get the buffet table ready the day before, all you'll have to do at party time is bring out the food and welcome your guests.

Tropical Fruit-Black Bean Salsa

✳

Add the kiwifruit just before serving so the salsa doesn't become too juicy.

- 1 cup canned black beans, rinsed and drained
- 1 small papaya or mango, peeled, seeded, and chopped (¾ cup)
- ½ cup finely chopped fresh pineapple or one 8-ounce can crushed pineapple (juice pack), drained
- 1 medium orange, peeled, sectioned, and finely chopped (⅓ cup)
- ¼ cup thinly sliced green onions
- ¼ cup finely chopped red sweet pepper
- 2 tablespoons snipped fresh cilantro
- 1 tablespoon lime or lemon juice
- 3 small kiwifruit, peeled and finely chopped (⅔ cup)
- Tortilla chips

Stir together black beans, papaya or mango, pineapple, orange, green onions, sweet pepper, cilantro, and lime or lemon juice in a medium mixing bowl. Cover and chill for 4 to 24 hours. Stir in kiwifruit. Transfer to serving dish using a slotted spoon. Serve with tortilla chips. Makes about 3½ cups salsa.

Nutrition facts per tablespoon (without tortilla chips): 8 cal., 0 g total fat (0 g sat. fat), 0 mg chol., 11 mg sodium, 2 g carbo., 0 g fiber, 0 g pro. **Daily values:** 1% vit. A, 12% vit. C, 0% calcium, 0% iron

---

Corn Bread Rounds With Jalapeño Jelly

✳

To make a colorful appetizer tray, top some of the corn bread rounds with red jelly and others with green jelly.

- ¾ cup all-purpose flour
- ¼ cup cornmeal
- 1 tablespoon sugar
- 1 teaspoon baking powder
- ¼ teaspoon salt
- ¼ cup butter
- ¼ cup milk
- 2 tablespoons canned diced green chili peppers, drained
- 1 tablespoon oil-packed dried tomatoes, drained and finely chopped
- 1 8-ounce tub cream cheese
- ¼ cup red and/or green jalapeño jelly, melted

Stir together flour, cornmeal, sugar, baking powder, and salt in a medium mixing bowl. Using a pastry blender, cut in the butter until mixture resembles coarse crumbs. Add the milk, chili peppers, and tomatoes all at once and stir until the mixture forms a ball.

Turn dough out onto a lightly floured surface and knead by gently folding and pressing dough for 8 to 10 strokes. Roll the dough until ¼ inch thick. Cut with a floured 2-inch round biscuit cutter, dipping cutter into flour between cuts. Place dough rounds on an ungreased baking sheet.

Bake in a 400° oven for 12 to 15 minutes or until golden. Remove and cool on a wire rack. (To make ahead, freeze baked rounds in freezer containers. Thaw before using.) To serve, spread cream cheese atop each round. Drizzle with melted jelly. Makes 18 rounds.

Nutrition facts per round: 109 cal., 7 g total fat (4 g sat. fat), 21 mg chol., 133 mg sodium, 10 g carbo., 0 g fiber, 2 g pro. **Daily values:** 8% vit. A, 2% vit. C, 3% calcium, 3% iron

Cranberry-Praline Mascarpone Spread

electric mixer on medium speed until combined. Stir in the dried cranberries or cherries.

Before serving, stir in finely chopped praline mixture and 1 tablespoon milk, if desired, to thin consistency of spread. Transfer to a serving bowl. If desired, garnish with orange peel curls. Serve with cookies and fruit. Makes 1½ cups.

Nutrition facts per tablespoon spread: 70 cal., 6 g total fat (3 g sat. fat), 13 mg chol., 11 mg sodium, 4 g carbo., 0 g fiber, 2 g pro. **Daily values:** 0% vit. A, 0% vit. C, 0% calcium, 0% iron

Turkey and Vegetable Tortilla Rolls

Vary the color of the sweet peppers, if you like (see photo, page 196).

- 12 asparagus spears
- 1 large red sweet pepper
- 1 8-ounce package cream cheese, softened
- 2 tablespoons milk
- 2 teaspoons snipped fresh rosemary or ½ teaspoon dried rosemary, crushed
- 1 to 2 teaspoons brown mustard
- 4 7- or 8-inch flour tortillas
- 2 6-ounce packages thinly sliced cooked smoked turkey
  Lettuce leaves

Cook asparagus in a small amount of boiling water for 4 to 8 minutes or until crisp-tender. Drain thoroughly on paper towels. Cut pepper into strips.

Beat cream cheese, milk, rosemary, and mustard together in a mixing bowl with an electric mixer until the mixture is smooth.

To assemble, place 1 tortilla on a flat surface. Spread one-fourth of the cream cheese mixture on the tortilla. Place one-fourth of the turkey on cream cheese mixture. Arrange 3 of the asparagus spears and several pepper strips over the turkey. Roll up tortilla. Repeat with remaining tortillas and filling ingredients. Wrap each tortilla roll in plastic wrap; chill up to 12 hours.

  PARTY PERFECT

Cranberry-Praline Mascarpone Spread

For make-ahead convenience, you can prepare the praline mixture up to 3 days ahead and store it at room temperature. The cheese mixture also can be made ahead and stored, covered, in the refrigerator. Just before serving, stir the two together.

- ⅓ cup finely chopped almonds or hazelnuts (filberts)
- ¼ cup sugar
- 1 tablespoon butter
- ¼ teaspoon vanilla
- 1 8-ounce carton mascarpone cheese or one 8-ounce package cream cheese, softened
- ½ teaspoon finely shredded orange peel
- 1 tablespoon Grand Marnier or orange juice
- ¼ cup dried cranberries or tart red cherries, chopped
- 1 tablespoon milk (optional)
  Orange peel curls (optional)
  Assorted crisp cookies (such as Pirouettes or shortbread)
  Fresh fruit (such as strawberries, apple slices, pear slices, and/or grapes)

Line a baking sheet with foil. Butter the foil and set aside.

Combine almonds or hazelnuts, sugar, butter, and vanilla in a heavy 8-inch skillet. Cook over medium heat (do not stir) until sugar begins to melt, shaking skillet occasionally. Reduce heat to low; continue cooking until sugar turns golden, stirring frequently with a wooden spoon. Immediately spread coated nuts on prepared baking sheet. Cool nuts and break into chunks; finely chop. Store in airtight container.

Beat cheese, orange peel, and Grand Marnier in a mixing bowl with an

To serve, remove plastic wrap and cut each tortilla roll into 1-inch-thick slices. Place, cut side up, on a lettuce-lined plate. Makes 24 to 28 slices.

Nutrition facts per slice: 86 cal., 6 g total fat (2 g sat. fat), 11 mg chol., 205 mg sodium, 4 g carbo., 0 g fiber, 4 g pro. **Daily values:** 5% vit. A, 17% vit. C, 1% calcium, 3% iron

Gunpowder Guacamole

Sugar-and-Spice Almonds

To make extra nuts for gift giving, prepare a separate batch instead of doubling the recipe. The nuts clump together if cooked in larger quantities (see photo, page 196).

½ cup sugar
½ teaspoon finely shredded orange peel
¼ teaspoon ground cinnamon
⅛ teaspoon salt
⅛ teaspoon ground allspice
⅛ teaspoon ground nutmeg
1 cup unblanched whole almonds

Line a baking sheet with foil. Butter the foil and set aside.

Combine sugar, orange peel, cinnamon, salt, allspice, and nutmeg in a heavy 10-inch skillet. Stir in almonds. Cook over medium-high heat (do not stir) until sugar begins to melt, shaking skillet occasionally (this will take 5 to 7 minutes). Reduce heat to low; continue cooking until sugar turns golden brown, stirring frequently with a wooden spoon (this will take 2 to 4 minutes).

Immediately pour nut mixture onto the prepared baking sheet. Spread into a single layer with a wooden spoon. Cool completely. Break apart, if necessary. Store in an airtight container. Makes 2 cups.

Nutrition facts per ¼ cup serving: 124 cal., 7 g total fat (1 g sat. fat), 0 mg chol., 34 mg sodium, 15 g carbo., 1 g fiber, 4 g pro. **Daily values:** 0% vit. A, 0% vit. C, 4% calcium, 5% iron

Gunpowder Guacamole

2 medium avocados, seeded, peeled, and cut up
1 tablespoon lime juice
1 medium red sweet pepper, roasted and chopped or ½ cup chopped purchased roasted red sweet peppers
3 green onions, finely chopped
1 to 2 tablespoons chopped jalapeño or serrano chili peppers*
¼ teaspoon salt
¼ teaspoon ground black pepper
⅛ teaspoon ground red pepper
Tortilla chips

Combine avocados and lime juice in a medium mixing bowl. Using a potato masher, coarsely mash avocado mixture (mixture should be slightly lumpy).

Stir roasted sweet pepper, green onions, jalapeño or serrano peppers, salt, black pepper, and red pepper into avocado mixture. Cover and chill until serving time. Serve with tortilla chips. Makes about 1⅔ cups.

*Note: When handling hot chili peppers, avoid touching your eyes; wear disposable gloves to protect your skin.

Nutrition facts per tablespoon (without tortilla chips): 26 cal., 2 g total fat (0 g sat. fat), 0 mg chol., 21 mg sodium, 2 g carbo., 1 g fiber, 0 g pro. **Daily values:** 3% vit. A, 12% vit. C, 0% calcium, 1% iron

timesaving tips

■ Choose a few "star" recipes, then round out your food table with purchased items, such as trays of cheeses, meats, fresh vegetable cruidités, and fruit pieces. Accompany these with baskets of crackers, baguette slices, and chips.

■ Plan your menu and grocery list one to two weeks in advance and include some make-ahead recipes.

■ If you love to entertain but have no time to cook, consider hiring a caterer or a friend who cooks to help with the food preparations. Often a caterer will let you supply the recipes, if desired.

■ Hire someone to help pour beverages and keep food trays replenished so you can enjoy your own party.

199

Three-Cheese Loaf

Three-Cheese Loaf

2 cups finely shredded
    cheddar cheese (8 ounces)
1 cup finely shredded Swiss
    cheese (4 ounces)
½ of an 8-ounce package
    cream cheese
⅓ cup dairy sour cream
2 teaspoons horseradish mustard
⅛ teaspoon onion powder
⅔ cup chopped pistachio nuts,
    walnuts, or pecans
    Assorted crackers and fruits

Bring cheddar cheese, Swiss cheese, and cream cheese to room temperature. Add sour cream, horseradish mustard, and onion powder. Beat until combined and mixture is slightly fluffy.

Line one 7½×3½×2-inch or two 5¾×3×2-inch loaf pan(s) with plastic wrap. Sprinkle half the nuts in the large pan or one-fourth of the nuts in each of the smaller pans. Spread half of the cheese mixture over nut layer (one-fourth in each of the smaller pans). Top with remaining nuts; spread with remaining cheese mixture, pressing into pan(s) to make an even layer. Cover and chill at least 2 hours.

To serve, unmold onto serving plate; remove plastic wrap and let stand 10 minutes before serving. Serve with crackers and fruits. Makes 20 servings.

Nutrition facts per serving spread: 120 cal., 10 g total fat (5 g sat. fat), 25 mg chol., 109 mg sodium, 2 g carbo., 0 g fiber, 6 g pro. **Daily values:** 8% vit. A, 0% vit. C, 12% calcium, 2% iron.

Nutty Blue Cheese Rolls

These flavorful appetizers get a head start with a refrigerated piecrust.

⅔ cup finely chopped walnuts
⅓ cup crumbled blue cheese
1 tablespoon finely snipped
    parsley
¼ teaspoon pepper
½ of a 15-ounce package (1 crust)
    folded refrigerated unbaked
    piecrust
1 tablespoon milk
2 teaspoons grated Parmesan
    cheese
    Finely snipped parsley

For filling, stir together walnuts, blue cheese, 1 tablespoon parsley, and the pepper in a medium bowl. Unfold piecrust on a lightly floured surface according to package directions. Spread filling evenly over the crust. Cut the pastry circle into 12 wedges. Starting at the wide ends, loosely roll up wedges. Place rolls, tip side down, on a greased baking sheet. (To make ahead, cover and chill rolls for up to 24 hours.)

Brush rolls lightly with milk before baking. Sprinkle with Parmesan cheese and additional parsley.

Bake in a 425° oven about 15 minutes or until golden. Cool slightly on a wire rack. Serve warm. Makes 12 rolls.

Nutrition facts per roll: 139 cal., 10 g total fat (1 g sat. fat), 8 mg chol., 130 mg sodium, 9 g carbo., 3 g fiber, 3 g pro. **Daily values:** 1% vit. A, 1% vit. C, 2% calcium, 1% iron

Nutty Blue Cheese Rolls

turkey *basics*

Because many of us save turkey and all the trimmings for a once- or twice-a-year feast, even experienced cooks can use a refresher course on buying, thawing, and cooking the traditional bird. Here are some tips. For recipes, see *pages 204–205.*

unstuffed* whole turkey roasting guide

Ready-to-cook turkey weight	Oven temperature	Roasting time
8 to 12 pounds	325°	2¾ to 3 hours
12 to 14 pounds	325°	3 to 3¾ hours
14 to 18 pounds	325°	3¾ to 4¼ hours
18 to 20 pounds	325°	4¼ to 4½ hours
20 to 24 pounds	325°	4½ to 5 hours

Stuffed birds generally require 15 to 45 minutes more roasting time than unstuffed birds.

buying and thawing a turkey

■ When buying a turkey, allow 1 pound per adult serving if the bird weighs 12 pounds or less. For larger turkeys, count on ¾ pound for each serving. If you want leftovers, buy a bird that's 2 to 4 pounds larger than the size you'll need for serving.

■ Although not all turkeys are labeled indicating whether the bird is a hen or tom, select a hen turkey if you want more white meat and a tom if you want more dark meat. Also check for the "sell by" date on the label of a fresh turkey. This date is the last day the turkey should be sold by the retailer. The unopened turkey should maintain its quality and be safe to use for one or two days after the "sell by" date.

■ If you buy a frozen turkey, look for packaging that is clean, undamaged, and frost free. Allow plenty of time to thaw a frozen turkey. For a whole frozen turkey, leave the bird in its wrapping and place it on a tray in the refrigerator. Plan on at least 24 hours for every 5 pounds and don't count the day you'll roast the bird. (Once thawed, turkeys will keep one or two days in the refrigerator.)

■ If you run short of time and the turkey isn't completely thawed the day you plan to roast it, place the bird in a clean sink full of COLD water and change the water every 30 minutes. Do NOT thaw turkey at room temperature or in warm water—these methods will allow harmful bacteria to grow quickly to dangerous levels. You'll know the bird is ready for roasting if the giblets can be removed easily and there are no ice crystals in the interior cavity. If the turkey is still frozen in the center, the bird will cook unevenly.

preparing a turkey for roasting

■ Once the turkey has thawed, release the legs from the leg clamp or the band of skin crossing the tail. Also remove the giblets and neck from cavities. Rinse the turkey inside and out, let it drain, and pat dry with paper towels.

■ If you don't have an accurate meat thermometer, cook the stuffing separately because there is no visual test for stuffing doneness. Mix the stuffing just before you stuff and roast the bird. Allow ¾ cup of stuffing per pound of bird. Spoon some stuffing loosely into the neck cavity. Pull the neck skin over the stuffing and fasten to the back with a short skewer.

■ Loosely spoon stuffing into the body cavity rather than packing it. Otherwise, it won't get hot enough by the time the turkey is cooked. Spoon any remaining stuffing into a casserole; cover and chill until ready to bake. Tuck the legs under the band of skin that crosses the tail or reset the legs into the leg clamp. Or, tie the legs with kitchen string to the tail. Twist the wing tips under the back.

■ Place the turkey, breast side up, on a rack in a shallow roasting pan. Insert a meat thermometer into the center of an inside thigh muscle so the bulb doesn't touch bone. Cover the turkey loosely with foil, leaving space between the bird and the foil. Press the foil over the drumsticks and neck. Roast in a 325° oven using the timings in the chart on *page 202* as a guide.

■ When the bird has been in the oven for two-thirds of the roasting time, cut the skin between the drumsticks but don't remove the clamp. Remove the foil the last 30 minutes to let the turkey brown.

■ When the turkey is done, the thigh meat should be 180° and the center of the stuffing should be at least 165°. (Check the temperatures with a thermometer—see tips *below*.) The drumsticks should move easily in their sockets, and their thickest parts should feel soft when pressed. In addition, juices from the thigh should run clear when it's pierced deeply with a long-tined fork. Remove the turkey from the oven and cover loosely with foil. Let stand for 20 minutes. Release the legs from the leg clamp. To avoid possible burns, don't remove the leg clamp until turkey has cooled.

■ Do not allow the turkey to remain at room temperature more than two hours after it comes out of the oven. Cooked turkey and stuffing may be refrigerated, separately, up to two days.

thermometer tips

■ Use a thermometer to ensure that the turkey and the stuffing have reached a safe temperature for consumption.

■ A meat thermometer is used for larger cuts of poultry (and meat). Insert the thermometer into the turkey at the beginning of the cooking time, making sure it doesn't touch bone or the pan.

■ An instant-read thermometer, also called a rapid-response thermometer, measures a wide range of temperatures. These thermometers are not designed to stay in food during cooking. Remove the food from the oven, then insert the thermometer into the thickest portion of the food, not touching bone or pan.

■ Check a thermometer for accuracy by submerging at least 2 inches of the stem of the thermometer in boiling water. It should read 212°F.

Roast Turkey with Bourbon-Butter Glaze

Part of the glaze is slipped under the turkey's skin and the rest is brushed over the turkey for a golden color. If the turkey is stuffed, add extra roasting time.

½ cup butter, softened
¼ cup packed brown sugar
2 tablespoons chopped fresh
  marjoram or 2 teaspoons
  dried marjoram, crushed
1 teaspoon finely shredded
  lemon peel
1 14- to 16-pound turkey
½ cup bourbon
  Salt
  Pepper

For glaze, combine butter, brown sugar, marjoram, and lemon peel in a small mixing bowl.

Rinse turkey and pat dry with paper towels. Place turkey, breast side up, on a rack in a shallow roasting pan. Using your fingers, separate turkey skin from breast meat, being careful not to tear skin or pierce meat. Spread about half of the butter mixture over the breast meat under the skin.

Melt remaining butter mixture; cool slightly. Stir in bourbon. Brush mixture over outside of turkey. Season turkey with salt and pepper. Pull neck skin to back and fasten to back with a short skewer. Tuck drumsticks under band of skin that crosses tail. If there isn't a band, tie drumsticks to tail. Twist wing tips under back.

Insert a meat thermometer into the center of one of the inside thigh muscles. The thermometer bulb should not touch the bone. Cover turkey loosely with foil. Roast turkey in a 325° oven for 3¾ to 4¼ hours or until meat thermometer registers 180°.

When turkey is two-thirds done, cut skin or string between drumsticks. Remove foil the last 30 minutes to let bird brown. Turkey is done when drumsticks move very easily in their sockets and their thickest parts feel soft when pressed. Remove turkey from oven and cover loosely with foil. Let stand 20 minutes before carving. Makes 12 to 15 servings.

Nutrition facts per serving: 432 cal., 23 g total fat (9 g sat. fat), 174 mg chol., 231 mg sodium, 4 g carbo., 0 g fiber, 45 g pro. **Daily values:** 18% vit. A, 0% vit. C, 4% calcium, 22% iron

Rich Pan Gravy

Pour pan drippings from roast turkey into a large measuring cup. Skim and reserve fat from pan drippings. Measure fat and add melted butter or margarine, if necessary, to make ½ cup. Add chicken broth to the skimmed drippings to measure 2½ cups total; set aside.

Pour the ½ cup fat into a medium saucepan (discard any remaining fat). Stir in ½ cup all-purpose flour, ¼ teaspoon salt, and ⅛ teaspoon pepper. Cook and stir over medium heat for 2 minutes. Gradually whisk broth mixture into flour mixture. Cook and stir until thickened and bubbly. Add ½ cup milk. Cook and stir 1 minute more. Makes about 3½ cups.

Nutrition facts per 2 tablespoons: 41 cal., 3 g total fat (2 g sat. fat), 9 mg chol., 57 mg sodium, 2 g carbo., 0 g fiber, 0 g pro. **Daily values:** 3% vit. A, 0% vit. C, 0% calcium, 0% iron

Herbed Roasted Turkey

¼ cup olive oil
1 tablespoon snipped fresh basil
1 tablespoon snipped
  fresh oregano
1 tablespoon snipped fresh
  parsley
2 cloves garlic, minced
¼ teaspoon salt
1 8- to 12-pound turkey

Combine olive oil, basil, oregano, parsley, garlic, and salt in a small bowl.

Rinse turkey and pat dry with paper towels. Place turkey, breast side up, on a rack in a shallow roasting pan. Using your fingers, separate turkey skin from breast meat, being careful not to tear skin or pierce meat. Spread about half of the oil mixture over the breast meat under the skin. Brush remaining mixture over outside of turkey. Pull neck skin to back and fasten with a short skewer. Tuck drumsticks under band of skin that crosses tail. If there isn't a band, tie drumsticks to tail. Twist wing tips under back.

Insert a meat thermometer into the center of one of the inside thigh muscles. The thermometer bulb should not touch the bone. Cover turkey loosely with foil. Roast turkey in a 325° oven for 2¾ to 3 hours or until meat thermometer registers 180°.

When turkey is two-thirds done, cut skin or string between drumsticks. Remove foil the last 30 minutes to let bird brown. Turkey is done when drumsticks move very easily in their sockets and their thickest parts feel soft when pressed. Remove turkey from oven and cover loosely with foil. Let stand 20 minutes before carving. Makes 8 to 12 servings.

Nutrition facts per serving: 526 cal., 28 g total fat (7 g sat. fat), 216 mg chol., 220 mg sodium, 0 g carbo., 0 g fiber, 64 g pro. **Daily values:** 15% vit. A, 1% vit. C, 5% calcium, 30% iron

Spice-Rubbed Turkey

¼ cup cooking oil
1 tablespoon chili powder
1 teaspoon ground cumin
1 teaspoon garlic salt
½ teaspoon ground coriander
1 12- to 14-pound turkey

Combine cooking oil, chili powder, cumin, garlic salt, and coriander in a small bowl.

Rinse turkey and pat dry with paper towels. Place turkey, breast side up, on a rack in a shallow roasting pan. Using your fingers, separate turkey skin from breast meat, being careful not to tear skin or pierce meat. Spread about half the oil mixture over the breast meat under the skin. Brush remaining mixture over outside of turkey. Pull neck skin to back and fasten with a short skewer. Tuck drumsticks under

band of skin that crosses tail. If there isn't a band, tie drumsticks to tail. Twist wing tips under back.

Insert a meat thermometer into the center of one of the inside thigh muscles. The thermometer bulb should not touch the bone. Cover turkey loosely with foil. Roast turkey in a 325° oven for 3 to 3¾ hours or until meat thermometer registers 180°.

When turkey is two-thirds done, cut skin or string between drumsticks. Remove foil the last 30 minutes to let bird brown. Turkey is done when drumsticks move very easily in their sockets and their thickest parts feel soft when pressed. Remove turkey from oven and cover loosely with foil. Let stand 20 minutes before carving. Makes 12 to 14 servings.

Nutrition facts per serving: 315 cal., 17 g total fat (4 g sat. fat), 126 mg chol., 267 mg sodium, 1 g carbo., 0 g fiber, 37 g pro. **Daily values:** 11% vit. A, 0% vit. C, 3% calcium, 20% iron

Corn Bread and Dried Peach Dressing

Southern-Style Corn Bread
½ cup chopped celery with leaves
½ cup chopped onion
⅓ cup butter
1½ cups chopped cooked ham
2 beaten eggs
¼ cup snipped fresh parsley
2 teaspoons dried sage, crushed
½ teaspoon pepper
¼ teaspoon salt
1½ cups chopped dried peaches
1 cup coarsely chopped pecans, toasted
1 to 1⅓ cups chicken broth

Prepare corn bread; cut into ½-inch pieces. Place in a large shallow baking pan. Bake in a 325° oven about 15 minutes or until bread pieces are slightly dry, stirring once. Transfer to a very large bowl.

Cook celery and onion in butter in a large skillet or saucepan over medium heat about 5 minutes or until vegetables are tender. Add to corn bread in bowl. Add ham.

Combine eggs, parsley, sage, pepper, and salt in a small bowl. Add to corn bread mixture; toss lightly until mixed. Add peaches and pecans. Drizzle with enough of the broth to moisten, tossing very lightly until mixed. Use to stuff a 14- to 16-pound turkey. Spoon any remaining stuffing into a casserole; cover and chill until ready to bake. The last 45 minutes of turkey roasting, add the casserole to the oven and bake, covered, until heated through. Makes 12 to 15 servings.

SOUTHERN-STYLE CORN BREAD: Stir together 2 cups yellow cornmeal, 1 cup all-purpose flour, 4 teaspoons baking powder, and ½ teaspoon salt in a mixing bowl. Lightly beat together 1½ cups buttermilk, 2 eggs, and ⅓ cup melted butter. Add to flour mixture and stir just until batter is smooth (do not overbeat). Pour into a greased 9×9×2-inch baking pan. Bake in a 425° oven for 25 to 30 minutes or until golden brown.

Nutrition facts per serving dressing: 370 cal., 20 g total fat (8 g sat. fat), 109 mg chol., 693 mg sodium, 38 g carbo., 3 g fiber, 12 g pro. **Daily values:** 17% vit. A, 11% vit. C, 14% calcium, 20% iron

205

▼ Before placing a serving on a dessert plate, stencil the plate, using a paper doily, a sieve, and cinnamon, cocoa powder, or powdered sugar. Place the doily on a plate and spray lightly with nonstick spray coating. Sift a topping over the stencil, then lift off the doily carefully. Stencil the dessert in the same way (omit the spray coating). Use cinnamon, unsweetened cocoa powder, or cinnamon-sugar mixture on cake with a light-colored frosting. Try powdered sugar on a chocolate-frosted cake.

▲ Decorate a pie, frosted cake, or cookie platter with chocolate stars. Spoon melted and cooled chocolate into a small, self-sealing plastic bag. Snip off one corner of the bag, and pipe the melted chocolate onto a waxed-paper-lined baking sheet, forming a square. Pipe a second square at a 45-degree angle to the first. Let chocolate stand until firm.

In a Twinkling:
Treats

◄ Freeze cranberries and use them instead of ice to cool the champagne. As the berries thaw, they take on a frosty charm.

For Sugared Cranberries, combine 2 tablespoons water and 1 tablespoon refrigerated egg product. Brush cranberries with the mixture, then roll in granulated sugar. Use within 2 hours to decorate desserts.

◀ For a simple but festive presentation, arrange loops of wired star garland in random curls around the base of a pedestal cake plate.

▲ To make small chocolate curls, draw a vegetable peeler across a bar of milk chocolate. The chocolate curls best if it is at room temperature. Use the narrow side of the chocolate bar for narrow curls and the broad surface for wide curls.

207

To make a **miniature herb bouquet** for decorating a serving plate or topping an appetizer tart, select three or four kinds of herbs with different textures and colors. Cut the stems about 4 inches long and arrange herbs to show off the different types before tying with a string. If you like, you can dye the string with tea.

▼

▲ Give your desserts a sophisticated look by pooling the sauce under the dessert instead of over it. Spoon 1 or 2 tablespoons of sauce on each dessert plate and tilt the plate to spread the sauce evenly. If you like, pipe a contrasting colored sauce to outline the edge, using a pastry bag with a round tip.

menu

Minestrone
or
Nacho Cheese and
Corn Chowder

✻

Citrus Tossed Salad
with Cranberry
Vinaigrette

✻

Sweet Potato-
Wheat Twist
or
Easy Herb Focaccia

✻

Pumpkin
Gingerbread

✻

Coffee and/or Milk

Minestrone

Sweet Potato-Wheat Twist
(see recipe, page 210)

*Citrus Tossed Salad with
Cranberry Vinaigrette*
(see recipe, page 211)

This is a season of stories. Whether it's the Christmas story of Christ's birth or one of the many secular poems and tales that have become Christmas traditions, stories are passed on from one generation to the next.

storyteller's *eve*

Give your family a special gift this year by setting aside an evening for storytelling, complete with a soup supper. Then gather in front of a toasty fire and take turns reading aloud from a favorite book.

Minestrone

Serve this vegetable-packed soup with an assortment of cold cuts, such as salami and ham, a variety of cheeses, olives, and pickled peppers.

6 cups water
1 28-ounce can tomatoes, cut up
1 8-ounce can tomato sauce
1 large onion, chopped
1 cup chopped cabbage
1 medium carrot, chopped
1 stalk celery, chopped
4 teaspoons instant beef bouillon
    granules
1 tablespoon dried Italian
    seasoning, crushed
1 teaspoon bottled minced garlic
    or 2 cloves garlic, minced
¼ teaspoon pepper
1 15-ounce can cannellini or
    great northern beans
1 10-ounce package frozen lima
    beans or one 9-ounce
    package frozen Italian-style
    green beans

4 ounces packaged dried linguine
    or spaghetti, broken
1 small zucchini, halved
    lengthwise and sliced
2 to 3 tablespoons purchased
    pesto (optional)
    Grated Parmesan cheese

Combine water, undrained tomatoes, tomato sauce, onion, cabbage, carrot, celery, bouillon, Italian seasoning, garlic, and pepper in a 5- to 6-quart Dutch oven. Bring to boiling; reduce heat. Cover and simmer 10 minutes.

Stir in undrained canned beans, lima beans, linguine, and zucchini. Return to boiling; reduce heat. Simmer, uncovered, 15 minutes. Serve in bowls. Top each serving with 1 teaspoon pesto, if desired. Pass Parmesan cheese to sprinkle over soup. Makes 8 servings.

Nutrition facts per serving: 177 cal., 3 g total fat (1 g sat. fat), 5 mg chol., 992 mg sodium, 32 g carbo., 5 g fiber, 10 g pro. **Daily values:** 33% vit. A, 41% vit. C, 14% calcium, 19% iron

Nacho Cheese and Corn Chowder

3 medium onions, chopped
    (1½ cups)
6 cups milk
¾ cup all-purpose flour
4½ teaspoons instant chicken
    bouillon granules

3 cups frozen whole kernel corn
3 cups shredded colby-and-
    Monterey Jack cheese
    (12 ounces)
3 cups shredded American
    cheese (12 ounces)
1 4½-ounce can diced green
    chili peppers, drained
½ cup thick and chunky salsa
    Tortilla chips (optional)
    Bottled hot pepper sauce
    (optional)

Combine onions and 3 cups water in a 4½- to 5-quart Dutch oven. Bring to boiling; reduce heat. Cover and simmer about 5 minutes or until onions are tender. *Do not drain.*

Gradually stir or whisk 2 cups of the milk into the flour until smooth. Stir into Dutch oven with remaining milk and bouillon granules. Cook and stir over medium heat until thickened and bubbly. Cook and stir 1 minute more.

Stir in corn, cheeses, and chili peppers. Cook over low heat, stirring frequently, until heated through. Garnish each serving with 1 tablespoon salsa and a few tortilla chips, if desired. Pass hot pepper sauce, if desired. Makes 8 servings.

Nutrition facts per serving: 485 cal., 27 g total fat (16 g sat. fat), 77 mg chol., 1,490 mg sodium, 37 g carbo., 1 g fiber, 27 g pro. **Daily values:** 36% vit. A, 24% vit. C, 66% calcium, 11% iron

Easy Herb Focaccia

This simplified version of focaccia (foh CAH chee ah) starts with a roll mix.

    1   16-ounce package hot roll mix
    1   egg
    2   tablespoons olive oil
    ⅔   cup finely chopped onion
    1   teaspoon dried rosemary,
          crushed
    2   teaspoons olive oil

Lightly grease one 15×10×1-inch baking pan, one 12- to 14-inch pizza pan, or two 9×1½-inch round baking pans. Set aside.

Prepare the hot roll mix according to package directions for basic dough, using the 1 egg and substituting the 2 tablespoons oil for the margarine. Knead dough; allow to rest as directed. If using large baking pan, roll dough into a 15×10-inch rectangle and carefully transfer to prepared pan. If using a pizza pan, roll dough into a 12-inch round. For round baking pans, divide dough in half; roll into two 9-inch rounds. Place in prepared pan(s).

Cook onion and rosemary in the 2 teaspoons oil in a skillet until onion is tender. With fingertips, press indentations every inch or so in dough. Top dough evenly with onion mixture. Cover; let rise in a warm place until nearly double (about 30 minutes).

Bake in a 375° oven for 15 to 20 minutes or until golden. Cool 10 minutes on a wire rack(s). Remove from pan(s) and cool completely. Makes 24 servings.

Nutrition facts per serving: 85 cal., 2 g total fat (0 g sat. fat), 9 mg chol., 133 mg sodium, 14 g carbo., 0 g fiber, 2 g pro. **Daily values:** 1% vit. A, 0% vit. C, 0% calcium, 4% iron

Sweet Potato-Wheat Twist

Wrap one loaf in heavy foil or place in a freezer bag and freeze up to 3 months (see photo, page 208).

    1¼ cups water
    1   cup chopped peeled sweet
          potato (1 medium)
    1   cup buttermilk
    2   tablespoons shortening,
          margarine, or butter
    2   tablespoons honey
    2   teaspoons salt
    4¾ to 5½ cups all-purpose flour
    2   packages active dry yeast
    1   egg
    1½ cups whole wheat flour

Combine water and sweet potato in a medium saucepan. Bring to boiling; reduce heat. Cover and simmer about 12 minutes or until very tender. *Do not drain.* Mash potato in the water. Measure potato-water mixture and, if necessary, add water to equal 1½ cups.

Return potato mixture to saucepan. Add buttermilk, shortening, honey, and salt. Heat or cool, as necessary, and stir until warm (120° to 130°).

Stir together 2 cups of the all-purpose flour and the yeast in a large mixing bowl. Add potato mixture and egg. Beat with an electric mixer on low speed for 30 seconds, scraping the sides of the bowl constantly. Beat on high speed for 3 minutes. Divide the batter in half.

To half of the batter, stir in the whole wheat flour and about ½ cup all-purpose flour, using a spoon. Turn out onto a lightly floured surface. Knead in enough flour (¼ to ½ cup) to make a moderately stiff dough that is smooth and elastic (6 to 8 minutes total). Shape into a ball. Place in a lightly greased bowl; turn once to grease surface. Cover and let rise in a warm place until double (about 45 minutes).

To the remaining batter, stir in as much of the remaining all-purpose flour as you can (about 2 cups), using a spoon. Turn out onto a lightly floured surface. Knead in enough of the remaining flour (¼ to ½ cup) to make a moderately stiff dough that is smooth and elastic (6 to 8 minutes total). Shape into a ball. Place in a lightly greased bowl; turn once to grease surface. Cover and let rise in a warm place until double (about 45 minutes).

Punch down each ball of dough and turn out onto a lightly floured surface. Divide each ball of dough in half. Cover and let rest for 10 minutes.

Roll each portion of dough into an evenly thick 10-inch-long rope. Loosely twist one plain and one whole wheat rope together; press ends together to seal. Place in a lightly greased 9×5×3-inch loaf pan. Repeat with remaining two ropes in another loaf pan. Cover and let rise in a warm place until nearly double (30 to 40 minutes).

Bake in a 375° oven about 40 minutes or until breads sound hollow when lightly tapped. If necessary, loosely cover bread with foil the last 10 minutes to prevent overbrowning. Remove from pans immediately. Cool on wire racks. Makes 2 loaves (32 slices).

Nutrition facts per slice: 103 cal., 1 g total fat (0 g sat. fat), 7 mg chol., 145 mg sodium, 20 g carbo., 1 g fiber, 3 g pro. **Daily values:** 8% vit. A, 1% vit. C, 1% calcium, 7% iron

210

Citrus Tossed Salad *with* Cranberry Vinaigrette

See photo, page 208.

8 cups torn mixed greens
2 cups orange sections and/or
   red grapefruit sections
2 cups jicama, cut into thin,
   bite-size strips
2 small red onions, sliced and
   separated into rings
   Cranberry Vinaigrette
   Croutons (optional)

Combine torn mixed greens, orange and/or grapefruit sections, jicama, and red onions in a large salad bowl. Shake Cranberry Vinaigrette well. Pour over salad. Toss lightly to coat. If desired, top with croutons. Serve immediately. Makes 8 servings.

CRANBERRY VINAIGRETTE: Combine ½ cup cranberry juice; 2 tablespoons salad oil; 2 tablespoons vinegar; 2 teaspoons snipped fresh basil or ½ teaspoon dried basil, crushed; and 1 teaspoon sugar in screw-top jar. Cover and shake well. Makes about ⅔ cup.

Nutrition facts per serving: 94 cal., 4 g total fat (1 g sat. fat), 0 mg chol., 6 mg sodium, 15 g carbo., 2 g fiber, 2 g pro. **Daily values:** 11% vit. A, 76% vit. C, 4% calcium, 7% iron

Pumpkin Gingerbread

1¼ cups all-purpose flour
1½ teaspoons grated fresh
    gingerroot or ½ teaspoon
    ground ginger
1   teaspoon finely shredded
    orange peel
¾   teaspoon ground cinnamon

Pumpkin Gingerbread

½ teaspoon baking powder
½ teaspoon baking soda
⅓ cup butter
⅓ cup packed brown sugar
1 egg
½ cup canned pumpkin
¼ cup mild-flavored molasses
¼ cup milk
   Whipped cream
   Orange peel curls (optional)

Stir together flour, gingerroot or ground ginger, finely shredded orange peel, cinnamon, baking powder, and baking soda in a medium mixing bowl. Set aside.

Beat together butter and brown sugar in a large mixing bowl with an electric mixer on medium to high speed until combined. Add egg and beat well. Beat in pumpkin and molasses on medium speed until smooth.

Alternately add flour mixture and milk to the pumpkin mixture, beating until smooth. Pour into a greased and lightly floured 8×8×2-inch baking pan.

Bake in a 350° oven for 35 to 40 minutes or until a wooden toothpick inserted near center comes out clean. Cool in pan on a wire rack 10 minutes. Serve warm with whipped cream. If desired, garnish with orange peel curls. Makes 9 servings.

Nutrition facts per serving: 233 cal., 13 g total fat (8 g sat. fat), 63 mg chol., 179 mg sodium, 27 g carbo., 1 g fiber, 3 g pro. **Daily values:** 44% vit. A, 1% vit. C, 5% calcium, 11% iron

211

Try These for a Good Read

If you don't have a favorite for family reading, try one of the following titles recommended by children's literature consultant Susannah Richards.

collections

A CHRISTMAS TREASURY selected by Stephanie Nettell, illustrated by Ian Penney (Penguin, 1997, all ages).
An appealing anthology of varied offerings, this collection can be read, enjoyed, and shared by adults and a wide age range of children. It includes poetry, songs, stories, and excerpts of longer works from both traditional and contemporary sources. The book is divided into sections emphasizing the religious aspects of Christ's birth, feasting, the joy of giving and receiving gifts, and reflections and experiences of the holiday from a variety of regions, times, and cultures.

MICHAEL HAGUE'S FAMILY CHRISTMAS TREASURY illustrated by Michael Hague (Henry Holt, 1995, all ages).
Hague, known for his illustrations of works such as *The Secret Garden*, has chosen 32 of his favorite stories, poems, and songs to present with his own illustrations. This well-stocked sampler includes excerpts from *A Christmas Carol*, Kenneth Grahame's *Wind in the Willows*, and *A Child's Christmas in Wales*, as well as O. Henry's "The Gift of the Magi."

CHILDREN JUST LIKE ME: CELEBRATIONS! by Barnabas and Anabel Kindersley (Dorling-Kindersley, 1997, all ages).
Children around the world celebrate 25 favorite holidays in this stunning photographic collection. The details and rituals of each holiday are shared by individual children who bring vibrancy and exuberance to the holiday descriptions.

THE FAMILY TREASURY OF JEWISH HOLIDAYS by Malka Drucker, illustrated by Nancy Patz (Little Brown, 1994, all ages).
This real treasure is not only for the children in the family but for the parents as well. A 10-chapter anthology of Jewish holidays, it is a rich resource that goes well beyond describing ritual to offer a wealth of Jewish history and symbolism. Additionally, it includes related songs, recipes, crafts, and read-along selections by Isaac Bashevis Singer and others.

christmas

SANTA'S BOOK OF NAMES by David McPhail (Little Brown, 1997 [1993], ages 4 to 8).
After Santa accidentally drops his very important list, Edward catches up with him and helps him decipher it. It's a wonderful story with equally delightful ink and watercolor illustrations.

SANTA CALLS by William Joyce (HarperCollins, 1993, ages 5 to 9).
The reader is a guest on an exciting journey to the North Pole. The final twists in this fantastic tale are revealed in two facsimile letters attached at the end of the book.

THE STORY OF CHRISTMAS by Barbara Cooney, illustrated by Loretta Krupinski (Dial, 1995 [1967], ages 3 to 6).
There are many different ways to celebrate Christmas, and Cooney explains the origins of the holiday and of the feasts and celebrations held at that time of year by different faiths and cultures. Many of these customs have been incorporated into Western Christmas traditions. The richness of the holiday is beautifully illustrated in gouache and colored pencil.

THE FIRST CHRISTMAS by Nonny Hogrogian (Greenwillow, 1995, ages 4 and up).
Using passages from the King James Version of the Bible, simple narration to connect them, and lavish oil paintings as illustrations, the author relates the story of the first Christmas. This beautiful retelling of a familiar tale is for readers young and old.

A CHRISTMAS CAROL by Charles Dickens, illustrated by Everett Shinn. (Stewart, Tabori & Chang, 1997, ages 9 and up).
Dickens' Christmas story has been in print for more than 150 years. In this version, his original text is accompanied by Everett Shinn's illustrations for the 1938 edition of *A Christmas Carol* and the 1941 *Christmas in Dickens*. The book's classic design and its time-honored story make this a wonderful family gift as well as a good choice for reading aloud.

THE TWELVE DAYS OF CHRISTMAS illustrated by Jan Brett (PaperStar/Putnam, 1997 [1986], all ages).
Vibrant illustrations and the delightful story-within-a-story make this two treasures in one. The center panels relate to the song while the side panels tell the story of a young couple and their family finding and decorating their holiday tree. An editor's note provides some background about the song, the text, and the music.

THE NIGHT BEFORE CHRISTMAS by Clement C. Moore, illustrated by Ted Rand (North-South, 1995, all ages).

The classic poem is presented in a large-format book with beautiful watercolor illustrations. A perfect version to share as an annual tradition.

hanukkah

HANUKKAH! by Roni Schotter, illustrated by Marylin Hafner (Little, Brown, 1990, ages 4 to 8).
This charming family story has everyone joining in to prepare the traditional Hanukkah foods and to participate in holiday activities. The book concludes with a brief overview of the holiday and definitions of some Hanukkah words.

A GREAT MIRACLE HAPPENED THERE: A CHANUKAH STORY by Karla Kuskin, illustrated by Robert Andrew Parker (HarperTrophy, 1995 [1993], ages 5 to 8).
A young Jewish boy shares the celebration of Chanukah with his non-Jewish friend and explains the meaning of the holiday to him. The Chanukah story is one of faith, courage in the face of insurmountable odds, and victory.

THE ADVENTURES OF HERSHEL OF OSTROPOL by Eric A. Kimmel, illustrated by Trina Schart Hyman (Holiday House, 1995, ages 5 and up).
Hershel's adventures are retold by the master storyteller Kimmel. Hershel actually lived in the last century, and stories about him have become folk tales of a Jewish trickster. He's never evil and is often laughed at as a fool; but Hershel is no fool, and stories about him have lasted for generations.

WHILE THE CANDLES BURN: EIGHT STORIES FOR HANUKKAH by Barbara Diamond Goldin, illustrated by Elaine Greenstein (Viking, 1996, ages 4 to 8).
This collection of Jewish stories weaves the traditional Hanukkah motifs of miracles and victory in with universal themes of peace, charity, and religious commitment. It is an elegant anthology that spans history, geography, and cultural tradition.

THE UGLY MENORAH by Marissa Moss (Farrar, Straus & Giroux, 1996, ages 4 to 8).
Rachel is spending Hanukkah with her grandmother to keep her company now that she is a widow. When Rachel sees her grandmother's very simple "ugly" menorah, she asks why her grandmother doesn't get a new one. What follows is a touching story that emphasizes warm family memories and the idea that beauty is indeed in the eye of the beholder.

kwanzaa

SEVEN CANDLES FOR KWANZAA by Andrea Davis Pinkney, illustrated by Brian Pinkney (Dial, 1993, ages 4 to 8).
This book presents a simple explanation of the principles of Kwanzaa, to be read while lighting the candles during the weeklong holiday.

KWANZAA: A FAMILY AFFAIR by Mildred Pitts Walter, illustrated by Cheryl Carrington (Lothrop, 1995, ages 7 and up).
This celebrated author provides background information and shares her own experiences of Kwanzaa. She also offers instructions for crafts and recipes for special holiday dishes.

THE CHILDREN'S BOOK OF KWANZAA: A GUIDE TO CELEBRATING THE HOLIDAY by Dolores Johnson (Aladdin, 1997, ages 7 and up).
Johnson's comprehensive book provides a brief history of Africans and Africans in America. Chapters detail the seven principles of Kwanzaa and how they are practiced, as well as cover the holiday's symbols and how they are used. Crafts, gift ideas, and recipes are also included.

A KWANZAA CELEBRATION by Nancy Williams, illustrated by Robert Sabuda (Little Simon, 1995, ages 2 and up).
Each spread in this pop-up book illustrates and describes one of the principles of Kwanzaa. The text teaches the symbols and words associated with the holiday.

CELEBRATING KWANZAA by Diane Hoyt-Goldsmith, photos by Lawrence Migdale (Holiday House, 1993, ages 8 to 12).
A Chicago African-American family celebrates Kwanzaa. The text explains the origin of the holiday, customs, and the seven principles. Color photographs complement the story.

WOOD-HOOPOE WILLIE by Virginia Kroll, illustrated by Katherine Roundtree (Charlesbridge, 1995, ages 4 to 8).
A young boy and his grandfather explore their African-American heritage. This upbeat, affirming intergenerational story ends with a Kwanzaa celebration.

Holiday Fruit Salad
(see recipe, page 219)

Company Scalloped Potatoes
(see recipe, page 217)

Green Beans with
Caramelized Onions
(see recipe, page 218)

Festive Pork Roast
(see recipe, page 216)

214

buffet dinner

Buffets are a great way to entertain large numbers of people when dining table space is limited. And buffet service allows you to relax with your guests.

Dilly Buns
(see recipe, page 219)

Shrimp with Mustard Cream Sauce

Fresh pea pods dress shrimp in style and make them easier to handle as a finger food (see photo, page 216).

1½ pounds medium shrimp (about 36), peeled and deveined*
36 fresh pea pods
2 tablespoons butter or margarine
4 teaspoons all-purpose flour
½ cup half-and-half or light cream
½ cup dairy sour cream
¼ cup white wine vinegar
2 tablespoons Dijon-style mustard
½ teaspoon pepper
1 tablespoon capers, drained (optional)
Romaine leaves (optional)

Cook shrimp, uncovered, in boiling water about 2 minutes or until opaque. Drain. Cook the pea pods, covered, in a small amount of lightly salted, boiling water for 2 to 3 minutes or until tender. Drain, rinse, and cool. Wrap a pea pod around each shrimp. Secure with a toothpick. Cover and chill.
For sauce, melt butter in a small saucepan. Stir in flour. Add cream all at once. Cook and stir over medium heat until thickened and bubbly. Reduce heat, cook and stir 1 minute more. Remove from heat.

Stir sour cream, vinegar, mustard, and pepper into cream mixture. Pour into a small serving bowl; cover and chill. To serve, sprinkle sauce with capers and serve with shrimp arranged on a platter lined with romaine leaves, if desired. Makes 36 (12 servings).
***Note:** Leave shell on the tails of the shrimp, if desired.

Nutrition facts per serving: 93 cal., 6 g total fat (3 g sat. fat), 77 mg chol., 168 mg sodium, 3 g carbo., 0 g fiber, 8 g pro. **Daily values:** 8% vit. A, 11% vit. C, 3% calcium, 8% iron

215

menu

Shrimp with Mustard Cream Sauce

Festive Pork Roast

Company Scalloped Potatoes

Green Beans with Caramelized Onions

Holiday Fruit Salad

Dilly Buns – Butter

Mocha-Ladyfinger Parfaits and/or Fruited Nut and Cream Cheese Tart

Choice of beverages

for twelve

Shrimp with Mustard Cream Sauce
(see recipe, page 215)

2 teaspoons curry powder
1 teaspoon ground ginger
½ teaspoon pepper
2 tablespoons cornstarch
  Kumquats (optional)
  Fresh herb sprigs (optional)

Place roast in a large plastic bag; set in a large deep bowl. For marinade, combine wine, brown sugar, vinegar, catsup, water, oil, soy sauce, garlic, curry powder, ginger, and pepper in a medium bowl. Pour marinade over meat; seal bag. Marinate in the refrigerator for 6 to 8 hours or overnight, turning the bag several times. Drain meat, reserving marinade in the refrigerator. Pat meat dry.

Place meat on a rack in a shallow roasting pan. Insert meat thermometer. Roast in a 325° oven for 2¼ to 2½ hours or until meat thermometer registers 155°.

About 25 minutes before the meat is done, make sauce. Stir cornstarch into reserved marinade in a medium saucepan. Cook and stir until thickened and bubbly. Cook and stir for 2 minutes more. Brush roast frequently with sauce during the last 15 minutes of roasting.

Let meat stand, covered, about 15 minutes before slicing. (Meat temperature should rise about 5° while standing.) Reheat remaining sauce to boiling and pass with meat. Garnish with kumquats and fresh herbs, such as rosemary, sage, marjoram, and thyme, if desired. Makes 12 to 15 servings.

Nutrition facts per serving: 344 cal., 17 g total fat (5 g sat. fat), 85 mg chol., 394 mg sodium, 16 g carbo., 0 g fiber, 27 g pro. **Daily values:** 1% vit. A, 4% vit. C, 1% calcium, 11% iron

216

buffet dinner tips

■ Enlisting help: Since buffets tend to be more casual than seated dinners, there's nothing wrong with allowing willing guests to help at any stage of the party. If you wish, assign mini tasks as people arrive. Everyone, including children, can be made to feel more a part of the gathering by being asked to help.

■ Savvy set-up: The more work you do before the party, the more smoothly the plans will flow. Arrange the table in a logical serving sequence starting with plates, followed by the main dish, vegetables, salad, bread, cutlery, and napkins. (To save space, tie cutlery and napkins together with a fancy ribbon.) Appetizers, beverages, and desserts are best set up on separate tables in various locations.

Festive Pork Roast

Ginger, curry, and soy sauce give this pork roast an Oriental accent, and kumquats, used as a garnish, underscore the effect (see photo, pages 214–215).

1 5-pound boneless pork top
  loin roast (double loin, tied)
1½ cups dry red wine
⅔ cup packed brown sugar
½ cup vinegar
½ cup catsup
½ cup water
¼ cup cooking oil
2 tablespoons soy sauce
2 cloves garlic, minced

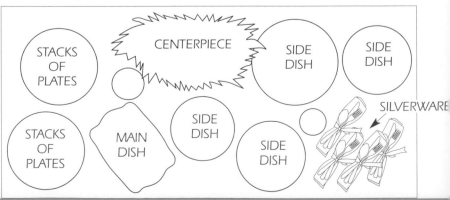

Company Scalloped Potatoes

See photo, pages 214–215.

1 cup chopped onion
¾ cup chopped red and/or green
 sweet pepper (1 medium)
4 cloves garlic, minced
2 tablespoons butter
 or margarine
2 10¾-ounce cans condensed
 cream of celery soup
2 cups milk
¼ teaspoon black pepper
8 cups sliced, peeled potatoes
 (about 2¾ pounds)
⅔ cup grated Parmesan cheese
1 cup soft bread crumbs
3 tablespoons butter
 or margarine, melted
 Green and/or red sweet
 pepper rings (optional)

Cook onion, chopped sweet pepper, and garlic in 2 tablespoons butter or margarine in a large saucepan about 5 minutes or until tender. Stir in soup, milk, and black pepper. Heat, stirring occasionally, until bubbly.

Layer half of the potatoes in a greased 3-quart oval or rectangular baking dish. Cover with *half* of the soup mixture. Sprinkle with *half* of the Parmesan cheese. Layer remaining potatoes and soup mixture atop. Cover dish with foil.

Bake in a 325° oven for 1½ hours or until nearly tender. Uncover and sprinkle with a mixture of bread crumbs, the remaining Parmesan cheese, and melted butter. Bake for 15 minutes more or until potatoes are tender and crumbs are golden. Let stand 15 minutes before serving. Garnish top with sweet pepper rings, if desired. Makes 12 servings.

Nutrition facts per serving: 232 cal., 10 g total fat (5 g sat. fat), 26 mg chol., 590 mg sodium, 30 g carbo., 2 g fiber, 7 g pro. **Daily values:** 11% vit. A, 22% vit. C, 13% calcium, 5% iron

MENU TIMETABLE

several days ahead:

■ Have plenty of ice on hand for the chilled beverages. Chill sparkling water, other beverages, and wine, if desired.
■ Make sure that the linens are ironed.
■ Prepare and freeze Dilly Buns.
■ Determine which serving containers will be used.

1 day ahead:

■ Prepare marinade; marinate meat.
■ Prepare mint dressing for Holiday Fruit Salad; cover and chill.
■ For Company Scalloped Potatoes, slice the potatoes and place in cold water in the refrigerator. Chop the onion and sweet pepper and refrigerate in sealed plastic bags. Prepare the crumb mixture and refrigerate in a plastic bag.
■ Prepare the Mocha-Ladyfinger Parfaits and/or the Fruited Nut and Cream Cheese Tart. Cover and chill.
■ Set out the plates, flatware, serving pieces, and glassware. Wrap flatware in napkins and tie with ribbon, if desired.
■ Arrange the centerpiece and gather candles and other table decorations.

up to 8 hours ahead:

■ Cook shrimp and pea pods for Shrimp with Mustard Cream Sauce; wrap shrimp with pea pods. Cover the wrapped shrimp and chill.
■ Prepare sauce for shrimp appetizer; cover and chill in serving bowl.
■ Wash and cut beans and cut onions for Green Beans with Caramelized Onions; refrigerate separately in plastic bags. Toast nuts.
■ Cut butter sticks into pats and place in serving bowl. Cover and chill.

4 hours ahead:

■ Section grapefruit and cut up jicama for Holiday Fruit Salad; cover and chill.

2¾ hours ahead:

■ Set out Dilly Buns to thaw.
■ Start roasting Festive Pork Roast.
■ Prepare Company Scalloped Potatoes, draining off the water in which potatoes were stored. Two hours before serving, add casserole to oven.
■ Arrange shrimp on serving platter; cover and chill until serving time.

1 hour ahead:

■ Cut up avocados and pears for Holiday Fruit Salad and brush with a little orange juice to keep pieces from turning dark. Arrange on romaine-lined platter(s) along with grapefruit and grapes, if desired. Cover and chill.

45 minutes ahead:

■ Prepare sauce for Festive Pork Roast.

30 minutes ahead:

■ Finish preparing Green Beans with Caramelized Onions.

just before serving:

■ Place Dilly Buns in napkin-lined basket or bowl.
■ Add kumquat and fresh herb garnish to the Festive Pork Roast.
■ Sprinkle toasted nuts and bacon over the beans.
■ Add pepper ring garnish to the Company Scalloped Potatoes.
■ Pour salad dressing over salad.
■ Prepare the coffee and/or tea and add any garnishes to the desserts.

217

Green Beans with Caramelized Onions

3 slices bacon

1 tablespoon butter or margarine

4 medium sweet onions, cut into thin wedges

2 cloves garlic, cut into thin slivers

2 teaspoons snipped fresh thyme or ½ teaspoon dried thyme, crushed

2 tablespoons cider vinegar

2 tablespoons brown sugar

2 pounds fresh green beans, washed, trimmed, and cut into 2-inch pieces

¼ cup chopped pecans or almonds, toasted

Cook bacon until crisp in a large skillet. Remove bacon, drain, and crumble, reserving 1 tablespoon of the drippings in the skillet.

Add butter to drippings in skillet. Cook and stir over medium heat until melted. Add onions, garlic, and thyme to skillet. Cover and cook over medium-low heat about 12 minutes or until onions are tender, stirring occasionally. Uncover; add vinegar and sugar. Cook and stir over medium-high heat about 4 minutes or until onions are golden.

Meanwhile, cook green beans in a large saucepan in a small amount of lightly salted water about 10 minutes or just until crisp-tender. Drain.

To serve, toss green beans and onion mixture together. Transfer mixture to a serving bowl. Sprinkle with nuts and crumbled bacon. Makes 12 servings.

Nutrition facts per serving: 73 cal., 3 g total fat (1 g sat. fat), 4 mg chol., 38 mg sodium, 10 g carbo., 2 g fiber, 2 g pro. **Daily values:** 5% vit. A, 14% vit. C, 3% calcium, 7% iron

Green Beans with Caramelized Onions

Dilly Buns

Decorate the tops of these rolls with fresh dill sprigs baked onto the rolls (see photo, pages 214–215).

2½ to 3 cups all-purpose flour
1 package fast-rising active dry yeast
2 teaspoons dillseed
¼ teaspoon baking soda
1 cup cream-style cottage cheese
¼ cup water
2 tablespoons butter or margarine
2 teaspoons sugar
½ teaspoon salt
¼ teaspoon pepper
1 egg
1 beaten egg
1 tablespoon water
Fresh dill sprigs (optional)

Combine ¾ cup of the flour, the yeast, dillseed, and baking soda in a large mixing bowl. Heat and stir cottage cheese, the ¼ cup water, butter or margarine, sugar, salt, and pepper in a small saucepan until warm (120° to 130°) and butter is almost melted.

Add cheese mixture to flour mixture. Add the first egg. Beat with an electric mixer on low speed for 30 seconds, scraping the sides of the bowl constantly. Beat on high speed for 3 minutes. Using a spoon, stir in as much of the remaining flour as you can.

Turn dough out onto a lightly floured surface. Knead in enough of the remaining flour to make a moderately soft dough that is smooth and elastic (3 to 5 minutes total). Cover and let rest for 15 minutes.

Lightly grease eighteen 2½-inch muffin cups. Shape the dough into 54 balls. (To make 54 equal-size balls, divide entire batch of dough into thirds; divide each portion in half making 6 portions. Divide each of the 6 portions into thirds for 18 portions, and divide each of those 18 portions into thirds, making 54 portions.) Place 3 balls in each muffin cup. Cover; let rise in a warm place until nearly double (20 to 30 minutes).

Combine the remaining beaten egg and 1 tablespoon water; brush onto rolls. Top each roll with a dill sprig, if desired; brush again with egg mixture. Bake in a 375° oven about 12 minutes or until golden. Makes 18 rolls.

Nutrition facts per roll: 93 cal., 2 g total fat (2 g sat. fat), 28 mg chol., 150 mg sodium, 14 g carbo., 1 g fiber, 4 g pro. **Daily values:** 2% vit. A, 0% vit. C, 1% calcium, 6% iron

Holiday Fruit Salad

If you cut up the pears and avocado ahead, be sure to brush with citrus juice to prevent them from browning (see photo, pages 214–215).

¼ cup lime juice
2 tablespoons water
2 tablespoons salad oil
2 teaspoons sugar
½ teaspoon celery seed
2 teaspoons snipped fresh mint
2 medium avocados
Romaine and/or salad greens
1 cup jicama cut into matchstick-size pieces
4 large pink grapefruit, peeled and sectioned
4 large pears, pared, cored, and sliced (4 cups)
Red or green grapes (optional)

For dressing, combine lime juice, water, oil, sugar, celery seed, and mint in a screw-top jar. Cover and shake to mix well. Set aside.

Cut avocados lengthwise through the fruit around the seed. Separate halves and remove seed. Peel and slice avocado. Line a large platter (about 16 inches in diameter) with romaine and/or salad greens. Place jicama strips in center of platter. Arrange grapefruit, pear, avocado, and grapes, if desired, around jicama. Shake dressing well; drizzle over salad. Makes 12 servings.

219

Nutrition facts per serving: 146 cal., 7 g total fat (1 g sat. fat), 0 mg chol., 4 mg sodium, 22 g carbo., 4 g fiber, 2 g pro. **Daily values:** 7% vit. A, 71% vit. C, 2% calcium, 5% iron

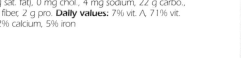

Dilly Buns

220

Fruited Nut and
Cream Cheese Tart

Mocha-Ladyfinger Parfaits

Mocha-Ladyfinger Parfaits

To provide guests with a choice, prepare both the tart and these parfaits.

  2 4-serving-size packages instant French vanilla pudding mix
  8 ounces mascarpone cheese or cream cheese
  1 cup whipping cream
 ⅔ cup strong coffee, cooled
  1 tablespoon coffee liqueur or hazelnut-flavored syrup (syrup used to flavor coffee)
  4 ounces milk chocolate or semisweet chocolate
  2 3-ounce packages ladyfingers (24 ladyfingers), cut crosswise into thirds
 12 fresh strawberries (optional)

Prepare pudding mixes according to package directions (*using 4 cups milk*). Cover and chill for 2 hours. Meanwhile, let cheese stand at room temperature for 30 minutes.

Stir cheese until smooth. Gradually stir *1 cup* of the pudding into cheese to lighten it. Fold that mixture into the remaining pudding. Beat whipping cream in a chilled small bowl with an electric mixer on medium speed or with a rotary beater just until soft peaks form. Fold whipped cream into pudding mixture; set aside.

Stir together coffee and the coffee liqueur or hazelnut-flavored syrup in a small bowl; set mixture aside. Shave enough curls from the chocolate to sprinkle over tops of the parfaits; finely chop the remaining chocolate.

To assemble parfaits, arrange *half* of the ladyfinger pieces in the bottoms of 12 goblets or glasses. Drizzle *half* of the coffee mixture over ladyfingers in goblets. Spoon *half* of the pudding mixture on top and sprinkle with chopped chocolate. Repeat with remaining ladyfinger pieces, coffee mixture, and pudding. Top with shaved chocolate curls. Cover and chill about 8 hours or overnight. Garnish each serving with a fresh strawberry, if desired. Makes 12 servings.

Nutrition facts per serving: 353 cal., 22 g total fat (13 g sat. fat), 109 mg chol., 310 mg sodium, 36 g carbo., 1 g fiber, 9 g pro. **Daily values:** 16% vit. A, 2% vit. C, 10% calcium, 5% iron

---

Fruited Nut and Cream Cheese Tart

The subtle flavors of dried apricots and nuts come together beautifully in this handsome tart.

     Orange Tart Pastry
  6 ounces cream cheese, softened
  1 egg
  3 tablespoons granulated sugar
 ¼ teaspoon vanilla
  2 eggs
 ⅔ cup light-colored corn syrup
 ⅓ cup packed brown sugar
 ¼ cup butter or margarine, melted and cooled
  1 teaspoon finely shredded orange peel
 ½ teaspoon vanilla
  1 cup coarsely chopped pistachio nuts and/or cashews
 ½ cup snipped dried apricots
     Whipped cream (optional)
     Pistachio nut halves (optional)

Prepare pastry. Use your hands to slightly flatten pastry dough on a lightly floured surface. Roll dough from center to edge into a 13-inch circle. Wrap pastry around rolling pin. Unroll into an ungreased 11-inch tart pan with a removable bottom. Ease pastry into tart pan, being careful not to stretch pastry. Press pastry into the fluted side of tart pan. Trim edge. Place a double thickness of foil over pastry in the bottom of tart pan. Bake in a 450° oven for 5 minutes; remove foil. Bake 5 minutes more; set aside.

Beat cream cheese, 1 egg, granulated sugar, and ¼ teaspoon vanilla in a small mixing bowl with an electric mixer on medium speed until combined. Cover and chill in refrigerator for 30 minutes. Spread in pastry-lined tart pan.

For filling, beat the 2 eggs slightly in a large mixing bowl with a rotary beater or a fork. Stir in the corn syrup. Add the brown sugar, butter, orange peel, and ½ teaspoon vanilla, stirring until sugar is dissolved. Stir in nuts and apricots.

Place pastry-and-cream-cheese-lined tart pan on a baking sheet on the oven rack. Carefully pour filling into pan. Bake in a 350° oven about 40 minutes or until a knife inserted near the center comes out clean. Cool for 1 to 2 hours on a wire rack. Refrigerate within 2 hours; cover for longer storage. Garnish with whipped cream and pistachio nuts, if desired. Cut into wedges to serve. Makes 12 servings.

ORANGE TART PASTRY: Stir together 1¼ cups all-purpose flour and ¼ cup granulated sugar in a medium mixing bowl. Using a pastry blender, cut in ½ cup cold butter until the pieces are pea-size. Stir together 2 beaten egg yolks, 1 tablespoon water, and 1½ teaspoons finely shredded orange peel in a small mixing bowl. Gradually stir egg yolk mixture into dry mixture. Using your fingers, gently knead dough just until a ball forms. If necessary, cover with plastic wrap and chill in refrigerator for 30 to 60 minutes or until dough is easy to handle.

Nutrition facts per serving: 398 cal., 24 g total fat (12 g sat. fat), 135 mg chol., 191 mg sodium, 42 g carbo., 2 g fiber, 7 g pro. **Daily values:** 28% vit. A, 2% vit. C, 4% calcium, 19% iron

221

Nothing quite spells decadence the way chocolate does. Richly gracing a multitude of forms and flavors—in cakes, cookies, beverages, and mousses, with fruit, nuts, and liqueurs—chocolate is heavenly in all its incarnations.

have yourself
a merry
chocolate
christmas

Chocolate Pots de Crème

Since this pudding dessert (poh duh KREM) is so rich, a small portion goes a long way. Spoon into tiny cups or dessert bowls. Then add a dollop of whipped cream to individual servings.

  1 cup half-and-half or light cream
  1 4-ounce package sweet baking
      chocolate, coarsely chopped
  2 teaspoons sugar
  3 beaten egg yolks
  ½ teaspoon vanilla

Combine cream, chocolate, and sugar in a heavy small saucepan. Cook and stir over medium heat for 10 minutes or until mixture reaches a full boil and thickens.

Gradually stir about *half* of the hot mixture into the beaten egg yolks. Stir egg yolk mixture into remaining hot mixture in pan. Cook and stir over low heat for 2 minutes more. Remove saucepan from heat.

Stir in vanilla until combined. Pour chocolate mixture into 4 to 6 pots de crème cups, demitasse cups, or small dessert bowls. Cover and chill for 2 to 24 hours. Makes 4 to 6 servings.

Nutrition facts per serving: 276 cal., 21 g total fat (11 g sat. fat), 182 mg chol., 31 mg sodium, 22 g carbo., 2 g fiber, 5 g pro. **Daily values:** 2% vit. A, 0% vit. C, 7% calcium, 7% iron

Chocolate-Raspberry Mousse Cake

When time is at a premium, dress up a cake mix with a mousse mix and ice cream topping. Although fresh raspberries may be costly at this time of year, you'll need only a few to decorate this simply elegant cake.

  1 package 2-layer-size devil's food
      cake mix
  2 2- to 2½-ounce packages
      chocolate mousse dessert
      mix

Chocolate-Raspberry Mousse Cake

⅔ cup cold milk

⅓ cup raspberry liqueur

1 11- to 12-ounce jar fudge ice
      cream topping or raspberry-
      fudge sauce
      Fresh raspberries
      Chocolate curls

Grease and lightly flour two
9×1½-inch round baking pans; set the
baking pans aside.

Prepare, bake, and cool cake mix
according to package directions.

Prepare mousse mixes according to
package directions *except* use the
⅔ cup cold milk and the ⅓ cup liqueur
for the total amount of liquid.

Split each cooled cake layer in half
horizontally using a serrated knife. To
assemble cake, place bottom of one
split layer on a serving plate. Spread a
thin layer of fudge topping (about
⅓ cup) over the bottom layer. Spread
about ½ cup of the mousse mixture
over the fudge topping. Repeat layering
twice with cake, fudge topping, and

mousse mixture. Top with the
remaining cake layer.

Frost top and sides with remaining
mousse mixture. Before serving,
decorate with fresh raspberries and
chocolate curls. Store cake in the
refrigerator. Makes 12 to 16 servings.

Nutrition facts per serving: 371 cal., 11 g total fat
(4 g sat. fat), 2 mg chol., 464 mg sodium,
63 g carbo., 1 g fiber, 6 g pro. **Daily values:**
2% vit. A, 0% vit. C, 8% calcium, 14% iron

223

Berry Chocolate

Serve immediately with dippers; swirl as you dip. If the fondue mixture thickens, stir in some additional milk. Makes 8 servings.

Nutrition facts per serving (without dippers): 302 cal., 14 g total fat (9 g sat. fat), 18 mg chol., 72 mg sodium, 45 g carbo., 2 g fiber, 6 g pro. **Daily values:** 5% vit. A, 2% vit. C, 14% calcium, 7% iron

Yule Street Truffles

- 1 cup semisweet chocolate pieces
- 2 tablespoons butter
- ¼ cup sifted powdered sugar
- 1 tablespoon brandy
- ½ cup chopped toasted almonds
- ½ cup flaked coconut
- ½ cup whole pitted dates, chopped
- ¼ cup red candied cherries, chopped
- 8 ounces chocolate-flavored candy coating, melted
  Ground toasted almonds (optional)
  Sliced or slivered almonds (optional)
  Toasted flaked coconut (optional)
  Cocoa powder (optional)
  Melted chocolate and/or chocolate-flavored candy coating (optional)

Combine chocolate pieces and butter in a microwave-safe 1-quart casserole. Microcook, uncovered, on 100% power (high) for 1 to 2 minutes or until melted.

Stir in powdered sugar and brandy. Add chopped almonds, the ½ cup coconut, dates, and cherries. Shape mixture into ¾-inch balls. Dip in melted candy coating. Decorate with ground almonds, sliced or slivered almonds, toasted flaked coconut, cocoa

Berry Chocolate

- 1 ounce (2 tablespoons) chocolate liqueur
- ½ ounce (1 tablespoon) Chambord or other raspberry liqueur
- 1 cup prepared hot chocolate
  Whipped cream
  Chambord or other raspberry liqueur or unsweetened cocoa powder (optional)

Pour liqueurs into a 10-ounce mug. Add hot chocolate. Garnish with whipped cream; drizzle with a little Chambord or sprinkle with cocoa powder, if desired. Makes 1 serving.

Nutrition facts per serving: 345 cal., 5 g total fat (3 g sat. fat), 18 mg chol., 154 mg sodium, 48 g carbo., 1 g fiber, 9 g pro. **Daily values:** 15% vit. A, 3% vit. C, 24% calcium, 0% iron

Chocolate Fondue

For a mocha-flavored fondue, substitute ½ cup strong brewed coffee for the milk.

- 8 ounces semisweet chocolate, coarsely chopped
- 1 14-ounce can (1¼ cups) sweetened condensed milk
- ½ cup milk
  Dippers such as angel food cake, pound cake, marshmallows, dried apricots, whole strawberries, banana slices, or pineapple chunks

Melt chocolate in a heavy medium saucepan over low heat, stirring constantly. Stir in the sweetened condensed milk and milk; heat through. Transfer to a fondue pot; keep warm over low heat of fondue burner.

powder, or melted chocolate or candy coating, if desired. Store in a sealed container in refrigerator. Makes about 40 pieces.

Nutrition facts per piece: 83 cal., 5 g total fat (2 g sat. fat), 2 mg chol., 6 mg sodium, 10 g carbo., 0 g fiber, 1 g pro. **Daily values:** 0% vit. A, 0% vit. C, 0% calcium, 1% iron

Fudge-Filled Thumbprints

Get the children involved with these cookie preparations. Let them make the thumbprint indentations for the fudge filling.

½ cup butter, softened
⅓ cup packed brown sugar
1 egg yolk
½ teaspoon vanilla
1 cup all-purpose flour
1 slightly beaten egg white
¾ to 1 cup finely chopped pecans
4 ounces semisweet chocolate
2 tablespoons butter
2 teaspoons seedless raspberry jam
½ cup sifted powdered sugar
2 to 3 teaspoons milk
¼ teaspoon vanilla

Beat the ½ cup butter in a large mixing bowl with an electric mixer on medium to high speed for 30 seconds. Add brown sugar and beat until combined. Beat in egg yolk and vanilla until combined. Beat in as much of the flour as you can with mixer. Stir in any remaining flour with a wooden spoon.

Shape dough into 1-inch balls. Roll balls in egg white and then roll in pecans. Place 1-inch apart on a lightly greased cookie sheet. Press your thumb into the center of each ball.

Bake in a 375° oven for 9 to 11 minutes or until edges are lightly browned. Transfer to a wire rack and let cool completely.

For filling, melt chocolate and 2 tablespoons butter in a small saucepan over low heat, stirring frequently. Remove from heat. Stir in raspberry jam until smooth. Let filling cool slightly. Spoon filling into the depressions in the cookies. Let stand until set. (Filled cookies may need to be refrigerated for 15 to 20 minutes to set the chocolate.)

For icing, combine the powdered sugar, 1 teaspoon milk, and ¼ teaspoon vanilla in a small mixing bowl. Stir in additional milk, 1 teaspoon at a time, until of drizzling consistency. Drizzle over cookies. If planning to store cookies, do not fill or add icing until just before serving. Makes about 24 cookies.

Nutrition facts per cookie: 127 cal., 9 g total fat (4 g sat. fat), 22 mg chol., 52 mg sodium, 12 g carbo., 1 g fiber, 1 g pro. **Daily values:** 5% vit. A, 0% vit. C, 0% calcium, 3% iron

Double-Chocolate Mocha Biscotti

Espresso adds to the flavor of these crunchy Italian confections, which are dipped in white chocolate.

1 12-ounce package (2 cups) miniature semisweet chocolate pieces
⅓ cup butter, softened
⅔ cup sugar
2 teaspoons baking powder
2 teaspoons instant espresso or coffee powder
2 eggs
1 teaspoon vanilla
2 cups all-purpose flour
1 cup (6 ounces) white baking pieces
1 teaspoon shortening

Set aside ½ cup of the miniature semisweet pieces. Melt remaining pieces in a small saucepan over low heat, stirring occasionally.

Meanwhile, beat butter in a large mixing bowl with an electric mixer on medium to high speed for 30 seconds. Add sugar, baking powder, and espresso or coffee powder; beat until combined. Beat in melted chocolate, eggs, and vanilla until combined. Beat in as much flour as you can with the mixer. Stir in any remaining flour with a wooden spoon. Stir in reserved chocolate pieces. Divide dough in half.

Using lightly floured hands, shape each portion into an 8-inch-long loaf. Place rolls about 5 inches apart on a lightly greased cookie sheet. Flatten to 2½ inches in width.

Bake in a 375° oven for 25 to 30 minutes or until firm and a wooden toothpick inserted in center comes out clean. Cool on cookie sheet for 1 hour.

Transfer to a cutting board. Cut each loaf diagonally into ½-inch-thick slices. Lay slices, cut sides down, on the cookie sheet. Bake in a 375° oven for 10 minutes. Turn slices over and bake for 10 to 15 minutes more or until dry and crisp. Remove from cookie sheet and cool on a wire rack.

Melt white baking pieces and shortening in a small heavy saucepan over low heat, stirring occasionally. Dip one corner of each cookie into melted mixture. Makes about 30 cookies.

Nutrition facts per cookie: 155 cal., 8 g total fat (3 g sat. fat), 22 mg chol., 56 mg sodium, 21 g carbo., 0 g fiber, 2 g pro. **Daily values:** 2% vit. A, 0% vit. C, 2% calcium, 4% iron

225

powder, and soda; beat until combined. Beat in egg and vanilla until combined. Gradually beat in flour mixture.

Shape dough into 1-inch balls; place on ungreased cookie sheet. Press down center of each ball with thumb. Drain maraschino cherries, reserving juice. Place a cherry in the center of each cookie. In a small saucepan combine the chocolate pieces and sweetened condensed milk; heat until chocolate is melted. Stir in 4 teaspoons of the reserved cherry juice.

Spoon about 1 teaspoon of the frosting over each cherry, spreading to cover cherry. (Frosting may be thinned with additional cherry juice, if needed.)

Bake in a 350° oven about 10 minutes or until done. Remove to wire rack; cool. Makes 48 cookies.

Nutrition facts per cookie: 81 cal., 3 g total fat (1 g sat. fat), 11 mg chol., 45 mg sodium, 12 g carbo., 0 g fiber, 1 g pro. **Daily values:** 2% vit. A, 0% vit. C, 1% calcium, 2% iron

Chocolate-Covered Cherry Cookies

Chocolate-Covered Cherry Cookies

Be sure to use real chocolate (not imitation) because the not-so-real product won't bake properly.

1½ cups all-purpose flour
½ cup unsweetened cocoa powder
½ cup butter, softened
1 cup sugar
¼ teaspoon salt
¼ teaspoon baking powder
¼ teaspoon baking soda
1 egg
1½ teaspoons vanilla
48 undrained maraschino cherries (about one 10-ounce jar)
1 cup semisweet chocolate pieces
½ cup sweetened condensed milk

Combine flour and cocoa powder in a mixing bowl; set aside. Beat butter in a large mixing bowl with an electric mixer on medium to high speed for 30 seconds. Add sugar, salt, baking

German Chocolate Cheesecake

With its nutty-coconut topping, this dreamy cheesecake will remind you of its old-fashioned namesake.

Coconut-Pecan Topping
1 cup graham cracker crumbs
2 tablespoons sugar
⅓ cup butter, melted
¼ cup flaked coconut
¼ cup chopped pecans
4 ounces semisweet chocolate, chopped
3 8-ounce packages cream cheese, softened

¾ cup sugar
½ cup dairy sour cream
2 teaspoons vanilla
2 tablespoons all-purpose flour
3 eggs
   Pecan halves (optional)

Prepare the Coconut-Pecan Topping; set aside.

For crust, combine graham cracker crumbs, the 2 tablespoons sugar, melted butter, coconut, and pecans in a mixing bowl. Press mixture into the bottom and ½ inch up sides of a 9-inch springform pan. Bake in a 350° oven for 8 to 10 minutes. Cool slightly.

Melt chocolate in a saucepan over low heat. Remove from heat and set aside to cool.

For filling, beat together the cream cheese, ¾ cup sugar, sour cream, and vanilla in a mixing bowl. Add flour and beat well. Add eggs and cooled chocolate; beat until just combined. Turn filling into the cooled crust.

Bake in a 375° oven for 45 to 50 minutes or until the center appears nearly set when you shake it. Cool for 15 minutes. Loosen sides of cheesecake from the sides of the pan. Cool 30 minutes. Remove sides of pan.

Spread Coconut-Pecan Topping over cheesecake. Cover and refrigerate 3 to 24 hours. If desired, garnish with pecan halves. Makes 12 to 14 servings.

COCONUT-PECAN TOPPING: Melt ½ cup butter in a small saucepan. Stir in ¼ cup packed brown sugar, 2 tablespoons half-and-half or light cream, and 2 tablespoons light-colored corn syrup. Cook and stir over medium heat until bubbly. Stir in 1 cup flaked coconut, ½ cup chopped pecans, and 1 teaspoon vanilla. Remove from heat; cool for 5 minutes. Spread over partially cooled cheesecake.

Nutrition facts per serving: 599 cal., 47 g total fat (27 g sat. fat), 155 mg chol., 365 mg sodium, 40 g carbo., 2 g fiber, 9 g pro. **Daily values:** 41% vit. A, 0% vit. C, 7% calcium, 14% iron

melting chocolate

Chocolate is heat-sensitive and burns easily, especially when it is melted alone. Containers and stirring utensils must be clean and perfectly dry. Small amounts of water may cause melted chocolate to lose its gloss instead of melting smoothly. Here are two ways to melt chocolate easily:

■ To melt on the rangetop: Place cut-up chocolate or chocolate pieces in a heavy saucepan. Melt the chocolate over low heat, stirring often to prevent scorching. Sometimes 1 teaspoon shortening is added for each ½ cup or 3 ounces of chocolate to help the chocolate set up.

■ To melt in a microwave oven: Place up to 6 ounces of chopped chocolate or chocolate pieces in a microwave-safe bowl or measuring cup. Microwave, uncovered, on 100% power (high) for 1½ to 2 minutes or until soft enough to stir smoothly. Stir after 60 seconds; the chocolate pieces or squares won't seem melted until stirred.

227

German Chocolate Cheesecake

Create a sense of occasion with imaginative table settings.

the art *of the* table

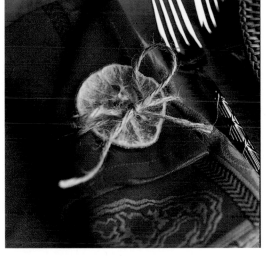

Laying on a holiday table doesn't require special china or linens. Use your collections—blue-and-white china, milk glass, or hotel silver, for example—as your starting point and let color create the mood. Add one element with a holiday motif, such as salad plates, to underscore the seasonal theme.

229

Autumn Spice

here's how...

Combine rich spice colors to create an autumn-harvest look for Thanksgiving. Start with a tablecloth or layered cloths in warm spice tones. To have extra fabric for catching up at the corners, choose a cloth that's one size larger than your table. Gather up the fabric at each corner and tie it tightly with a long piece of twine. Assemble wheat and cinnamon sticks into four small bouquets and bind them with rubber bands. Tie one bouquet at each corner with the twine, then thread the twine through three dried orange slices and tie in a knot.

Dress the napkins to match by layering each one with an orange slice and tying it in place with twine. For an easy, casual centerpiece, fill three baskets of graduated sizes with fresh and dried fruits and stack them. Use dark wicker chargers under the dinner plates to frame the plates and repeat the texture of the baskets.

You can find dried citrus and dried orange slices at crafts stores or florist's supply shops. Or, dry your own slices. Choose firm, good quality fruits. Cut them into slices ¼ inch thick and arrange them on a cooling rack in a 200-degree oven. Let the slices dry for several hours, turning them every hour. After the slices are dry and leathery, turn off the oven, open the oven door slightly, and let the slices cool overnight.

Kwanzaa

～ Celebrate history and heritage with a focus on family.

This holiday, observed from December 26 to January 1, celebrates African-American heritage and the strengthening of community through principles of mutual commitment and responsibility. Decorations incorporate symbolic elements, such as the seven-branched candelabrum (called a *kinara*), a straw mat, vegetables, ears of corn, and a communal unity cup.

here's how...

To set a Kwanzaa table, start with the straw mat, which represents tradition as the foundation on which cultural values rest. Vegetables, mounded in shallow baskets, recall the Swahili origins of the word "kwanzaa," which means first fruits of the harvest.

Ears of corn symbolize children and therefore posterity and the future, so they're a perfect base for photo place cards. To make the place cards, start with 18-gauge paper-wrapped florist's wire from a crafts store or florist's supply shop. Thread on decorative

beads, then use pliers to bend the wire into geometric shapes at one end, using bends in the wire to space the beads and hold them in place. Trim the straight end of the wire to the desired length. Make a hole in one end of a piece of dried corn (sold as bird or squirrel feed); you may need to use an ice pick for this. Insert the straight end of the place card holder in the hole and secure it with a drop of glue if the wire seems wobbly.

Take pictures with a Polaroid camera of each family member or guest, then insert his or her photo between the bent wires and set the ear of corn at the appropriate place at the table. Or, use the photos as part of the centerpiece, placing them among the fruits and vegetables on the table.

As an added flourish at each place setting, curl a banana leaf or an aspidistra leaf into a cone shape and tie it with raffia. Tuck in a few stems of alstroemeria, a florist's flower that looks like a small lily.

230

232

Winter Green

Bring your love of the garden to the table with pots of evergreens, jute placemats, and dinnerware in soft green tones. Instead of laying the placemats out in the usual way, turn them so the long sides hang over the table's edge; to suggest the effect of a tablecloth and create a formal feeling. Soft green dinner plates pick up the green in the holiday salad plates, but you could use plain white dinner plates instead. A simple white napkin with a green organdy edge reinforces the natural color scheme.

To make the place card holders and centerpiece, use either aged terra-cotta pots or add age to new pots by applying a thin coat of green or blue-green acrylic paint and quickly wiping off

233

some of the paint before it dries. You also can let the paint dry, then scuff off paint from the sides and edges with sandpaper. Wedge a piece of water-soaked floral foam into each pot. Stuff in pine tips, holly, or boxwood to make a bouquet. For place settings, use garden markers and write each person's name on the metal marker with an indelible marking pen.

Crocheted toppers for tumblers originally protected iced tea or lemonade from curious insects at outdoor parties or picnics. Bring them indoors for a charming garden touch. To make your own, use a purchased doily and thin jeweler's wire to string red and green beads through the points. You can find doilies, wire, and beads at crafts stores.

234

Red and White

Mix and match milk glass, patterned china, and hobnail glass to create a cottage-style Christmas tabletop. Spread a red quilt or cloth over the table (make sure the quilt is machine washable in case of spills). Stack red-and-white patterned china and pink hobnail glass plates at each place, and welcome each guest to the table with an individual arrangement of roses in a milk-glass cup, sugar bowl, or creamer. Fill the containers with fresh cranberries to hold the rose stems in place. Add a little water but not enough to make the berries float.

Mix and match flatware too. Check estate sales and antiques shops for inexpensive odd pieces of sterling silver or vintage flatware and combine them for a collected look.

For the centerpiece, create your own epergne by stacking footed candy dishes or vases on a footed cake plate. Combine Red Delicious apples, lady apples, red plums and red currants with pink and red roses to emphasize the color theme. (For a striking color accent, add purple plums and grapes.)

Dress up the backs of chairs with strands of cranberries and tiny red glass balls. Thread fresh or frozen cranberries on dental floss, using a tapestry needle. Since the berries may bleed if they're left out for several hours, tie the garlands to the chairs at the last minute, and remove them promptly after dinner. Or substitute red wooden beads for the cranberries.

235

Blue and White

here's how...

Put your collection of blue-and-white china in a candy-cane-color setting, and you have a merry Christmas breakfast table. A white quilt on the table creates touchable texture; to protect it from spills and add holiday color, layer a swath of gingham taffeta over the top. Don't cut or sew the taffeta; just buy a length of fabric that's three times the diameter of your table. Fold the fabric in half and lay it across the table, spreading out the two halves on the diagonal to cover the tabletop. Bunch the edges to form poufs below the table edge.

Use a large blue-and-white platter to organize a centerpiece of cyclamen and candy-striped candles or slip the cyclamen pots into blue-and-white cachepots or silver plated buckets (available at home furnishings stores).

Add orange fruit, such as persimmons or oranges, around the base of the buckets for a jolt of unexpected color.

Tie napkins with red-and-white gingham ribbon and place a red beaded pear or apple in each coffee cup for a good-morning gift. Place cards certainly aren't necessary, but they can be fun, adding to the sense of occasion. Use rattan balls with pink bows to prop up the place card.

Lunar Liftoff!

here's how...

Greet the New Year with a glittering futuristic tablescape that suggests rocket ships and moon landings. Spot mirrors from an auto-parts store create the lunar surface.

Layer silver tulle over a white cloth (or if your table is a light color, just use the tulle). Buy blind-spot mirrors in three sizes (2-inch, 3-inch, and 3¾-inch in diameter)—you'll need two or three of each, more if you have a long table. At a discount auto-parts store, the smallest ones cost about $1.50 and the largest about $2.50. Arrange them randomly on the tabletop, along with small votive candles in silver containers.

For a focal point, arrange white flowers in tall, trumpet-shape vases; if you don't have silver, use sleek, clear glass. Choose flowers such as alstroemeria, freesia, or other trumpet-shape flowers and arrange them in simple, rounded bunches to suggest a spray of fireworks. To reinforce the theme, purchase party horns and champagne flutes with elongated shapes and party favors with silver and gold metallic streamers. White napkins and white-and-gold dinner plates complete the lunar look.

GIVING

What better occasion for sentimental gifts that celebrate family and friendship than the holiday season? If gift-giving sometimes feels like a duty rather than a pleasure, turn it into an adventure by matching your recipients' interests to a theme. Does your sister-in-law like to relax in a long, hot bath? Give her homemade herbal spa treatments. Does your neighbor love to garden? Pot up amarylis bulbs or tree seedlings. When you put your heart into it, it's as much fun to give as it is to receive.

from the HEART

Convey your heartfelt feelings with a handmade gift. If you're pressed for time, assemble an instant gift tailored to the recipient's tastes and interests; see *pages* 252–253 for ideas.

tokens of *affection*

see *pages* 252–253 for ideas.

family traditions

My husband and I were anticipating our baby's first Christmas when we realized opening gifts wouldn't be that much fun—our infant was too young to be excited about the toys, and we'd know everything our child was getting. We decided to divide the Christmas allowance between us, shop separately, and keep the baby's presents a secret from each other. We had so much fun surprising each other that we've decided to continue this method until the baby is older.
— *Sandi Hutchinson, Stillwell, Kansas*

241

SHOPPING LIST

From a crafts store:
  decorative 16-ounce
    bottle with cork
  assorted dried flowers
  raffia
From a bed-and-bath
  shop, nature store, or
  gift shop:
  16 ounces of almond
    oil (for Soothing
    Bath Oil)
  16 ounces of soy oil,
    safflower oil,
    sunflower oil, olive
    oil, or wheat-
    germ oil (for
    Stimulating Bath Oil)
  essential oils: lavender,
    rose, rosemary,
    juniper
  vitamin E capsules
  funnel, large coffee can,
    and saucepan
  paraffin (available in grocery
    stores)

Aromatic Bath Oils

❧ Choose lavender for a soothing bath oil or juniper for one that leaves you feeling invigorated. The dried flowers are just for looks—the fragrances come from the essential oils.

here's how...

1 Wash the bottle in hot, soapy water, rinse, and let it dry. Stuff dried flowers into the bottle for decoration.

2 Blend the oils in a separate container. For Soothing Bath Oil, mix the almond oil with 24 drops of lavender essential oil and 8 drops of rose essential oil. For the Stimulating Bath Oil, blend the carrier oil (soy oil or one of the suggested substitutes) with 24 drops of rosemary essential oil and 8 drops of juniper essential oil. For each mixture, break open 8 capsules of vitamin E and stir the contents into the oil mixture.

3 Using the funnel, pour the oil mixture into the bottle and cork it. To seal the cork with paraffin, place the wax in the coffee can and stand the can in a saucepan with several inches of water. Bring the water to simmering and let the paraffin melt. Dip the corked top into the melted paraffin several times to seal it and to keep the closure airtight. Tie additional dried flowers to the neck of the bottle with raffia.

Basket of Flowers

Give a living gift of potted plants in a moss-covered basket.

～ It makes a wonderful fresh arrangement, and the potted plants can be replaced to change with the seasons.

here's how...

Use the hot-glue gun to attach pads of sheet moss to the sides and top edges of the pot.

3

Bend the rope over the pot, positioning each end flush with the bottom of the pot. Hold it in place by wrapping the pot and sticks with spool wire.

5

243

Wire additional stems of herbs to the basket handle, and cover the wire with ribbon.

2

To make the basket handle, cut long flexible branches ¼ inch or less in diameter (willow and birch are especially easy to work with). Weave the branches together or align several and wrap them with spool wire to make a rope 6 to 8 feet long.

4

Use spool wire to tie bunches of herbs into bouquets, assembling three or more kinds of herbs with contrasting textures in each bundle. Position the potted plants in the moss-covered pot. Wrap the stem ends of the herb bouquets in damp moss, then tuck them in among the potted plants.

Recipe Box

Fill this easy-to-make box with your favorite recipes for a wonderful keepsake gift.

❧ Be sure to include old family recipes—the collection will make a cherished gift for children or grandchildren setting up housekeeping.

here's how...

1 Following the diagram *below right,* draw a pattern on tracing paper. Cut out and trace onto the wrong side of the corrugated paper. Cut out the shape.

2 Lightly score the paper along the dashed lines by lightly drawing a crafts knife across the right side of the paper, using a ruler as a guide. Indent the paper to make a sharp fold, but don't cut all the way through. Fold the paper along the scored lines.

3 Glue the red card stock onto the bottom of the box. Glue one 6½-inch flap to the sides to create a pocket for the recipe cards.

4 Using the hole punch, make holes where indicated by Xs on the pattern. Place a cinnamon stick in the center of a 5-inch piece of raffia and wrap the raffia around the stick twice. Center the stick between the holes on the right side of one flap and slip the raffia ends through the holes to the inside. Knot the raffia ends and clip the excess. Repeat for the remaining flap. After you fill the box with recipe cards, close the flaps, and wrap the 16-inch length of raffia figure-eight style around both cinnamon sticks.

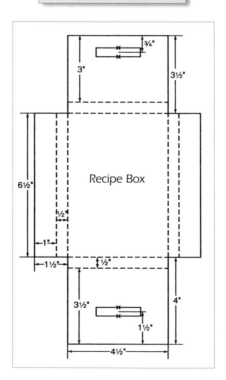

Recipe Box

244

SHOPPING LIST

From an art-supply store:
  one sheet of handmade
    paper 20×30 inches
  eight 20×26-inch sheets
    of heavy art paper
  spray adhesive
  scraps of black and
    gold art papers
From a crafts store:
  crafts knife and
    hole punch
  2¾×9-inch scrap
    of leather
  white glue
From a hardware store:
  ⅞-inch diameter
    O rings
  16-inch length of brass
    rod or tubing,
    cut in half
  two 9×12-inch envelopes
  4 feet of ¼-inch-wide
    grosgrain ribbon
  old family photo
  crochet hook

family traditions

E very year on January 1, we spend the day putting the past year's photographs into an album. It's hard to keep up with this job during the year, but New Year's Day is usually a stay-at-home day for us, so it's fun to look over the year's events while organizing the photos and putting them in the album.

— *Linda Gnesin*
Cherry Hill, New Jersey

Memory Album

Along with pages for photos, this album includes envelopes that hold memorabilia— theater tickets, greeting cards, letters, pressed flowers, and other mementoes.

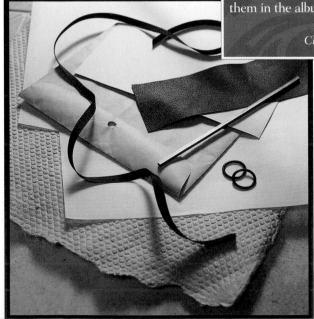

246

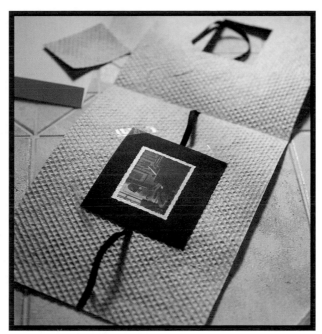

For the bound-in envelopes, use purchased 9×12-inch envelopes, or make your own from art paper. Open up a purchased envelope and use it as a pattern. Glue hook-and-loop fastening-tape dots to the flap and envelope.

here's how...

1 To make the album pages, cut the heavy art paper into 12 sheets measuring 9×14 inches. On each page, score 1 inch in from one short edge by, drawing the crafts knife lightly across the surface of the paper, using the ruler as a guide. Fold the paper to the front along the scored line. To deckle the opposite short edge, hold the ruler firmly on the paper about 2 inches from the edge and carefully tear the paper along the ruler.

2 To make the covers, cut two 9×24½-inch rectangles from the hand-made paper. Fold each piece in half to make a doubled, 9×12¼-inch rectangle. Score each cover 1 inch from the cut edge to make the spine.

3 To make a window for the front-cover photo, open out one cover and draw a 2¾×3½-inch rectangle centered on the right side (see the photo *top right*). Cut out the window with a crafts knife. Make a ¼-inch slit in the fold for the ribbon, centering the slit. Thread a

24-inch piece of ribbon through the slit. Glue one end of the ribbon at the back edge of the front cover and leave the remaining end free, beyond the fold (see the photo *top right*).

4 From the black and gold art papers, cut rectangles slightly larger than the family photo; the black rectangle should be larger than the window opening. Use spray adhesive to mount the photo on the gold paper and then attach the gold rectangle to the black one. Center the photo on the left half of the inside front cover over the ribbon, and secure it in the corners with small pieces of tape. Apply spray adhesive to the right inside front cover (the window side), then refold the cover along the fold line and press in place.

5 For the back cover, open out the folded 9×12¼-inch rectangle and cut a slit in the fold at the center to match the slit on the front cover. Thread ribbon through, securing one end at the back edge with a dot of glue. Apply spray adhesive to one side of the inside back cover and press the two sides together.

6 To make the leather spine wrap, cut a 2¾×9-inch rectangle from soft leather or suede. Make a template for punching the holes from a 1×9-inch piece of heavy paper. Use the hole punch to make holes 1½ inches from the top and bottom edges and ½ inch in from one long edge of the template. Attach the template to one long edge of the leather spine wrap and punch two holes; repeat for the opposite edge.

7 Working with one page or envelope at a time, clip the template to the folded tab edge of each sheet of paper and the bottom of each envelope, and punch the holes.

247

8 To assemble the album, stack the back cover, pages, envelopes, and front cover, lining up the holes. Wrap the spine with the leather strip, aligning the holes. Using a crochet hook, pull an O ring through each hole, then push a rod through the O rings on the front and back of the album. The rod and O rings hold the book together and can be reassembled to add more pages.

Slipcovered Photo Album

〜 Turn an ordinary purchased photo album into a keepsake with a silvery organza slipcover.

Go one step further and make the album an extraordinary gift for a landmark birthday, an anniversary, college graduation, or retirement by filling it with photos of the recipient's family, friends, or activities.

here's how...

1 Measure the album from edge to edge across the spine and add ½ inch. Measure the album from top to bottom and add ½ inch. Cut a rectangle this size from newsprint or newspaper for the album-cover pattern.

2 Cut two pieces of fabric 1 inch larger all around than the pattern.

Center the pattern on the wrong side of one piece of fabric and hold it in place with a book or other weight. Following the manufacturer's instructions, iron the ⅞-inch-wide fusible tape to the fabric along all four sides of the pattern. (This will be the flange that extends beyond the edges of the album.)

4 Remove the pattern. Peel the backing from the fusible tape along the top edge of the slipcover only. Lay the remaining fabric rectangle over the first, wrong sides facing and aligning raw edges. Press to fuse the two fabric rectangles together along the top edge. To make the pocket for the photo, cut a

piece of fabric 1½ inches larger than the photo. Following the manufacturer's instructions, iron a strip of ⅝-inch-wide fusible tape along each edge of the pocket. Position the pocket on the front cover (the right half of the top fabric rectangle). Peel the backing from the fusible tape on three sides of the pocket and iron to adhere the pocket to the cover. Insert the photo, then peel the backing from the remaining edge and iron to adhere.

6 Using metallic thread in both the needle and bobbin, stitch around the photo with a straight stitch.

7 With the front of the slipcover faceup, fold the slipcover in half and press along the fold. Unfold the slipcover and place it with the front (photo side) facedown and cut a slit in the lining between the top and bottom strips of fusible tape. Cut small horizontal slits at

the top and bottom of this slit to equal the width of the album spine. Fold under the raw edges along the slit and fuse them in place with ⅝-inch fusible tape for a neat, finished appearance.

8 Fuse the remaining three edges of the slipcover. Stitch around the inner edge of the fusible tape, using a zig-zag stitch and metallic thread. Trim the raw outer edges even with the outside edge of the fusible tape.

Fold the album covers back and slide the slipcover onto the covers.

*The album shown here is a post-bound album, which can be disassembled to add more pages. The organza slipcover is best for albums with slender spines.

250

Christmas Memory Tray

❧ Preserve holiday mementoes inspired by a poem or song in a frame that doubles as a serving tray.

here's how...

1 Carefully remove the backing and glass from the frame.

2 Use sandpaper to roughen the surface of the frame if it's varnished or painted. Wipe off the sanding dust.

3 Paint the frame silver, applying two or more coats if necessary. Smooth the painted surface as needed by rubbing it with a grocery bag or kraft paper.

4 Apply the crackle finish, following the manufacturer's directions.

5 Lightly brush on gold paint, then rub off the excess, leaving gold highlights. Brush gold paint on the silver pulls and rub off for similar highlights on the pulls.

6 Center one pull on each short side of the frame, as shown in the photo, and attach with screws.

7 Secure the handmade paper to the frame backing with double-sided adhesive tape. Arrange memorabilia on top of the paper until you are pleased with the design. To hold large pieces in place, use small pieces of double-sided adhesive tape or dots of glue. Anchor large ribbons in the same manner. Arrange baby's breath and ferns, and scatter shredded paper bits across the design.

8 Place the glass on top and clip the backing and glass together around the edges with the clothespins to allow you to hold it in place as you turn it over to set it in the frame. With the back of the frame facing you, place the piece, glass side down, in the frame, carefully removing one clothespin at a time as you ease the glass and backing into the frame. Push the

pins or brads that came with the frame back in place.

9 If desired, secure a felt rectangle to the back of the frame with double-sided adhesive tape.

Note: Choose a wooden frame with a flat outside edge that is at least ¾ inch wide. When purchasing the pulls, take the frame to the hardware store so you can be sure the pull fits the edge.

Very Personal Gift Tags

here's how...

There's no mistaking who the gift is from when you attach tags like these. Look for sturdy 2×3-inch tags at office supply shops, or cut your own from construction paper. For the photo, write a message in large letters on a piece of construction paper: "From Me," "Happy Holidays," or "Love, Grandma and Grandad." Take a picture of the gift giver holding the paper. A head and chest shot works best. After you have the film developed, take the print to a Kodak copier (they're usually in the film department of a drug store or discount store) and follow the instructions to make nine wallet-size copies. The copier reduces your original image to this size and makes multiple images all at the same time. One sheet costs about $7. If you need more tags, make color photocopies at a copy center for $1 each. Cut away the background, and use a glue stick to attach the photo image to the gift tag.

Other options

The stamp-size photos that accompany a full set of portrait photos from some photo studios are perfect for gift tags. Simply cut them out and glue them onto construction paper. Another option is the sticker film from Polaroid. Look for the cameras and film at discount stores and drug stores. Each photo comes out as a small sticker that you can apply directly to the gift tag.

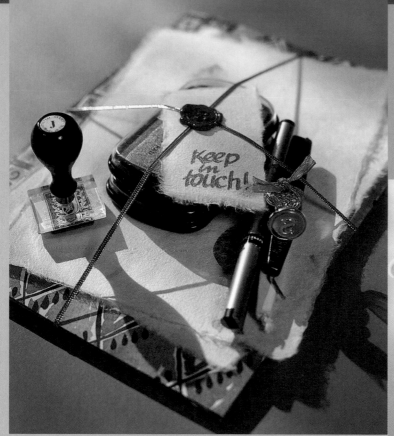

It's the next best thing to being there. Keep in touch with faraway friends with a gift pack of stationery supplies, such as note paper, postcards, postage stamps, a pen, and sealing wax and a stamp. Also include a prepaid phone card, available from post offices, grocery stores, and discount stores.

In a Twinkling:
Instant Gifts

▲ Present a bouquet of memories with film, an album, storage box, and frame. For the film "flowers," cut a ⅛-inch-diameter dowel into 10-inch lengths, and paint each one green. Use a crafts knife or paring knife to make a small slit in the bottom of each plastic film container. Slip a dowel through the slit and into the center of the roll of film.

◀ For friends headed to the beach or on a cruise, fill a straw hat with sunglasses, magazines or books about their destination, sun block, a disposable camera (panoramic for scenic areas, underwater for scuba divers, or outdoors for the beach), and a travel umbrella for an occasional rainy day.

Inspire a would-be gardener with a pot full of gardening tools and supplies, such as a trowel, pruning shears, gloves, and seed packets for the coming season. For an indoor gardener, fill a terra-cotta saucer with gravel or small pebbles, add a few narcissus bulbs, and wrap the saucer in clear cellophane. Remember to include instructions for forcing: Place the saucer in a sunny spot and add water to just below the base of the bulbs. Keep the water at this level.

Encourage a budding artist with a gift certificate for a class at your local art center or art museum. Assemble the certificate, a class schedule, and a few supplies, and present them on a "palette" made from cardboard (a pizza box works well) and covered with a second copy of the class schedule. Cut two slits in the palette and thread a ribbon through to tie the supplies in place.

Please a pet owner (or the owner's pet) with a new bowl and an assortment of pet treats, toys, grooming supplies, and even a new leash.

Pamper your friends with the luxury of a spa retreat at home.

spa *gifts*

Long soaks in warm, herb-infused waters can relax tense muscles and relieve stress. So treat the people on your gift list to the pleasures of fragrant herbal bath products with bath tea bags, herbal hair rinse, and green-tea body wash. Make the oversize tea bags from interfacing and fill them with herbs to steep in the bathwater. For your friends who prefer showers, mix green tea with unscented body wash for an invigorating cleanser. An herbal hair rinse to use after shampoo leaves hair smelling fresh and fragrant.

Present this at-home spa in a wire basket with a few washcloths or a big fluffy bath towel. Tuck in the hair rinse, tea bags, and body wash, and stitch a bath glove from a pair of washcloths to complete the gift.

bath tea bag

HERBAL MIXES: Shop for dried herbs at health-food stores. Don't use crushed herbs intended for cooking; they'll leak out of the tea bag material.

STIMULATING: equal amounts of rosemary leaves, marjoram leaves, peppermint leaves, lavender flowers, and chamomile flowers

RELAXING: equal amounts of lavender flowers, basil, thyme, sage leaves, and rosemary leaves

Add a small amount of oatmeal to each mixture for its skin-softening effects.

here's how...

1 For each bag, cut a 10×16½-inch piece of interfacing. Stitch the long edges together, using a ¼-inch seam. Press the tube so that the seam falls in the center of one side (this will be the wrong side). Press the seam allowances to one side.

2 To make the bottom pleat, fold the tube in half, right sides facing, and press; fold each half again 1 inch away from the center fold, creasing in the opposite direction so the open ends of the tube meet. (The seam will now be on the inside.) Using a paper funnel, fill each side of the bag with about ¼ cup of the desired herb mixture.

3 Align the edges at each end of the tube and fold the corners to the center, making a point. Fold the points down, then fold one point over the other. Staple a loop of string over the folded points.

4 Staple a paper tag to the top of the loop and attach a piece of double-sided adhesive tape to the back of the tag. (Don't remove the backing on the side of the tape facing you.) On the tag, write the ingredients in the herbal mix and include instructions for using the tea bag: Hang the bag over the faucet by the loop. If necessary to keep the tea bag in place while water runs through it, peel off the back of the double-sided tape and press it to the faucet. After bathing, rub the tea bag over your skin for extra soothing benefits.

green tea body wash

here's how...

1 Brew one 8-ounce cup of green tea, letting it steep until it is full strength. Pour the tea and leaves into a blender and blend well. Pour the mixture through a sieve to strain out most of the leaves.

2 Add the mixture to the body wash by teaspoonfuls until you like the color.

herbal hair rinse

here's how...

1 Bring 4 cups of distilled water to a boil, then add the desired mixture of herbs and allow to steep for 20 minutes.

2 Strain the mixture into a decorative, shatterproof bottle. Keep refrigerated and use within one week.

bath mitt

here's how...

1 To make a pattern, trace around your hand and wrist on the scrap paper, spreading your fingers slightly. Add ¼ to ½ inch all around the hand and add at least 1 inch on each side of the wrist. Cut out the pattern.

2 Place the pattern on one washcloth, positioning it so the wrist edge falls at the cloth's trimmed edge. Trace around the pattern with a water-soluble marker. Repeat for the remaining washcloth.

3 Cut two pieces of elastic ½ inch shorter than the wrist width. Stitch one piece of elastic to each washcloth at the wrist (in the cloth's trim area). The elastic should extend ¼ inch beyond the traced wrist lines.

4 From the bias tape, cut an 8-inch length. Stitch the long open edges together, then fold to make a loop.

5 Pin the washcloths together with the elastic aligned and facing out. Sandwich the bias-tape loop between the cloths, with the raw edges at the seam. Stitch around the traced lines, being sure to catch the bias tape loop.

6

Cut out the glove ½ inch beyond the stitching line. Zigzag stitch around the cut edges. Turn the glove inside out. Add a felt leaf at the wrist, if desired.

How can dreams help but be sweet when bed linens are suffused with the fragrance of lavender?

lavender dreams

E veryone appreciates the gift of a good night's sleep. According to traditional Asian medicine, buckwheat-hull pillows help promote rest. The pillow conforms to your head and neck, supporting them comfortably and relieving neck pain and stress. Add lavender buds to encourage relaxation; stitch up a pillowcase to coordinate with the recipient's bedroom colors. For a lighter fragrance, mix up a lavender spray for linens—the pleasure of laying your head on a crisply pressed pillowcase is worth the extra minute or two it takes to spritz and iron the case.

lavender pillow
here's how...

If your pillow has a zipper closure, simply unzip and add the cup of lavender flowers. If it doesn't have a zipper, carefully clip the stitches in one seam for about 2 inches. Add the lavender, using a paper funnel, then restitch the opening closed with small blind stitches.

2 Use the plain pillowcase that comes with the pillow for your pattern. Cut one piece of fabric twice the width of the case, adding ½ inch for seam allowances.

3 Encase one long edge of the fabric in the edging lace and stitch; pin the ribbon over the edging on the right side of the case, and stitch close to each edge of the ribbon.

4 Fold the case in half, right sides facing and aligning the raw edges. Stitch the bottom and side seams. Zigzag stitch over the raw edges, then turn the case to the right side and press.

lavender laundry spritz
here's how...

To make the lavender laundry spray, mix 4 ounces of alcohol-based lavender-scented toilet water or room freshener with 24 ounces of distilled water. (Don't use oil-based room sprays as the oil may damage fabric.) Pour the mixture into a clear spray bottle, and make a label from typing paper. Glue it to the bottle with spray adhesive. Include instructions to use the spray on pillowcases or linens just before pressing.

257

Present your host or hostess with one of these handmade gifts, and your creativity and thoughtfulness will be remembered long after the holidays are over.

thoughtful tokens

Turn pinecones into topiaries to display singly or in a group. These are small enough that your hostess can easily find a spot for one. They're also great to have on hand when you need a gift in a hurry.

Although etiquette books advise against showing up at a party with cut flowers—it's inconvenient for the hostess to stop and find a vase for them—it's okay to send them afterward to express your thanks. To give the

flowers a personal touch, deliver them yourself in a thrift-shop vase you've painted with Christmas designs. Edible or drinkable gifts are good, too. For a more memorable presentation, offer baked goods on a plate you've etched yourself, or wrap up wine or sherry in a "cozy" or wine scarf.

Painted Vase

here's how...

1 Referring to the photograph *at left,* paint rows of lines, squiggles, dots, spirals, and squares onto the vase. Follow any embossed lines as a guide in creating a repeating pattern. Don't worry about making the lines uniform: if they're thick and thin, it adds to the whimsical charm of the design. If you want a more controlled pattern, draw your design on tissue paper and tape it to the inside of the vase. Paint over the designs, then move the pattern to the next area and repeat.

2 To heat-set the paint and make it permanent and waterproof, bake the finished vase in the oven, following the manufacturer's instructions.

Mini-Topiaries

here's how...

1 Following the manufacturer's instructions, use adhesive size to paint designs on the terra-cotta pots. When the adhesive is tacky to the touch, apply the metal leaf. Spritz the pinecones with bright-gold spray paint.

2 Place gravel or small rocks in the bottom of the pot to balance the weight of the pinecone. Push the plastic foam ball into the pot so it fits snugly.

3 To make a topiary with a trunk, cut a twig to the desired length and sharpen one end to a point with a knife. Use hot glue to attach the pinecone to the blunt end. Push the pointed end into the plastic foam ball.

4 To make a trunkless topiary, glue the pinecone directly to the plastic foam.

5 Cover the plastic foam ball with sheet moss or sphagnum moss. For the tall topiary, spray a few tiny pinecones gold and glue them around the base.

SHOPPING LIST

clear glass vase
    (ours is from a
    secondhand shop)
From a crafts store:
    Delta CeramDecor
    paints: red, green,
    and white
    paintbrush

From a hardware store:
  assorted small terra-cotta
    pots with saucers
  gravel or small rocks
From a crafts store:
  composition metal leaf
    and adhesive size or a
    gilding kit
  plastic foam ball
  bright-gold spray paint
  sheet moss or sphagnum
    moss
  hot-glue gun and
    glue sticks
From your yard:
  assorted large and
    small pinecones
  ¼-inch-diameter twigs

Wine Bottle Cozies

SHOPPING LIST

¾ yard green loose-weave cotton fabric
⅜ yard batting
thread to match fabric
2 yards of piping cord
silver cording
silver metallic thread
lightweight aluminum wire

Christmas Tree
here's how...

1 Enlarge the pattern below. Cut two tree shapes each from the fabric and batting. Baste the batting to the wrong side of the fabric.

2 To cover your own piping, cut the remaining fabric on the bias into 2½-inch-wide strips. Stitch the strips together to form a straight 55-inch-long strip. Center the piping cord on the wrong side of the strip; fold the strip over the cord and stitch as close to the cord as possible, using the zipper foot on your sewing machine.

3 With right sides facing and raw edges aligned, stitch the piping to the front of the tree. Stitch the two tree shapes together, right sides facing and piping sandwiched in between. Leave the bottom edge open. Turn the tree right side out and stuff the points with additional batting to fill out the shape.

4 Turn under the bottom edge of the tree back and topstitch the hem in place.

5 Arrange silver cording on the tree front as desired and tack it in place with the silver metallic thread.

SHOPPING LIST

purchased cloth napkin
lightweight aluminum wire
silver buttons
matching thread
small beads

Napkin Drape
here's how...

1 Place the wine bottle in the center of the napkin. Bring the napkin up around the bottle and wrap it with aluminum wire to hold it in place. Wrap wire several times along the length of the bottle, crisscrossing the wire.

2 Where the wires cross, hand-sew a button, then sew a bead on top.

3 Sew a button, topped by a bead, to each corner of the napkin.

Wine Scarf
here's how...

1 From the rayon fabric, cut two 6½x23-inch strips.

2 From the tracing paper, cut a small freehand star. Using the paper as a pattern, cut the star from the 3-inch square of coordinating fabric, adding ½ inch all around. Turn under the ½-inch allowance and press. Blind-stitch the star to the right side of one strip of rayon in one corner.

3 Pin the two rayon strips together, right sides facing. Stitch, leaving a small opening for turning. Turn and press; whip-stitch the opening closed.

SHOPPING LIST

½ yard of 45-inch-wide rayon
matching thread
3-inch square of tracing or typing paper
3-inch square of coordinating fabric

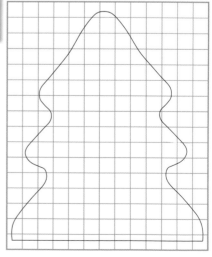

1 SQUARE = 1 INCH

260

glass plate or platter
clear self-adhesive shelf
   covering
fine-tip permanent
   marking pen
From a crafts store:
glass cleaner made to
   work with acid (sold
   with or alongside the
   etching cream)
crafts knife
burnisher or an old
   credit card
foam paintbrush
etching cream
lint-free cloth

Etching Precautions:

1 Make sure the room temperature is above 70 degrees.

2 Provide good ventilation.

3 Cover the work area with newspapers.

4 Work near a source of running water.

5 Wear a long-sleeve garment and rubber gloves to protect your skin from the etching cream. Protect your eyes from possible splashes by wearing glasses or goggles.

261

Etched-Glass Plates

➻ Etch a clear or colored glass plate with the words of a Christmas carol or other holiday greeting, then mound cookies or candy on the plate to leave with your hostess.

here's how...

1 Clean the glass plate with the special glass cleaner. (It is important to use the special glass cleaner because it won't leave a film.)

2 Create words on a computer, and use the printout for your pattern. Tape the pattern to the back of the plate.

Cover the plate with clear self-adhesive shelf paper, piecing strips as needed to cover the surface completely. Trace the words with the permanent marking pen, then remove the pattern from the back of the plate.

Cut out the letters using the crafts knife. Press the edges of the letters firmly, using the burnisher or an old credit card to seal the edges. (Don't use your fingers—the oil from your skin may interfere with the action of the etching cream.)

5 To prepare the plate for etching, lightly reclean the exposed glass with the special glass cleaner. Use a damp, not wet, cloth. Pat dry.

Check the list of precautions, above, before you begin working with the etching cream. Using the foam paintbrush, apply a thick layer of etching cream over the stencil cutouts. Gently move the cream around the area to eliminate air bubbles. Wait 5 to 6 minutes, then rinse off the etching cream.

7 Remove the contact paper to expose the etching.

Blooming bulbs make glorious holiday gifts to enjoy right away. Or, for a present that looks to the future, pot evergreen seedlings for your gardening friends.

gifts that *grow*

Blooming Amaryllis

SHOPPING LIST:
amaryllis bulb
potting soil
terra-cotta pot (about 2 inches wider than the bulb)

Paperwhite narcissus and amaryllis are two classics for forcing into early bloom for the holidays, and you can also force hyacinths, crocuses, certain daffodils, tulips, and irises. Check bulb catalogs or your local nursery for selections recommended for forcing. If your friends have brown thumbs, they'll appreciate a pot of bulbs at the point of blooming—follow the instructions at right to bring amaryllis to the perfect stage for presentation. If your friends are do-it-yourselfers, package the bulbs with a container, potting soil, and instructions so they can enjoy the process themselves.

here's how...

1 Soak the roots of the amaryllis bulb in a small dish of water for about an hour.

2 Put a few inches of the potting soil in the bottom of the terra-cotta pot and firmly tap.

3 Set the bulb in the center of the pot. Make sure it sits high enough so that the neck of the bulb will protrude just above the rim of the pot.

4 Fill in around the bulb with potting soil, firming the soil with your fingertips. Water thoroughly. Keep the potted bulb in a warm, bright spot, and rotate it often.

SPLITTING BULBS: If another growth appears after your amaryllis has flowered, you can slice or break off the bulblet and its greenery from the main bulb. Be sure to keep a healthy handful of roots attached.

tips for other bulbs

■ Tulips, hyacinths, muscari, and crocuses can be forced into early bloom as well. Use a container with drainage holes. Add enough soil so that when you position the bulbs, the tips are about even with the rim of the pot. It's okay to crowd the bulbs, but they shouldn't touch. Fill in around them with soil to within ¼ to ½ inch of the rim. Water the soil, then put the pots in a dark place where temperatures stay between 40 and 50 degrees Fahrenheit. A basement, unheated garage, or refrigerator works well—just be sure the bulbs don't freeze. Check the soil from time to time and water as necessary to keep it damp. Roots will be forming, and the soil should not dry out. Let the bulbs chill for 8 to 16 weeks or until 1 inch of growth appears. Then move the pots to a brightly lit location where the temperature remains between 50 and 60 degrees Fahrenheit. Water often enough to keep the soil moist. The bulbs should bloom in a month or so.

■ Paperwhite and Soleil d'Or narcissus don't need to be chilled. Plant them in soil or nestle them into a 2- to 3-inch deep layer of pebbles, marbles, or gravel in a watertight container (such as a glazed ceramic dish or a brass box). The bulbs should be one-half to one-third submerged among the pebbles. Keep the water level just below the bottoms of the bulbs.

■ Hyacinths will root in water; purchase hyacinth glasses in garden centers and nursery catalogs. Fill the glass to the neck, then position the bulb in the top portion of the glass. Place the glass in a cool, dark spot until the roots reach about 4 inches, then move the glasses to a sunny location.

■ Any bulbs you force in soil can be planted outdoors in spring. Remove the spent flowers and continue watering the potted bulbs until you can plant them outdoors. It may take a couple of years for the bulbs to bloom again, and the flowers may be smaller than they were the first year. Bulbs forced in water will be completely spent after blooming and won't rebloom outdoors.

Reblooming Tips:

1 Pinch off the blossoms as soon as they start to droop and wither so that the plant won't waste energy trying to produce seeds.

2 After flowering, cut flower stalks so that only 2 to 4 inches remain. Place the pot in a warm, sunny spot. Water the stalks whenever the top of the potting soil feels dry. Fertilize once or twice a month with a balanced soluble fertilizer.

3 Put the plant outside in full to nearly full sun when spring warms up.

4 As cold weather approaches, stop watering and feeding to force the plant into dormancy. Turn the pot over so that the plant doesn't receive any rainfall.

5 Remove the foliage only after it turns yellow and dies.

6 Before the first frost, place the potted bulb in a cool (50 to 60 degrees), dark, dry place, such as a basement.

7 In November, bring the plant into light, and resume watering and feeding.

8 There's always a chance that the amaryllis won't rebloom the first year, so be prepared to give it at least one more opportunity.

Little Trees

 Give a gift of future Christmas trees with evergreen seedlings. Choose spruce, pine, or fir, according to the species recommended for your area. Check with a local nursery for seedlings. Plant them in potting soil in terra-cotta pots; the ones shown *at right* are Italian rose pots, available from specialty garden centers and garden catalogs. Cover the soil with pads of reindeer moss, which is available from floral-supply shops and crafts stores. If it's dry when you buy it, place the moss in a plastic bag and sprinkle it with water. Seal the bag and let the moss absorb moisture until it's soft. Tie organdy ribbon around each little tree and attach a card with the name of the species and instructions for its care—for example, "Set the pot in a sunny place and water the soil well once a week. In the spring, plant the seedling outdoors."

265

For the true book lover, assemble a few treats to enhance his or her enjoyment of a favorite pastime. Box up some bookmarks, highlighters, a protective book cover, and a small dictionary to keep handy by the bed. Book plates and an embossing tool let your friend give favorite books a personal stamp. A small portable readinglight makes reading in bed easy.

In a Twinkling:
Custom Gifts

▲ If the song your favorite handyperson most often sings is "If I Had a Hammer," answer the plea with a backup tool kit to store in the kitchen or den. Fill a rectangular plastic basket with a small hammer, various screwdrivers (Phillips, slot, large and small), a tape measure, and pliers, both needle-nose and plain. Tools will always be handy when they're needed.

◀ Give a relaxing night at the movies with all the comforts of home: package a tub of microwaveable popcorn with a videotape of a favorite movie and perhaps a certificate for a movie rental. Some candy, bottles of soda, and a copy of a comprehensive movie guide complete the gift.

267

▲ For friends or family members who usually eat lunch at their desks, make the experience more civilized with a lunch-for-one set that fits into a desk drawer. Camp flatware, a microwave-safe plate, mini salt and pepper shakers, and a place mat and napkins can all be stored in a small plastic box, along with a small bottle of dishwashing liquid for cleanup.

▲ If someone on your gift list is likely to make (again) that most common New Year's resolution, help him or her put a best foot forward with a "bouquet" of athletic socks, wrist bands, wrist or ankle weights, shoelaces, and a certificate for a visit to a local health club for a class or fitness evaluation.

▶

For the tiny tots on your list, make bath time a rub-a-dub good time with a net bag full of bubble bath, floating toys, a spout protector (shaped like a friendly animal), and children's soap in fun shapes.

268

Cookies-in-a-Jar

A gift made by hand travels most quickly to the heart (and in this case, to the stomach too). Whether it's something to munch on, hot soup for a cold winter's night, or delicious, homemade candy, a gift of good taste is always the right present.

gifts *from* *the* kitchen

Cookies-in-a-Jar

Long after all of the holiday treats have been eaten, this prett, layered, cookie-mix-in-a-jar holds sweet promise for a leisurely day of winter baking. Next time, vary the mix by substituting ⅔ cup candy-coated milk chocolate pieces or ⅔ cup semisweet and/or white baking pieces for the cherries and raisins.

- ¾ cup all-purpose flour
- ½ teaspoon baking powder
- ⅛ teaspoon baking soda
- ⅛ teaspoon salt
- ½ cup butter-flavored or regular shortening
- ½ cup packed brown sugar
- ⅓ cup dried tart cherries
- ⅓ cup golden raisins
- 1 cup rolled oats
- ¼ cup chopped pecans or walnuts
- ¼ cup flaked coconut

Stir together the flour, baking powder, baking soda, and salt in a small mixing bowl. Using a pastry blender, cut in shortening until pieces are pea size.

Starting with the flour mixture, layer the ingredients in a clean 1-quart glass canning jar in the following order (from bottom to top): flour mixture, brown sugar, cherries, raisins, oats, pecans or walnuts, and coconut.

Cover jar and attach a card with the directions for mixing and baking (see sample in box below).

Nutrition facts per cookie: 108 cal., 6 g total fat (1 g sat. fat), 9 mg chol., 30 mg sodium, 13 g carbo., 0 g fiber, 1 g pro. **Daily values:** 1% vit. A, 0% vit. C, 1% calcium, 3% iron

---

Fruit and Nut Oatmeal Drops
(Mix in this jar will keep for 2 weeks.)

Empty contents of the jar into a large mixing bowl. Stir the mixture until combined, using a wooden spoon. Stir in 1 egg and 1 teaspoon vanilla until mixture is well combined. Drop dough by rounded teaspoon 2 inches apart on an ungreased cookie sheet. Bake in a 375° oven for 8 to 10 minutes or until edges are lightly browned. Transfer cookies to a wire rack; cool. Makes about 24 cookies.

---

two gifts in one

■ Package homemade treats (or purchased gourmet specialties) in collectible containers that can be put to other uses after the holidays. Some ideas:

■ Carefully stack cookies in an ironstone tureen. Place the lid on the tureen, then slip ribbon through the handles and tie in a bow over the lid.

■ Fill a vintage carnival-glass bowl with homemade candy, then wrap the dish in opalescent cellophane and tie with ribbon.

■ Fill antique celery glasses or goblets with fudge or truffles.

■ Shop flea markets and antiques stores for enamelware. Small pots with lids are perfect for snack mix or nuts. Slip a bag of biscotti and specialty coffees into an enamelware coffeepot that can hold flowers after the holidays.

peel for the fruit in the cordial recipe (reserve remaining oranges for another use). Steep mixture for 3 weeks.

BANANA CORDIAL: Peel and thinly slice 1 large ripe *banana*. Steep the mixture for 1 week.

MANGO CORDIAL: Peel, pit, and chop 2 ripe *mangoes*. Steep the mixture for 1 to 2 weeks.

PEAR CORDIAL: Peel, core, and thinly slice 6 medium *pears*. Steep the mixture for 3 weeks.

Nutrition facts per ¼ cup: 148 cal., 0 g total fat (0 g sat. fat), 0 mg chol., 1 mg sodium, 14 g carbo., 0 g fiber, 0 g pro. **Daily values:** 0% vit. A, 0% vit. C, 0% calcium, 0% iron

Berry Cordials
※

1 cup vodka or gin
1½ cups sugar
2 cups fresh berries (may substitute a 12- to 16-ounce package frozen unsweetened berries, such as strawberries, blackberries, boysenberries, or lightly sweetened red raspberries, or pitted, dark sweet cherries or tart red cherries)

Heat vodka and sugar in a small saucepan over low heat, stirring just until sugar is dissolved. Remove from heat. Place warmed liquor mixture into a 2-quart glass jar or ceramic container. Stir in berries and cover. Let stand in a cool dark place for 2 to 4 weeks, swirling once a week. Strain as directed in the Fruit Cordials recipe at left. Or, use liquid and berries as a dessert topping. Makes 1⅔ cups cordial and 1¼ cups berries.

Nutrition facts per ¼ cup cordial: 243 cal., 0 g total fat (0 g sat. fat), 0 mg chol., 1 mg sodium, 41 g carbo., 0 g fiber, 0 g pro. **Daily values:** 0% vit. A, 0% vit. C, 0% calcium, 0% iron

Berry Cordials
Fruit Cordials

270

Fruit Cordials
※

For an easy, elegant gift, pour these beautiful cordials into inexpensive cut-glass bottles or unusual decanters. Embellish them with a handmade gift tag and tiny ornaments or holly sprigs tied around the bottle necks. Each fruit will give your cordial a different soft hue.

1½ cups sugar
1 cup water
Desired fruit (see suggestions at right)
1 750-ml bottle vodka (3½ cups)

Heat sugar and water in a small saucepan over low heat, stirring until sugar is dissolved. Remove from heat; cool. Pour sugar syrup into a 2-quart glass jar. Add desired fruit and vodka; stir gently. Cover the jar with a tight-fitting lid. Let stand (steep) in a cool dark place for the time suggested for each fruit, swirling every few days to distribute the ingredients.

To strain, set a wire strainer, lined with several thicknesses of 100-percent-cotton cheesecloth, over a large bowl or wide-mouth jar. Pour fruit mixture through. If liquid needs further clarifying, pour through a coffee funnel lined with a paper filter. Transfer the strained liquid to a clean, dry bottle using a funnel. Seal bottle tightly and label with contents so you'll be able to identify the flavor. Store at room temperature. Makes about 5 cups.

ORANGE CORDIAL: Remove a thin layer of peel from 3 *oranges* using a sharp knife or vegetable peeler. Take care to avoid the bitter white part. Use

Tomato Split Pea Soup

For a welcome gift of a cold winter night's supper, package the split peas in a glass jar together with the recipe for Tomato Split Pea Soup in a basket lined with a colorful kitchen towel. Add a pretty ladle for serving the finished soup and a package of Cracker Mix.

- 1 cup dry split yellow or green peas
- 1¼ to 1½ pounds meaty smoked pork hocks or one 1- to 1½-pound meaty ham bone
- 2 14½-ounce cans reduced-sodium chicken broth
- 1 cup chopped celery
- ¾ teaspoon snipped fresh tarragon or ¼ teaspoon dried tarragon, crushed
- ¼ teaspoon pepper
- 1 bay leaf
- ⅓ cup tomato paste
- 1 cup sliced carrot
- ½ cup chopped onion
- 1 cup Cracker Mix (see recipe, at right)

Rinse peas. Combine peas, pork hocks or ham bone, chicken broth, 1 cup *water*, celery, dried tarragon (if using), pepper, and bay leaf in a large saucepan or Dutch oven. Bring to boiling; reduce heat. Cover and simmer for 1¼ hours. Remove pork hocks or ham bone; set aside to cool.

Stir tomato paste, carrot, and onion into saucepan. Return to boiling; reduce heat. Cover and simmer for 20 minutes or until vegetables are tender.

Meanwhile, cut meat off bones; coarsely chop meat, discarding bones. Stir meat and fresh tarragon (if using) into saucepan; heat through. Discard bay leaf. Sprinkle each serving with some of the Cracker Mix. Makes 4 to 6 servings.

Nutrition facts per serving: 364 cal., 9 g total fat (2 g sat. fat), 25 mg chol., 1,267 mg sodium, 48 g carbo., 15 g fiber, 25 g pro. **Daily values:** 84% vit. A, 16% vit. C, 7% calcium, 20% iron

Cracker Mix

This fun, crunchy cracker mix is great as a go-with for hot soup (see Tomato Split Pea Soup at left). Or, spice up the mix to munch with a mug of hot cider or a cold beverage—use 2 teaspoons Worcestershire sauce and ¼ teaspoon bottled hot pepper.

- 1 cup bite-size fish-shaped pretzel or cheese-flavored crackers
- 1 cup oyster crackers
- 1 cup bite-size shredded wheat biscuits
- 1 cup bite-size rich round crackers
- 2 tablespoons cooking oil
- ½ teaspoon Worcestershire sauce
- ¼ teaspoon garlic powder
  Dash bottled hot pepper sauce
- 2 tablespoons grated Parmesan cheese

Combine all crackers in a large bowl. Combine cooking oil, Worcestershire sauce, garlic powder, and bottled hot pepper sauce in a small bowl. Pour over cracker mixture, tossing to coat. Sprinkle cracker mixture with Parmesan cheese; toss to coat. Spread mixture in a shallow baking pan.

Bake in a 300° oven for 10 to 15 minutes or until golden, stirring once. Cool completely. Store in an airtight container. Makes 4 cups.

Nutrition facts per ¼ cup: 77 cal., 4 g total fat (0 g sat. fat), 1 mg chol., 113 mg sodium, 10 g carbo., 1 g fiber, 2 g pro. **Daily values:** 0% vit. A, 0% vit. C, 1% calcium, 3% iron

Cracker Mix

271

Cashew-White Fudge Bites

A festive way to package these sweet somethings is to wrap them in clear plastic wrap, then carefully overwrap in foil paper to avoid squashing the cashew toppers.

- 2 cups sugar
- 1 5-ounce can (⅔ cup) evaporated milk
- ½ cup butter
- 1 6-ounce package white chocolate baking squares, chopped, or one 6-ounce package white baking bars, chopped
- ½ of a 7-ounce jar marshmallow creme
- ½ cup chopped cashews
- ½ teaspoon vanilla
  Cashew halves (optional)

Line an 8×8×2-inch baking pan with foil, extending foil over edges of pan. Butter foil; set pan aside.

Butter the sides of a heavy 2-quart saucepan. Combine sugar, evaporated milk, and butter in the saucepan. Cook and stir over medium-high heat until mixture boils. Clip a candy thermometer to side of pan. Be sure the bulb is well covered and not touching bottom of pan. Reduce heat to medium; continue cooking and stirring until temperature registers 236° (7 to 10 minutes). Mixture should boil gently over entire surface.

Remove saucepan from heat; remove thermometer. Add chopped white chocolate; stir until melted. Stir in marshmallow creme, chopped cashews, and vanilla until mixture is combined. Beat by hand for 1 minute.

Pour into prepared pan. Allow fudge to cool and become somewhat firm on the surface (10 to 20 minutes).

Score into four large squares. When candy is firm, use foil to lift it out of pan. Use a knife with a long blade to cut each large square into 4 smaller squares. Then cut diagonally to make a total of 8 triangles for each large square. Repeat with remaining large squares. Lightly press a cashew half into each piece, if desired. Store tightly covered. Makes about 1¾ pounds (32 pieces).

Nutrition facts per piece: 132 cal., 6 g total fat (3 g sat. fat), 10 mg chol., 57 mg sodium, 19 g carbo., 0 g fiber, 1 g pro. **Daily values:** 3% vit. A, 0% vit. C, 2% calcium, 1% iron

Jamaican Jerk Seasoning Mix

Give this versatile spice mix in a small, decorated jar and attach a tag indicating possible uses.

- ¼ cup sugar
- 3 tablespoons onion powder
- 3 tablespoons dried thyme, crushed
- 2 tablespoons ground allspice
- 2 tablespoons ground black pepper
- 3 to 4 teaspoons ground red pepper
- 1 tablespoon salt
- 1½ teaspoons ground nutmeg

Combine all ingredients and store in an airtight container. To make ahead, store at room temperature up to 6 months. Makes about 48 teaspoons seasoning mix.

Use to sprinkle or rub over chicken, seafood, meats, or vegetables for grilling or broiling. Or, use the seasoning to spice up simple bean and rice dishes.

Nutrition facts per teaspoon: 8 cal., 0 g total fat (0 g sat. fat), 0 mg chol., 134 mg sodium, 2 g carbo., 0 g fiber, 0 g pro. **Daily values:** 0% vit. A, 0% vit. C, 0% calcium, 1% iron

272

Cashew-White Fudge Bites

Pear-Berry Gingerbread Loaves

Wrap these diminutive gingerbread loaves in plastic wrap and tie with a yarn bow embellished with small decorative fruits and berries.

    3 cups all-purpose flour
    2 teaspoons baking powder
 1½ teaspoons ground cinnamon
    ½ teaspoon baking soda
    ½ teaspoon salt
    2 beaten eggs
    ⅔ cup light-flavored molasses
    ⅔ cup cooking oil
    ½ cup packed brown sugar
    ⅓ cup milk
 1½ teaspoons grated gingerroot
    2 medium pears, peeled, cored,
        and finely chopped
        (about 1 cup)
    ½ cup dried cranberries
        Pear Icing

Grease bottoms and halfway up sides of four 5¾×3×2-inch individual loaf pans or eight 4-inch individual fluted tube pans*; set aside.

Combine flour, baking powder, cinnamon, baking soda, and salt in a large mixing bowl. Make a well in the center of flour mixture; set aside. Stir together eggs, molasses, oil, brown sugar, milk, and grated gingerroot in a medium mixing bowl. Add egg mixture all at once to the flour mixture. Stir just until moistened. Fold pears and dried cranberries into batter. Spoon batter into prepared pans.

Bake in a 350° oven for 35 to 40 minutes for loaf pans or about 25 minutes for fluted tube pans, or until a wooden toothpick inserted near the center comes out clean. Cool in pans on wire racks 10 minutes. Loosen and remove from pans. Cool completely on wire racks. Drizzle with Pear Icing. Makes 4 or 8 loaves (16 servings).

PEAR ICING: Stir together 1¼ cups sifted *powdered sugar*, 2 tablespoons *pear liqueur or pear nectar*, and ½ teaspoon *vanilla* in a small mixing bowl. If necessary, stir in a few drops of *milk* to make an icing that is easy to drizzle.

***If your set of fluted tube pans** includes only six, chill the remaining batter while the first batch bakes.

Nutrition facts per serving: 291 cal., 10 g total fat (2 g sat. fat), 27 mg chol., 168 mg sodium, 47 g carbo., 1 g fiber, 3 g pro. **Daily values:** 1% vit. A, 1% vit. C, 7% calcium, 13% iron

---

Hot and Spicy Nuts

Package these easy-to-make (and easy-to-eat) nuts for gift-giving in a jar. Tie on a chili pepper decoration and label with a personalized stick-on label.

    1 teaspoon ground coriander
    1 teaspoon ground cumin

Hot and Spicy Nuts

    ½ teaspoon salt
    ¼ teaspoon black pepper
    ⅛ teaspoon ground red pepper
    2 cups raw peanuts (or raw
        cashews, almonds, or
        macadamia nuts)
    1 tablespoon cooking oil

Stir together coriander, cumin, salt, black pepper, and red pepper in a small bowl; set aside. Place nuts in a 13×9×2-inch baking pan. Drizzle with cooking oil, stirring to coat. Sprinkle with spice mixture; toss lightly.

Bake in a 300° oven about 20 minutes or until lightly toasted, stirring once or twice. Cool in pan for 15 minutes. Turn out onto paper towels; cool completely. Store, covered, in a cool place. Makes 2 cups.

Nutrition facts per ¼ cup: 225 cal., 20 g total fat (3 g sat. fat), 0 mg chol., 153 mg sodium, 6 g carbo., 3 g fiber, 10 g pro. **Daily values:** 0% vit. A, 0% vit. C, 4% calcium, 9% iron

Pear-Cranberry Conserve
(*see recipe,* page 276)

Hot Fudge Sauce

Caramel-Rum Sauce

274

Cook and stir over medium heat until thickened and bubbly (mixture may look curdled). Cook and stir 2 minutes more. Remove from heat. Stir in butter, rum, and vanilla. Let mixture stand at room temperature until cool.

FOR GIFT GIVING: Pour into half-pint jars. Seal and label. Store sauce in the refrigerator up to 2 months. Makes 4 half-pints (about 3½ cups).

Nutrition facts per tablespoon: 52 cal., 1 g total fat (1 g sat. fat), 4 mg chol., 15 mg sodium, 9 g carbo., 0 g fiber, 0 g pro. **Daily values:** 1% vit. A, 0% vit. C, 1% calcium, 1% iron

Orange-Pistachio Muffin Mix

This recipe makes two batches of muffin mix.

- 3 cups all-purpose flour
- 1 cup sugar
- ½ cup nonfat dry milk powder
- 4 teaspoons baking powder
- 2 teaspoons dried grated orange peel
- ¾ teaspoon salt
- ⅔ cup shortening (that does not need refrigeration)
- 1 cup chopped pistachios or toasted almonds

Combine flour, sugar, milk powder, baking powder, orange peel, and salt in an extra-large mixing bowl. Using a pastry blender, cut in shortening until mixture resembles coarse crumbs. Stir in nuts. Divide mixture in half (each about 3⅓ cups) and place in 2 airtight containers or self-sealing storage bags. Store up to 6 weeks at room temperature or 6 months in the freezer. Each mix makes 12 muffins.

TO BAKE MUFFINS FROM ONE MIX: Place one mix in a large mixing bowl. Make a well in the center of the dry mixture. Combine 1 beaten egg and ¾ cup water in a small bowl. Add all at once to the dry mixture. Stir just until moistened (batter should be somewhat

Hot Fudge Sauce

- 8 ounces semisweet chocolate pieces (1⅓ cups)
- ½ cup butter
- 1⅓ cups sugar
- 1⅓ cups whipping cream

Melt chocolate and butter in a heavy medium saucepan over low heat, stirring frequently. Add sugar. Gradually add whipping cream. Bring to boiling; reduce heat. Boil gently over low heat for 8 minutes, stirring frequently. Remove from heat. Let stand at room temperature until cool.

FOR GIFT GIVING: Pour into half-pint jars. Seal and label. Store sauce in the refrigerator up to 2 months. On the gift tag or label, include directions to reheat the fudge sauce in a small saucepan over medium-low heat and serve over ice cream. Makes 4 half-pints (about 3½ cups).

Nutrition facts per tablespoon: 71 cal., 5 g total fat (2 g sat. fat), 12 mg chol., 19 mg sodium, 8 g carbo., 0 g fiber, 0 g pro. **Daily values:** 3% vit. A, 0% vit. C, 0% calcium, 0% iron

Caramel-Rum Sauce

Pair a jar of this sauce with one of the Hot Fudge Sauce for a double treat.

- 2 cups packed brown sugar
- ¼ cup cornstarch
- 1⅓ cups half-and-half or light cream
- 1 cup water
- ½ cup light-colored corn syrup
- ¼ cup butter
- ¼ cup rum
- 2 teaspoons vanilla

Combine brown sugar and cornstarch in a heavy large saucepan. Stir in cream, water, and corn syrup.

lumpy). Spoon into twelve 2½-inch greased or paper bake cup-lined muffin cups, filling each ⅔ full. Sprinkle lightly with a mixture of 1 tablespoon sugar and ⅛ teaspoon ground nutmeg.

Bake in a 375° oven for 20 to 25 minutes or until golden. Cool in muffin cups on wire rack for 5 minutes. Remove muffins; serve warm.

FOR GIFT GIVING: Label each package and include baking directions. To wrap the gift, see the packaging idea *below*.

Nutrition facts per muffin: 182 cal., 9 g total fat (2 g sat. fat), 18 mg chol., 141 mg sodium, 23 g carbo., 1 g fiber, 4 g pro. **Daily values:** 1% vit. A, 2% vit. C, 7% calcium, 7% iron

To package Orange-Pistachio Muffin Mix for gift giving, center one bag of mix

e's how...

on a square of green cellophane (available from crafts stores and art supply stores). Pull the cellophane up around the bag and secure it with a rubber band. Cut a square of white tulle 2 to 3 inches larger than the cellophane square. Center the cellophane-wrapped muffin mix on the tulle and tie the tulle with a bow. Attach purchased snowflake stickers to the tulle. Present the mix with a cast-iron or novelty muffin pan.

Almond-Chocolate Cups

Look for small foil candy cups at gourmet cooking shops or paper-supply store.

1   3-ounce package cream
        cheese, softened
¼ to ½ teaspoon almond extract
3   cups sifted powdered sugar
¼   cup finely chopped
        toasted almonds

1   12-ounce package (2 cups)
        semisweet chocolate pieces
16   ounces chocolate-flavored
        candy coating, cut up
        Small foil candy cups

Beat cream cheese and almond extract in a medium mixing bowl until smooth. Gradually add powdered sugar, stirring until mixture is thoroughly combined. (If necessary, knead in the last of the powdered sugar by hand.) Stir or knead in chopped almonds.

Divide mixture into four equal portions. On a cutting board roll one portion at a time to a 12-inch-long rope; cut crosswise into ½-inch pieces. Cover with plastic wrap to prevent drying out as you work with candy.

Melt together chocolate pieces and candy coating in a heavy medium saucepan over low heat, stirring just until smooth. Remove from heat. Place foil cups in large shallow pan. Spoon some of the melted chocolate mixture into one-fourth of the candy cups, filling each cup about ⅔ full.

Press a piece of cheese mixture in center of each cup (chocolate will not completely cover the cheese mixture). Repeat with remaining filling and chocolate, working with one-fourth at a time. If chocolate starts to set up, reheat over low heat just until smooth. Drizzle any remaining chocolate over white portion of candies, if desired.

Set cups aside until firm at room temperature (about 30 minutes) or in refrigerator about 10 minutes. Store in a tightly covered container in the refrigerator. Makes about 96 pieces.

FOR GIFT GIVING: Arrange candy cups in a box or decorative plate with instructions to store in the refrigerator.

Nutrition facts per piece: 60 cal., 3 g total fat (2 g sat. fat), 1 mg chol., 3 mg sodium, 9 g carbo., 0 g fiber, 0 g pro. **Daily values:** 0% vit. A, 0% vit. C, 0% calcium, 0% iron

Sugar Cookie Snowflakes

⅓   cup butter
⅓   cup shortening
¾   cup sugar
1   teaspoon baking powder
1   egg
1   tablespoon milk
1   teaspoon vanilla
2   cups all-purpose flour
        Powdered Sugar Glaze
        Decorations (optional)

Beat butter and shortening with an electric mixer on medium to high speed 30 seconds. Add sugar, baking powder, and dash salt; beat well. Add egg, milk, and vanilla; beat until well combined. Beat in as much flour as you can. Stir in any remaining flour. Divide dough in half. Wrap; chill dough for 3 hours.

Roll half of the dough at a time ⅛ inch thick on a lightly floured surface. Cut with 3- to 3½-inch cookie cutters into 6- or 8-pointed star shapes or scalloped rounds. Using tiny hors d'oeuvres cutters or a sharp knife, cut small shapes from cutouts to make snowflake designs. Place on ungreased cookie sheet. Bake in a 375° oven for 7 to 8 minutes or until edges are firm and bottoms are very lightly browned. Transfer to a wire rack and cool.

To decorate, dip tops in Powdered Sugar Glaze. If desired, sprinkle with edible glitter, colored decorating sugar, and/or tiny white decorative candies. Makes 36 to 48 cookies.

POWDERED SUGAR GLAZE: Stir together 1 cup sifted powdered sugar, ¼ teaspoon vanilla, and milk (3 to 4 teaspoons) to make glazing consistency.

Nutrition facts per cookie: 85 cal., 4 g total fat (2 g sat. fat), 11 mg chol., 33 mg sodium, 12 g carbo., 0 g fiber, 1 g pro. **Daily values:** 1% vit. A, 0% vit. C, 1% calcium, 2% iron

275

Pesto Popcorn Seasoning Mix

extract in a medium mixing bowl; mix well. Add all at once to the dry mixture. Stir just until moistened (batter should be lumpy). Fold in cherries and nuts. Spoon into prepared muffin cups, dividing batter evenly (cups will be full). **Bake in a 400° oven** for 12 to 15 minutes or until golden brown. Cool in muffin cups on wire rack for 5 minutes. Remove muffins. Brush lightly with Lemon Glaze. Makes 36.

LEMON GLAZE: Stir together ¾ cup sifted powdered sugar, 2 teaspoons lemon juice, and enough water (2 to 3 teaspoons) to make a glaze.

FOR GIFT GIVING: Prepare and bake muffins as directed; cool completely. Do not glaze. Place in a freezer container or bag; freeze for up to 3 months. Before serving or giving as a gift, remove from freezer and thaw at room temperature. Prepare Lemon Glaze; brush muffins lightly with glaze.

Nutrition facts per muffin: 91 cal., 4 g total fat (1 g sat. fat), 14 mg chol., 42 mg sodium, 13 g carbo., 0 g fiber, 2 g pro. **Daily values:** 3% vit. A, 0% vit. C, 2% calcium, 2% iron

Pesto Popcorn Seasoning Mix

Give this seasoning mix with a jar of unpopped popcorn.

- 3 tablespoons butter-flavored sprinkles
- 2 tablespoons grated Parmesan cheese
- 1 teaspoon dried basil, crushed
- ½ teaspoon dried parsley flakes, crushed
- ⅛ to ¼ teaspoon garlic powder

Combine all ingredients in a small bowl. Store mix in the refrigerator. Seasoning mixture will coat about 10 cups of popped popcorn.

FOR GIFT GIVING: Pour the seasoning mix into a 4-ounce-size bottle. Include instructions to keep refrigerated.

Nutrition facts for entire seasoning mix: 133 cal., 4 g total fat (2 g sat. fat), 10 mg chol., 1,853 mg sodium, 19 g carbo., 0 g fiber, 5 g pro. **Daily values:** 3% vit. A, 1% vit. C, 15% calcium, 3% iron

Sour Cream-Cherry Muffins

Only one mini-muffin pan? Keep the remaining batter refrigerated while baking each batch (see photo, page 277).

- 2 cups all-purpose flour
- ½ cup sugar
- 2 teaspoons baking powder
- ¼ teaspoon salt
- 2 eggs
- ½ cup dairy sour cream
- ½ cup milk
- ¼ cup cooking oil
- ½ teaspoon finely shredded lemon peel
- ¼ teaspoon almond extract
- 1 cup dried tart red cherries, coarsely chopped
- ½ cup chopped almonds Lemon Glaze

Grease thirty-six 1¾-inch muffin cups or line with miniature paper bake cups. Stir together flour, sugar, baking powder, and salt in a large mixing bowl. Make a well in the center of the dry mixture. Combine eggs, sour cream, milk, oil, lemon peel, and almond

Pear-Cranberry Conserve

Try this freezer spread on toasted English muffins (see photo, page 274).

- 1 cup cranberries
- ½ cup water
- 6½ cups sugar
- 1½ to 2 pounds pears, cored, peeled, and finely chopped (3 cups)
- ¾ cup finely chopped walnuts or pecans
- 2 teaspoons finely shredded lemon peel
- 1 6-ounce package liquid fruit pectin (2 foil pouches)
- ⅓ cup lemon juice

Combine cranberries and water in a 4-quart Dutch oven. Bring to boiling.

276

Cover and cook for 2 minutes or until cranberries begin to pop. Stir in sugar; gently simmer for 10 minutes or until sugar dissolves. Remove from heat.

Add pears, nuts, and lemon peel. Let stand 10 minutes, stirring occasionally. Combine pectin and lemon juice in a mixing bowl; add to pear mixture. Stir 3 minutes. Ladle at once into clean, half-pint jars or freezer containers, leaving ½-inch headspace. Seal and label. Let stand for several hours until set. Store up to 3 weeks in the refrigerator or 1 year in the freezer. Makes 8 half-pints.

FOR THE GIFT TAG: Keep conserve frozen until ready to use; thaw in the refrigerator overnight before serving.

Nutrition facts per tablespoon: 54 cal., 1 g total fat (0 g sat. fat), 0 mg chol., 0 mg sodium, 13 g carbo., 0 g fiber, 0 g pro. **Daily values:** 0% vit. A, 1% vit. C, 0% calcium, 0% iron

Coffeehouse
Chocolate Spoons

Sour Cream-Cherry
Muffins

Coffeehouse Chocolate Spoons

Use plastic spoons or collect metal spoons from flea markets or antique shops to make these flavorful gifts.

   6 ounces semisweet
      chocolate pieces
   4 ounces milk chocolate pieces
      or white baking bar
20 to 24 spoons

Place semisweet chocolate pieces in a heavy saucepan over low heat, stirring constantly until the chocolate begins to melt. Immediately remove from heat and stir until chocolate is smooth. Dip spoons into chocolate, draining off excess chocolate (see photo, *right*). Place spoons on waxed paper; refrigerate for 30 minutes to allow chocolate to set up.

Place milk chocolate pieces or white baking bar in a heavy saucepan over low heat, stirring constantly until chocolate begins to melt. Immediately remove from heat and stir until smooth. Cool to room temperature. Place the melted chocolate in a small self-sealing plastic bag. Using scissors, make a small cut in the corner of the bag; drizzle one or both sides of the chocolate-coated spoons with the melted milk chocolate or white baking bar. Refrigerate spoons for 30 minutes to allow chocolate to set up.

FOR GIFT GIVING: Wrap each spoon separately and store in a cool dry place for 2 to 3 weeks until ready to give as gifts. If desired, bundle a week's worth in a jumbo holiday coffee mug. Makes 20 to 24 spoons.

Nutrition facts per spoon: 69 cal., 4 g total fat (3 g sat. fat), 0 mg chol., 6 mg sodium, 8 g carbo., 1 g fiber, 1 g pro. **Daily values:** 0% vit. A, 0% vit. C, 1% calcium, 2% iron

here's how...

For chocolate-coated spoons: Dip a plastic or metal spoon into the melted semisweet chocolate. Tap the handle of the spoon on the edge of the saucepan to remove excess chocolate. Place spoons on a tray lined with waxed paper and chill until set.

Buttery Cashew Brittle

Buttery Cashew Brittle

Add a small container of this candy to a cookie tray for a special treat. The recipient will find that cashews are a wonderful replacement for the more expected peanuts. This candy also can be made with peanuts, almonds, or macadamia nuts.

 2 cups sugar
 1 cup light-colored corn syrup
 ½ cup water
 1 cup butter
 3 cups (about 12 ounces)
   raw cashews
 1 teaspoon baking soda, sifted

Combine sugar, corn syrup, and water in a 3-quart saucepan. Cook and stir until sugar dissolves. Bring mixture to boiling; add butter and stir until butter is melted. Clip a candy thermometer to side of pan. Reduce heat to medium-low; continue boiling at a moderate, steady rate, stirring occasionally, until thermometer registers 280°, the soft-crack stage (about 35 minutes).

Stir in cashews; continue cooking over medium-low heat, stirring frequently until thermometer registers 300°, the hard-crack stage (10 to 15 minutes more).

Remove pan from heat; remove thermometer. Quickly stir in the baking soda, mixing thoroughly. Pour mixture onto 2 buttered baking sheets or 2 buttered 15×10×1-inch pans.

As the cashew brittle cools, stretch it out by lifting and pulling with 2 forks from the edges. Loosen from pans as soon as possible; pick up sections and break them into bite-size pieces. Store tightly covered. Makes about 2½ pounds (72 servings).

Nutrition facts per serving: 90 cal., 5 g total fat (2 g sat. fat), 7 mg chol., 47 mg sodium, 11 g carbo., 0 g fiber, 1 g pro. **Daily values:** 2% vit. A, 0% vit. C, 0% calcium, 3% iron

Cracker Snack Mix

Pack the mix in a decorative tin or tightly covered bowl that also can be used as a serving container.

 ½ cup butter or margarine
 1 tablespoon Worcestershire
   sauce
 1 teaspoon chili powder
 ¼ teaspoon bottled hot
   pepper sauce
 5 cups oyster crackers
 3 cups corn chips
 3 cups pretzel sticks
 2 cups shelled raw pumpkin
   seeds (pepitas)
 ⅓ cup grated Parmesan cheese

Cook and stir butter, Worcestershire sauce, chili powder, and hot pepper sauce in a medium saucepan over medium-low until butter melts. Combine crackers, corn chips, pretzel sticks, and pumpkin seeds in a large roasting pan. Drizzle butter mixture over cracker mixture; toss to coat.

Bake in a 300° oven for 30 minutes, stirring once. Sprinkle with Parmesan cheese; toss to mix. Spread on foil and cool. Store in an airtight container. Makes 24 (½-cup) servings.

Nutrition facts per serving: 179 cal., 12 g total fat (2 g sat. fat), 6 mg chol., 273 mg sodium, 15 g carbo., 1 g fiber, 5 g pro. **Daily values:** 4% vit. A, 2% vit. C, 2% calcium, 10% iron

Cranberry Brioche

Include freshly baked brioche with packets of dried cranberries or cherries, assorted preserves, and brioche pans in a basket lined with a holiday kitchen towel or napkin.

 1 package active dry yeast
 ¼ cup warm water (105° to 115°)
 ½ cup butter or margarine,
   softened

⅓ cup sugar

1 teaspoon salt

4 cups all-purpose flour

½ cup milk

4 eggs

½ cup dried cranberries or tart red cherries

¼ cup chopped candied citron (optional)

¼ cup dried currants or snipped raisins

1 tablespoon sugar

Dissolve yeast in warm water in a small bowl. Beat butter, the ⅓ cup sugar, and salt in a large mixing bowl with an electric mixer on medium to high speed until fluffy. Add 1 cup of the flour and the milk to beaten mixture. Separate 1 of the eggs. Add the egg yolk and 3 whole eggs to flour mixture. (Chill remaining egg white.) Add dissolved yeast to flour mixture; beat well. Stir in cranberries or cherries, citron, and currants or raisins. Stir in remaining flour with a wooden spoon.

Place dough in a greased bowl. Cover and let rise in a warm place until double (about 2 hours). Refrigerate for 6 to 24 hours.

Grease 24 individual brioche pans or 2½-inch muffin pans; set aside. Stir down dough. Turn out onto a floured surface. Divide into 4 equal portions. Set 1 portion aside. Divide remaining 3 portions into 8 pieces each. Shape each piece into a ball, pulling edges under to make a smooth top. Place a ball in each prepared brioche pan or muffin cup. Divide remaining dough into 24 pieces; shape into small balls. Make a deep indentation in middle of each large ball with your thumb. Press a small ball into each indentation.

Combine reserved egg white and the 1 tablespoon sugar in a small bowl. Brush mixture over rolls. Cover and let rise in a warm place until nearly double (about 45 to 60 minutes).

Bake in a 375° oven for 13 to 15 minutes or until tops are golden. Remove from pans or muffin cups; cool on wire racks. Makes 24 brioche.

Nutrition facts per brioche: 144 cal., 5 g total fat (3 g sat. fat), 46 mg chol., 142 mg sodium, 22 g carbo., 1 g fiber, 3 g pro. **Daily values:** 5% vit. A, 0% vit. C, 1% calcium, 7% iron

---

Tomato-Cheese Spread Appetizer

Pack the cheese mixture into a small crock and decorate the top of the cheese with additional onion slices and a snip of dried tomato. Present it with a plastic bag of toasted bread rounds or include some purchased crackers or melba toast.

2 8-ounce packages cream cheese, softened

2 tablespoons milk

2 teaspoons Worcestershire sauce

¼ cup oil-packed dried tomatoes, drained and finely chopped

¼ cup chopped pitted ripe olives

3 tablespoons thinly sliced green onions with tops

Toasted Bread Rounds

For spread, beat cream cheese in a large mixing bowl with an electric mixer until smooth. Beat in the milk and Worcestershire sauce until creamy. Stir in the tomatoes, olives, and onion until combined. Store, tightly covered, in the refrigerator up to 5 days. Serve the spread with Toasted Bread Rounds. Makes 2½ cups spread.

TOASTED BREAD ROUNDS: Cut one 16-ounce loaf baguette-style French bread into about forty ¼-inch-thick slices. Place slices in a single layer on baking sheets. Bake in a 400° oven about 8 minutes or until crisp and light brown, turning once halfway through baking. Cool. Store in a tightly covered container at room temperature.

Nutrition facts per tablespoon with bread: 74 cal., 5 g total fat (3 g sat. fat), 13 mg chol., 111 mg sodium, 6 g carbo., 0 g fiber, 2 g pro. **Daily values:** 5% vit. A, 2% vit. C, 1% calcium, 2% iron

279

Cranberry Brioche

Gingerbread Scone Mix

Lemon Curd

blender until mixture resembles coarse crumbs. Store in an airtight container up to 6 weeks at room temperature or up to 6 months in the freezer.

For each gift, measure about 1¾ cups mixture into a container. Include a recipe for Gingerbread Scones with each gift. Makes 3 gifts.

GINGERBREAD SCONES: Place gingerbread mix in a medium bowl. Make a well in center of dry mixture. Combine 2 tablespoons milk, 1 tablespoon molasses, and 1 beaten egg; add to dry mixture. Stir just until moistened. Turn dough out onto lightly floured surface. Quickly knead dough by folding and pressing it gently for 10 to 12 strokes or until dough is nearly smooth. Pat or lightly roll dough into a 6-inch circle. Cut into 6 wedges. Place wedges 1 inch apart on an ungreased baking sheet. Brush with a little milk and sprinkle with coarse or granulated sugar. Bake in a 400° oven for 10 to 12 minutes or until bottoms are brown. Serve warm. Makes 6 scones.

Nutrition facts per scone (¹⁄₁₈ of recipe): 207 cal., 10 g total fat (3 g sat. fat), 36 mg chol., 213 mg sodium, 26 g carbo., 1 g fiber, 4 g pro. **Daily values:** 1% vit. A, 0% vit. C, 11% calcium, 11% iron

Gingerbread Scone Mix

Place the scone mix in a tightly covered container or a plastic bag and wrap it with colorful fabric. Tie the fabric with raffia and attach a new wooden spoon and a recipe card with directions for preparing the mix.

  3¾ cups all-purpose flour
  ½ cup packed brown sugar
  2 tablespoons baking powder
  2 teaspoons ground ginger
  1 teaspoon ground cinnamon
  ½ teaspoon salt
  ¼ teaspoon baking soda
  ¼ teaspoon ground cloves
  ¼ teaspoon ground nutmeg
  ¾ cup shortening

Combine flour, sugar, baking powder, ginger, cinnamon, salt, baking soda, cloves, and nutmeg in a large mixing bowl. Cut in shortening with a pastry

Lemon Curd

Accompany the Gingerbread Scone Mix with a jar of this lemon spread. It's similar in consistency and flavor to the lemon layer in a lemon meringue pie.

  1 cup sugar
  1½ teaspoons cornstarch
  ⅓ cup lemon juice
  ¼ cup butter, cut up
  3 beaten eggs
  4 teaspoons finely shredded lemon peel

Combine sugar, cornstarch, and lemon juice in a medium saucepan. Add butter. Cook and stir over medium

heat until thickened and bubbly. Cook and stir for 2 minutes more.

Stir about half of the mixture into beaten eggs. Return all to saucepan. Reduce heat; cook and stir 1 to 2 minutes more or until mixture begins to thicken. *Do not boil.* Strain to remove any egg particles. Gently stir lemon peel into hot mixture and pour into small jars. Cool. Cover and refrigerate up to 1 month. Makes 1¾ cups spread.

Nutrition facts per tablespoon: 51 cal., 2 g total fat (1 g sat. fat), 27 mg chol., 23 mg sodium, 8 g carbo., 0 g fiber, 1 g pro. **Daily values:** 2% vit. A, 3% vit. C, 0% calcium, 0% iron

Anise Candy Crystals

Fill a candy jar or an antique container with these colorful, licorice-flavored candy pieces.

  2 cups sugar
  ½ cup light-colored corn syrup
  ½ cup water
  ½ teaspoon oil of anise
     Several drops red food coloring

Line an 8×8×2-inch baking pan with foil, extending the foil up the sides of the pan. Lightly butter the bottom of the foil-lined pan; set aside.

Stir together sugar, corn syrup, and water in a medium saucepan. Cook and stir over medium-high heat until mixture boils, stirring to dissolve the sugar. Clip a candy thermometer to side of the pan. Reduce heat to medium; continue boiling at a moderate, steady rate, stirring occasionally, until thermometer registers 290°, the soft-crack stage (about 25 minutes). Remove pan from heat; remove thermometer.

When boiling stops, quickly stir in the oil of anise and red food coloring and pour into the prepared pan. Let stand 5 to 10 minutes or until a film forms over the surface of the candy. Using a broad spatula or pancake turner, begin marking candy by pressing a line across surface ¾ inch from edge of pan. Do not break film on surface. Repeat along other 3 sides of pan, intersecting lines at corners to form squares. (If lines do not remain in candy, it is not yet cool enough to mark.) Continue marking lines along all sides ¾ inch apart, until you reach the center. Repeat scoring. Cool completely.

Use foil to lift candy out of pan; remove foil from back and break candy into square pieces, tapping on back with a knife blade. Store in a jar. Makes about 100 pieces (18 ounces).

Nutrition facts per piece: 20 cal., 0 g total fat (0 g sat. fat), 0 mg chol., 1 mg sodium, 5 g carbo., 0 g fiber, 0 g pro. **Daily values:** 0% vit. A, 0% vit. C, 0% calcium, 0% iron

Nut Bread

Wrap the loaf in plastic wrap and place it in a ceramic container. Tie it up with wide organdy ribbon and a few small ornaments for a festive presentation.

 3 cups all-purpose flour
 1 cup sugar
 1 tablespoon baking powder
 ½ teaspoon salt
 ¼ teaspoon baking soda
 1 beaten egg
 1⅔ cups milk
 ¼ cup cooking oil
 ¾ cup chopped almonds, pecans, or walnuts

Grease bottom and ½ inch up sides of a 9×5×3-inch loaf pan; set aside.

Stir together flour, sugar, baking powder, salt, and soda. Make well in center; set aside. Combine egg, milk, and oil in a bowl. Add egg mixture all at once to flour mixture. Stir just until moistened (batter should be lumpy). Fold in nuts. Spoon into prepared pan.

Bake in a 350° oven for 1 to 1¼ hours or until a wooden toothpick inserted in center comes out clean. Cool in pan on a wire rack 10 minutes. Remove loaf from pan. Cool completely on a wire rack. Wrap and store overnight before slicing. Makes 1 loaf (18 servings).

Nutrition facts per serving: 187 cal., 7 g total fat (1 g sat. fat), 14 mg chol., 153 mg sodium, 28 g carbo., 1 g fiber, 4 g pro. **Daily values:** 1% vit. A, 0% vit. C, 7% calcium, 7% iron

281

Nut Bread

282

SHOPPING LIST
FOR MESH BOW:
6 feet of fiberglass
    screening (window
    screening), available at
    hardware stores
gold spray paint
floral wire or crafts wire

SHOPPING LIST
FOR TIN STAR:
6-inch square piece of
    28-gauge tin
tracing paper
6-inch square of
    lightweight cardboard
    for pattern
scrap of wood at least
    7 inches square
tin snips
roofing nails
16d (sixteen-penny) nail or
    small nail punch
cold chisels in $\frac{3}{16}$- and
    $\frac{3}{8}$-inch widths
rubber or wooden mallet
fine steel wool
nonglossy primer or
    paint for metal
lightweight floral wire

A beautifully wrapped gift is a treat to receive—and a treat to give. With just a little creativity, you can turn ordinary materials into extraordinary packaging.

wrap it up

For a homespun look, use brown wrapping paper and add a punched-tin star or a bow of fiberglass window screening. For a more celestial effect, use rubber stamps and embossing powder to transform plain paper bags into elegant containers. Adorn Hanukkah gifts with glittering Stars of David. If you have a large or odd-shaped gift, try the creative cover-up on *page 285*.

tin star

here's how...

1 Enlarge the half-star pattern on *page 285* by 200 percent and trace it (including the dots and lines) onto the tracing paper. Flip the paper to trace the other half, making a complete star.

2 Tape the tracing paper to the cardboard and press over all marks with a pencil to transfer the shape. Cut out the cardboard star and punch through the dots and along the interior lines. Trace around the template on the tin with an awl or pencil, and mark the dots and lines for the design.

Cut out the star with tin snips. Use caution; the edges will be sharp. You may want to wear heavy gloves. Also clip off the tip of each point to lessen the chance of cutting yourself.

Fasten the star to the wood scrap by tacking roofing nails along the edges in several spots. To make the design, pierce the star at each dot, using a 16d nail or a nail punch and hammer. Practice on a scrap of tin first. To cut the slots, pierce the tin at each line with the appropriate-size chisel.

5 If the star bends as you work on it, gently flatten it from the back with a mallet. Buff both sides with steel wool. Work carefully; the edges of the punched lines and holes are sharp.

6 Either leave the tin its natural color or paint it with a nonglossy primer or paint for metal. Thread wire through two holes, bringing both ends to the back, to attach the star to a package.

mesh bow

here's how...

1 Spray each side of the screening gold, letting the paint dry between coats. Cut the screening into strips 3 to 5 inches wide and about 6 feet long. The wider the strip, the bigger and showier the bow will be.

2 Wrap one strip around a package; cut off the excess. Loop and twist a strip to make a bow, securing the loops with wire. Trim the streamers as desired.

3 To make the center rosette, use a strip about 3 inches wide by 2 feet long. Gathering up one long edge with your fingers, roll the strip loosely, pinching together the gathered edge as you work. Let the top edge fan out slightly. When the rosette reaches the desired size, cut off the excess material and wrap the base of the rosette tightly with wire. Wire the rosette to the center of the bow and wire the bow to the package. If you wish, glue pine, dried leaves, and pinecones under the bow. To give the materials a verdigris look, mist them with patina-green and gold spray paints.

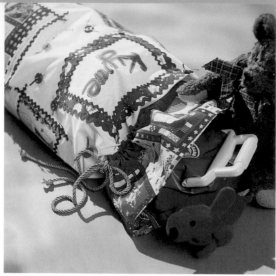

Hanukkah Surprises

Gifts sparkle with star-shape confetti.

Dress up packages with white wire-edge ribbon tied into fluffy bows, and attach Star-of-David confetti with dots of hot glue. (Check paper- and party-goods stores for the confetti.) Drop a handful of the stars into a clear cellophane bag with menorah candles and tie the bag closed with silver cording. To make the standing star, brush clear-drying glue on a blue plastic star and sprinkle it with silver glitter. Glue the star to a bow.

284

gift sack

(shown on *page 282*)

■ Spray the screening gold as for the mesh bow. Cut a strip wide enough for your gift to fit and twice as long. Fold the strip in half so the folded edge is the base of the bag.

■ Using yarn, floss, or ribbon and a large-eye needle, blanket-stitch the edges of the screening together. Blanket-stitch around the opening. Tie the bag closed with yarn.

Santa's Sack

Turn a king-size pillowcase into a personalized bag from Santa.

here's how...

1 Wash and dry all fabrics, trims, and the pillowcase. To make the band for the top of the sack, use the holiday-print fabric and cut a strip 14 inches wide and twice the width of the pillowcase opening plus 1 inch. To make the best use of the fabric's design, position the band so it shows one or more rows of the design. With right sides facing, stitch the short ends of the strip together with a ½-inch seam. Trim the seam allowances. Iron fusible web to the wrong side of the fabric, following the manufacturer's instructions and piecing as necessary.

2 Fold the band in half lengthwise, wrong sides facing, and finger press. Fuse the band to the top of the pillowcase, enclosing the pillowcase's decorative edge. On some pillowcases, the decorative edge is slightly shaped so the top is wider than the case. You will need to make small pleats at the bottom of the band to fit it to the pillowcase.

3 To make the drawstring casing, center the narrow grosgrain ribbon on the wide grosgrain ribbon and stitch it in place close to the edges of the narrow ribbon. Pin the casing to the pillowcase, overlapping the raw edges of the band. Turn under and overlap the raw ends of the casing, leaving the ends of the narrow ribbon open to receive the cord. Stitch the casing in place.

4 Paint or write the child's name on the pillowcase with a fabric marker or fabric paint. An easy way to do this is to use a computer to print the name, then place the pattern under the pillowcase as a guide. Heat-set the paint or ink if necessary, following the manufacturer's instructions. Outline the letters with the fine-point permanent marker.

5 Cut a frame for the name from the companion fabric, making the inside dimensions of the frame 1 inch larger on all sides than the name and 1¼ inches wide on all sides. Use fusible web to attach the frame to the fabric. Cut rickrack to fit the inside and outside dimensions of the name frame, and glue the rickrack in place with fabric glue.

6 Iron fusible web to the remaining decorative fabric and cut the fabric into blocks. Fuse the blocks to the pillowcase, placing them randomly. Cut lengths of rickrack 2½ inches longer than each side of the blocks, and glue the rickrack to the blocks, letting the ends hang free.

7 Using narrow satin ribbon and the large-eye needle, sew buttons to each corner of the name frame. Tie the ribbon ends over the center of each button and trim the ends to 1 inch. Sew the remaining buttons randomly to the pillowcase in the same way. Run the cord through the casing; knot the ends and dip them in fabric glue to keep them from fraying.

285

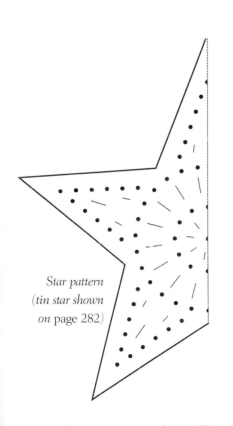

Star pattern (tin star shown on page 282)

Canvas Cover-Up

Transform an ordinary canvas drop cloth into a whimsical wrap for large or unwieldy gifts.

The lucky recipient can use the cloth as a holiday table covering!

here's how...

1 Draw a star (or enlarge the one *at left* and use as a guide) and trace it onto the sponge. Cut out the shape with the utility knife. To make the dot stamp, trace the top of the paint container on a scrap of sponge, and cut it out.

2 Spread the plastic drop cloth on your work surface, then lay the canvas drop cloth over it. Lightly mark the canvas to indicate where the zigzags will go. Pour a small amount of paint into a pie pan or disposable plate, and thin it with a few drops of water so the sponge can easily absorb it.

3 Begin stamping the stars in the center of the canvas and work out

toward the edges, placing the stars randomly. For each image, dip the star sponge into the paint, then press it onto the canvas.

4 Using the polyester brush, paint zigzag lines along the border. Stamp red dots along the edges of the canvas under every other zigzag.

5 After the paint has dried, use the green marker to draw swirls randomly among the stars. Also outline the red zigzags along the borders and write "Merry Christmas" as often as desired in the remaining spaces between the stars.

6 Drape or wrap the cloth over your gift and tie it with upholstery cord or wide ribbon.

Festive Package Trims

Make the gift wrap as special as the gift by topping packages with these creative bows and tags that are made quick as a wink.

here's how...

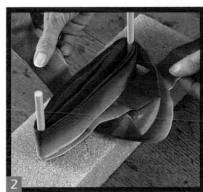

Push dowel pieces into floral oasis about 5 inches apart. Holding the ribbon end on top of the oasis, wrap dowels at least three times. For larger bows, wrap four to six times.

Cut the ribbon, leaving about an 8-inch tail. Slip tail of ribbon underneath loops, continuing to hold the starting end of the ribbon.

Secure the loops by tying the ribbon ends firmly into a knot in the center of the loops. Carefully slide the bow loops off the dowels.

Tie the bow atop intersecting ribbons that wrap around the package. Separate and fluff the loops. Fold ribbon ends in half and trim on the diagonal. If desired, glue or wire a trim to the center of the bow.

5 For tag, cut a small paper piece to fit on a section of ribbon as shown in the photograph, *opposite.* Glue the paper tag atop the ribbon. Insert the tag under the bow or punch a hole and add cording to tie it onto the package.

287

design tips...

■ For extra-special center trims, use coins or wrapped candies.
■ Make several bows to trim a tree or to tuck among greenery on a banister or mantel.

Recycle holiday greeting cards to make these petite gift boxes. They're perfect for holding jewelry or other small items— a rich piece of candy, a poem, or a personal message.

little *boxes*

For Christmas, you can hang these boxes on the tree as little surprises to hand out on Christmas morning. For Hanukkah or Kwanzaa, use heavy paper or greeting cards to make the boxes and put one at each place setting for the family meal.

Tube Pillow Packet

here's how...

1 Cut away the back of the card, except for a 1-inch-wide flap next to the fold. This is the gluing flap.

Working on the wrong side of the card, mark the center of the front panel at the top and bottom edges. Fold the sides to the center marks (the glue flap should be folded).

3 Open out the glue flap. Glue the flap to the inside of the card, creating a flat tube.

4 Mark down ⅝ inch from the center top and up ⅝ inch from the center bottom of the tube. Note: This distance can vary, depending on the size of the card.

On the right side of the tube, draw, then lightly score, an arc at the top and bottom. To draw the arc, use a round cup, glass, or bottle with a

diameter about 1 inch bigger than the width of the flat, folded card. Use the crafts knife or empty ballpoint pen to make the scoring line. Turn the tube over and repeat on the opposite side.

Insert a small gift, then push the scored arcs in to close the top and bottom of the packet.

Folded Purse Box

here's how...

1 On the wrong side of the card front, draw a square, centering the card's design. At the center of one side, draw a ¾x1⅝-inch rectangle for the tab. Cut out the shape.

2 Make a folding gauge as follows: cut a strip of paper the length of one side of the square and fold it into thirds. Also mark the center of the strip by folding it in half.

3 Using the gauge and a pencil and working on the wrong side of the card, mark thirds on all four sides of the square. Mark the center on two opposite sides (not the tab side—see *Diagram 1*).

4 With the empty ballpoint pen, score the thirds lines, creating a tic-tac-toe grid (*Diagram 1*). Also, score the grid with diagonal lines. On the side opposite the tab, cut a

⅞-inch slit about ⅜ inch from the edge.

5 Fold the card along the horizontal and vertical lines, then along the diagonal lines (*Diagram 2*). Fold all edges up, interlocking the diagonal folds.

6 To close the box, gently bend the tab and insert it into the slit (*Diagram 3*).

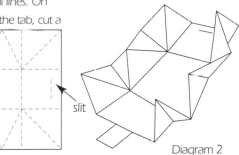

slit

Diagram 1

Diagram 2

Diagram 3

▶ Using a hot-glue gun, glue dried bay leaves from the grocery store in a wreath shape to the top of a package. Add two star anise for the bow. Dress up a plain brown box with cinnamon sticks and a large or medium-size jingle bell, tied in place with wire-edge organdy ribbon. Make a gift tag from art paper; cut a small slit in the top of the tag and tie short cinnamon sticks to the top of the tag with gold ribbon or cord.

In a Twinkling:
Packages

◀ Instead of a bow, top a package with inexpensive glass ball ornaments. Use three different sizes and attach them to the package with a hot-glue gun. Add curls of wired star garland for a festive finish.

▲ Put odds and ends to creative use to give packages an elegant look. Use scraps of ribbon and cording to make a bow and glue it to the box. Spray silk ivy leaves silver and glue them over the bow.

▲ Your packages will jingle all the way when you decorate them with bells in assorted sizes. Use a hot-glue gun and glue sticks to attach the jingle bells in a free-form design, and add a knotted ribbon for an accent.

▲ Instead of tying packages with ribbon, use shoelaces! Braid three pairs of neon-colored shoelaces together and wrap the braid around the box. Secure it with a rubber band, then unbraid the ends up to the rubber band and loop the tails through it to make a bow. Or tie metallic shoelaces around a box. Cut a free-form star from heavy paper and punch two holes in the center. Pull the shoelaces through the holes and tie them in a knot.

►
Purchased white boxes become dazzling gift containers when you add simple designs in gold rick-rack. Use small dabs of crafts glue to hold the rickrack in place. Line with gold tissue paper before filling it up.

Make the gift wrap a gift in itself. Match the fabric to the package contents to give a tantalizing hint of what's inside.

two gifts in one

Cotton holiday tea towels are perfect for presenting baked goods such as bread or pans of cookies or gingerbread. And what else should a well-dressed gift of jewelry or clothing wear but a coordinating silk scarf?

Tea Towel Wraps

here's how...

Bread Wrap

1 Place the towel right side down on a flat surface.

2 Fold in the towel's long edges until the width equals the length of the loaf plus about ½ inch. Position the loaf crosswise in the center of the towel.

3 Bring the short, unfolded edges together over the top of the bread. Holding the two edges together as one, fold them down a couple of times to make a snug wrapping around the bread.

4 Wrap the ribbon around the center of the loaf and tie it into a bow. Trim with a sprig of fresh Christmas greenery and artificial berries.

Pan Wrap

1 Place the towel right side down on a flat surface.

2 Cover the pan with plastic wrap, if necessary, to preserve the freshness of your baked goods. Center the pan on one half of the towel. Bring the other half of the towel over the top of the pan so the short end extends beyond the pan's edge by about 1 inch. Adjust the position of the pan, if necessary, to center the holiday motif on the top. Open out the towel.

3 Fold the bottom short end of the towel over the pan of cookies.

4 Fold the long sides of the towel over the sides of the pan, then fold the top of the towel over the pan.

5 Pinch the towel at each corner around the top of the pan, temporarily holding it in place with twist ties.

6 Cut the ribbon into quarters. Tie a ribbon around each corner, and remove the twist ties.

Scarf Wrap

here's how...

1 Place the scarf right side down on a flat surface.

2 Place the gift box in the center with its corners pointing toward the scarf's sides.

3 Gather the corners of the scarf together at the center top of the box and temporarily secure with a twist tie. Tie the

7¼x7¼x¾-inch gift box, wrapped in silver paper
square red silk scarf (about 15x15 inches)
twist tie
⅓ yard of ⅛-inch-wide red double-face satin ribbon
four polished Chinese coins *(see the note below)

ribbon around the gathers, and remove the twist tie.

4 Slip one Chinese coin onto each corner of the scarf and knot the scarf to hold the coin in place.

***Note:** Check bead stores, coin dealers, or stamp and coin shops for Chinese coins; they're also available at some import shops. For a similar effect, use copper or gold washers from a hardware store, or use large pony beads from a crafts store.

293

Silk Bow

here's how...

1 To give the tissue paper texture, crumple it and then smooth it out before wrapping it around the gift box (save the

excess tissue paper for stuffing the loops of the bow later).

2 Wrap the scarf around the length of the gift box and temporarily hold it in place at the top with the rubber band. Set the box aside.

3 Knot the ends of the gold elastic cord. Fold the cord in half, creating a doubled strand. Wrap the doubled strand around the rubber band, slipping the knotted ends through the loop of the cord. Pull tight.

4 Thread the Chinese coin over both knotted ends of the cord and push it up to the rubber band. Knot the cord next to the coin to hold it in place. Remove the rubber band.

5 Tie the scarf into a bow. To give the loops more body, lightly stuff them with scraps of the gold tissue paper.

4x4x12-inch gift box
gold tissue paper
long silk scarf (about 13x53 inches)
rubber band
15 inches of narrow gold elastic cord
one polished Chinese coin *(see the note above)

Turn family photos into gift wrap for small packages. Arrange the color snapshots on a piece of 11×17-inch white paper and tack them in place with loops of adhesive tape. Copy the collage on a color copier as many times as desired for gift wrap. (Remember to choose the 11×17-inch paper tray when you begin copying.)

In a Twinkling:
Gift Wraps

▲ Wrapped packages that have to be shipped don't have to be boring just because they shouldn't have bows. Use a decorative paper from an art supply store to wrap the box. Then wrap two lengths of ribbon around the box, leaving enough room for a second wider ribbon to be centered between them. Glue the ribbons to the box, then layer a third ribbon over these.

◄ Here's a gift that comes complete with treats. Wrap the box with bright red paper, then glue layers of ribbon in graduated sizes around the center of the box. Use thick white crafts glue or hot glue to attach wrapped peppermint candies to the box top. (If you use shiny paper, glue the candies with crafts glue rather than hot glue.)

◀ Present a small package in a botanical print. Make a color copy of a print (be sure to use noncopyrighted images), and wrap the box. For larger boxes, enlarge the image on the copier as needed.

▲ Use a hot-glue gun to attach vintage buttons (or other buttons collected from flea markets and garage sales) to the top of a package in a tree shape. Ivory-color vintage buttons on natural or brown wrapping paper make a stylish yet romantic combination; for a more colorful effect, combine jeweled buttons on colored paper. To remove the buttons from the paper, place the discarded gift wrap in a plastic freezer bag in the freezer; the buttons will pop off.

▲ Wrap a square box with parchment paper, then use 1½-inch-wide velvet ribbon to tie a 6-inch-diameter vine wreath to the top. Glue one end of a piece of ribbon around the wreath, pull the ribbon taut around the box, and glue the remaining end around the wreath. Repeat for the second ribbon. Glue velvet millinery leaves to the wreath, if desired.

Start a new tradition this year and set aside an afternoon for family creativity. A few hours spent crafting can be lots of fun—and kids will take pride in being able to say "I made it myself" when they present gifts to neighbors, teachers, or friends. Cooking can form the centerpiece of a holiday party, too. Decorating gingerbread house fronts like those on pages 160–163 makes a good holiday party project for pre-teens or teens. The holidays are also an excellent time to teach "an attitude of gratitude." To underscore the message that receiving a gift calls for a response, help kids make their own note cards. It's a great way to turn writing thank-you notes into an afternoon of fun.

KIDS'

STUFF

Keep little hands busy before the holidays by making ornaments, cards, and treats from the kitchen. Crafts give kids of all ages an opportunity to share the spirit of the season.

crafts *for* kids

Ice Cream Ornaments

Glue glass balls into real sugar cones to make these Christmas confections for the tree.

here's how...

1 For each ornament, spray the cone with two or more coats of clear spray varnish and let it dry. Glue the ornament into the cone so the hanger is centered on the top.

2 String jute or twine between two chairs to hang the ornaments for painting, and protect the floor with newspapers. Thin the paint with water, if necessary, so it's the consistency of half-and-half cream. Starting at the hanger, spoon paint over the ornament, allowing it to drip like chocolate sauce. Before the paint dries, drop sprinkles over the ornament. The dried paint will hold the sprinkles in place.

SHOPPING LIST

ice cream cones (sugar or waffle or waffle bowls)
clear spray varnish
plain glass ball ornaments to fit cones
thick white crafts glue
acrylic paint (brown and white)
plastic spoons
sprinkles (from the cake decorating section of a grocery store)

For the Birds

Remember our feathered and furry friends with these winter treats.

here's how...

sunflower-seed hearts

Use a heart-shape cookie cutter to cut shapes from stale bread. Make a hole in the top and thread raffia or twine through it to make a hanger. Cover the shape with peanut butter, then push sunflower seeds and other birdseed into the peanut butter.

orange baskets

Scoop out the pulp from an orange half. Pierce a hole near the rim on each side and thread a piece of raffia through each hole. Knot each piece, then tie them together to make a hanger. Fill the basket with dried cranberries and raisins.

fruits and veggies

Cut thin slices of apples and oranges and hang them outdoors with raffia loops. Buy cobs of dried corn from a birdfood-supply shop, slice them into sections, and hang each section from a tree branch with a raffia loop.

SHOPPING LIST

- heart-shape cookie cutter
- stale bread
- peanut butter
- sunflower seeds or mixed birdseed
- twine or raffia
- oranges, raisins, dried cranberries, and apples
- dried corn cobs

Handmade-Paper Star Garland

This elegant-looking garland is easier to make than you might think.

here's how...

Start with an ordinary papermaking kit, available at crafts stores, to make these paper stars. Use an old blender to make the pulp. Add gold glitter to the pulp, then press it into a sheet following the kit manufacturer's instructions, and let it dry.

Use a cookie cutter to trace stars on the paper and cut them out. String gold beads onto sewing thread or heavy carpet thread, adding a star every few inches. To attach each star, take a stitch in one point, knot the thread, and cut it. Make a stitch in the opposite point and continue adding beads.

Marbleized-Paper Ornaments

Liquid starch and acrylic paints make this ancient
craft accessible to kids—and adults.

here's how...

1 Use the plastic spoon to mix
2 tablespoons of paint with 2 tablespoons
of distilled water in a paper cup. Add
more paint or water as necessary to make
a creamy mixture.

2 Pour enough starch into the baking
pan to measure 1 to 1½ inches deep.
Skim the surface with a paper towel to
remove any air bubbles.

Dribble several
drops of the paint
mixture onto the
starch. If the paint
sinks below the
starch surface, add
a little more
distilled water to
the paint and
dribble a few
more drops onto
the starch. Use a
comb or feather to
swirl the paint on
the surface.

Lay a sheet of construction
paper on top of the paint,
letting the middle of the
page touch first. After about
15 seconds, lift the paper
from the paint. Lay it, paint
side up, on paper towels.

5 Lay a paper towel on
top of the paper. With the
heel of your hand, press
down on the paper towel to
remove excess
paint. Pull off the
paper towel and
repeat with another
paper towel. Lay
aside the marbled
paper, paint side
up, and let it dry.
Repeat this
procedure to marbleize a
second sheet of paper.

6 To make the ornaments,
draw a star, tree, or bell shape
onto tracing paper; cut it out.
Rub the glue stick over the
unpainted side of one sheet
of marbled paper; press it to
the unpainted side of the
remaining sheet.

7 Trace the
pattern twice onto the marbled paper
and cut out the shapes. Starting from the
bottom of one cutout, cut a slit two-
thirds of the way up the shape. Pierce a
small hole at the top of the shape;
thread a ribbon hanger through the
hole, and knot the ends.

8 Starting at the top of the second
cutout, cut a slit one-third of the way
down. Hold the shapes perpendicular
to each other, and slip the one with
the hanger over the top of the
second shape.

301

Catnip Toys

here's how...

1 Turn the bootie heel-side-up. Just above the toe seamline, pinch about ¼ to ⅜ inch to form a nose. Wrap embroidery floss around the base of this pinched area 8 times, then tie it off to form a nose. This also makes the toe seamline curve upward to form a smile. In the same way, make 2 ears in front of the bootie heel.

2 Lightly stuff the bootie with fiberfill, leaving room in the center of the bootie for a small amount of catnip. Add the catnip, then finish stuffing the bootie.

3 Cut the yarn into three 1-yard lengths. Fold the yarn in half and tie the top of the bootie closed. Using overhand knots, tie the 6 strands of yarn together about every inch. Trim the yarn tails after the final knot.

4 Using the fabric marker, make eyes and outline the smile.

5 For the whiskers, thread 12 inches of embroidery floss onto a blunt-tip needle. Stitch through the snout area to

the other side, then back to the first side, taking a very small stitch. The needle should exit the snout just a few threads away from where it entered. Pull the floss tightly and knot it, drawing in the snout to form a narrower nose. Repeat with a second color of floss. Make whiskers on the other side of the face in the same manner. Trim the whiskers as desired.

Crafts Stick Ornaments

💫 Set aside an afternoon to make these ornaments with your children or grandchildren. They'll make wonderful teachers' gifts or package toppers.

basic directions:

here's how...

An adult should do all cutting, using scissors or pruning shears to cut the crafts sticks. Apply paint to the back and side edges as well as to the front of each stick. For the hanging loop, glue the ends of an 8-inch-long piece of jute or ribbon to the back of the ornament at the top.

nutcracker

1 Use one jumbo and two narrow crafts sticks and a star sticker. Cut one narrow stick in half for the arms. Cut a 1-inch piece from each end of the second narrow stick for the boots.

2 Measure from the top of the jumbo stick and make tiny marks at 1 inch, 2 inches, and 3¾ inches. Paint the sticks as follows: apply flesh-tone paint between the 1-inch and 2-inch marks and to the rounded ends of the arm sticks; apply red paint from the 2-inch mark to the 3¾-inch mark. Paint the remaining sections of the arm sticks red. Paint the remaining areas of the jumbo stick blue. Paint the boots black.

3 Paint the face and uniform details as shown, using yellow, white, and black opaque paint markers. Adhere a star sticker to the hat.

4 Glue the arms to the body, allowing them to extend beyond the body about ¼ inch. Glue the boots to the bottom of the body, allowing the ends to extend slightly beyond the bottom of the body stick.

reindeer

1 Use one jumbo crafts stick. You'll also need a small piece of brown crafts foam, ⁵⁄₁₆-inch beady eyes, black dimensional paint, one red mini pompom, a small jingle bell, and narrow red ribbon.

2 Cut the jumbo stick in half to about 3 inches long. Paint the stick brown.

3 Transfer the antler pattern at *bottom right* to the crafts foam and cut two. Glue the antlers to the back of the head.

4 Glue the beady eyes about 1 inch from the top. Use black dimensional paint to draw the nose and mouth line, then glue the red pompom as shown. Glue the hanger to the back of the head. Tie the small jingle bell to the hanger with ribbon.

penguin

1 Use one jumbo and one narrow crafts stick; you'll also need orange crafts foam, ³⁄₁₆-inch beady eyes, narrow ribbon, and felt.

2 Paint the jumbo stick white and let it dry. Cut 1½ inches from each end of the narrow stick for the wings (discard the rest). Paint the wings black. Also paint a

narrow line of black along the edges of the white jumbo stick.

3 Transfer the beak and feet patterns below to orange crafts foam and cut them out. Glue the beady eyes, beak, and feet to the body. Glue the wings to the back of the stick, about 2 inches from the top of the head.

4 To make the hat, cut a 1×4-inch strip of felt. Fold it in half and tie a narrow ribbon ½ inch from the fold to gather the top of the hat. Clip the fold, then cut the felt to fringe it. Glue the penguin head inside the open ends of the hat. Cut a long, narrow strip of matching felt for the scarf. Fringe the ends and glue it in place.

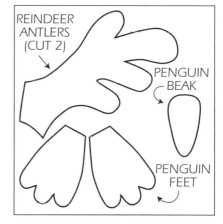

REINDEER ANTLERS (CUT 2)

PENGUIN BEAK

PENGUIN FEET

303

Family Game

 Playing board games is a great way to nurture togetherness, and this game should keep everyone talking. Use your own family's history to make up the questions and have every family member help. When everyone gathers for the holidays, bring out the game and enjoy an afternoon of laughter, sharing memories, and passing along family stories to the next generation.

here's how...

1 With a pencil, draw a heart shape on the drawing paper, nearly filling the paper. Erase the line in the upper left hand section to make the starting point of the game. Lightly draw a pair of spiral lines from the starting point to the center, creating a path that's at least 1½ inches wide. At the center, mark the end of the path with a small heart.

2 Divide the path into spaces no smaller than 1 inch. Draw over all pencil lines with the broad-tip marker. With the fine-tip marker, write on random spaces a variety of game actions such as "Lose 1 turn" or "Jump ahead 3 spaces." Other ideas for game actions include: Blow a kiss to each player, hug each player, give the player on your right a high-five, trade places with another player, dance a jig, take an extra turn, or sing a song.

3 Print "Draw 1 card" on eight or more spaces along the path.

4 Print your family's name at the center of the heart shape.

5 With the crayons or colored pencils, color the center heart red; color all "Draw 1 card" spaces turquoise; color all spaces with game actions orange. Randomly color the remaining spaces with four to six other colors of your choice. Each color will represent a topic for the game. You may want to leave two or three colors as free spots without a topic. For durability, use rubber cement to attach the paper to a piece of foam-core board, then cover it with clear self-adhesive shelf liner.

6 Make up four to six topics and assign each one a color (see the Topics Key for ideas). Write this key on the game board or on a separate piece of paper.

7 For the game cards, draw a heart on the back of each 3x5 note card. Before you begin to play, give each player several note cards and ask him or her to write down something about a family member on each card but not to write that person's name. (For example, "This person was in World War II," "This person won a prize at a horse show," "This person broke a leg," "This person plays the violin.") Stack the cards facedown near the game board.

To play, each person chooses a game piece and places it at the starting point. Players take turns flipping the coin. Heads means move the game piece ahead one space; tails means move ahead two spaces. The youngest person goes first. When you land on a colored space, do what the Topics Key tells you. When you land on a turquoise space, draw the top card, read it out loud, and try to guess whom it describes. If you guess correctly, you stay where you are; if you guess incorrectly, you lose your next turn. The first person to reach the heart of the family wins.

SHOPPING LIST

large sheet of white drawing paper or construction paper
black permanent markers, broad-tip and fine-tip
crayons or colored pencils
3x5-inch note cards
old buttons or other small objects for game pieces
one coin
optional: foam-core board, rubber cement, clear self-adhesive shelf liner

topics key

■ Yellow: player must
tell about something
that makes him happy
■ Pink: player must tell
about something for
which she is thankful
■ Green: player must
tell something funny
■ Purple: player must
share a long-ago
memory
■ Orange: player
must do whatever the
space indicates
■ Turquoise: player
must draw a card

305

A Gift of Charity

The Hebrew word for charity is *tzedakah*, and the tzedakah box is one that Jewish children pass around in class or keep at home to add contributions throughout the year. When the box is full, the children usually help choose the charity to which the money goes. These boxes are easy for children to make and are appropriate for exchanging with friends as Hanukkah gifts.

here's how...

1 Carefully open out the carton top and wash and dry it thoroughly.

2 Cut construction paper to fit around the carton, allowing for a slight overlap at the beginning and end. Wrap the paper around the carton and mark the corners, then remove the paper and fold it along these lines.

3 Using markers or crayons, decorate the paper to resemble a temple, home, or other building. Tape and glue the paper around the carton. Cut a slit in one side for inserting coins.

4 Fold the carton top closed and punch two holes through the top flange. Run ribbon through the holes and tie the carton closed. Add stickers or other decorations.

Autographed Overnight Bag

Start with a plain pillowcase to make a carryall for slumber parties.

Fabric paints take the place of a buttonhole attachment to edge the buttonholes on this bag. Give a laundry marker or fabric marker with the bag, so the recipient can collect her friends' autographs at each party.

here's how...

1 Place the pillowcase on a flat surface. Mark the center of the hemmed edge. Make another mark 2 inches on each side of the center. Position the plastic lid between the marks and trace around the lower half. Cut along the line through all layers of fabric. This will be the opening for the handle.

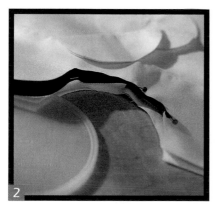

2

Separate the curved cut edges. Bind each edge with double-fold bias tape. Use a running stitch through all layers close to the outer edges of the binding.

3 Sew a button at the center of one side near the stitching on the hem. Sew an additional button 1½ inches in from each side of the pillowcase.

4 Fold the bottom of the pillowcase toward the hem with the side edges even. The pillowcase bottom should extend at least ½ inch beyond the top of the buttons. With chalk, mark the center top of each button on the pillowcase

SHOPPING LIST

plain pillowcase in a pastel color
plastic 4-inch margarine lid
scrap of cardboard
From a fabric store:
    thread to match pillowcase
    double-fold bias tape
    3 large buttons
    dressmaker's chalk
From a crafts store:
    dimensional paints
    acrylic crafts paint in the desired color
    clear acrylic spray, laundry markers, or colored fabric markers (optional)
From a hardware store or crafts store:
    ¼ inch diameter wooden dowel cut into two 16-inch pieces (lumber-supply companies will make the cuts for you)

bottom. Draw a vertical line where the buttonhole will be. Make the line at least ¼ inch longer than the button's diameter.

5

Cut the buttonhole openings with a sharp scissors through both layers of fabric. Slip buttons through the holes to check the fit. Cut three strips of cardboard to fit through the buttonholes. Insert a strip through each buttonhole and tip it sideways. Paint along the cut edge of each buttonhole with dimensional paint. Let dry, then paint the remaining cut

edges. Repeat on the opposite side of the pillowcase and use enough paint to make the fabric layers adhere to each other.

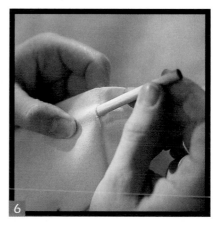

6

Paint the dowels. Let dry. To insert them in the pillowcase, make a small slit at one side near the top edge. Slide the dowels through the slit and into the hems on each side of the opening.

7 To use, put pajamas and other overnight essentials into the open bag. Fold it in half and button it up to carry it. To launder, hand-wash and air-dry.

307

Get your kids involved in crafting for the holidays with cards and gifts for teachers, friends, or siblings.

cards *for kids*

It's never too early for children to learn good manners, and writing thank-you notes after the holidays is a good place to start. Turn the task into a craft with rubber stamps, paper punches, and blank card stock.

Mittens Card

here's how...

1 Stamp two mittens in black ink on the red card stock or heavy paper. Cut them out.

2 Position the right mitten on the card to determine where to glue one end of the yarn. Remove the mitten and glue the yarn in place. Glue the mitten over the end of the yarn.

Glue two foam dots to the wrong side of the left mitten, and glue the foam dots to the card.

4 Stamp "Thanks" in red ink on the card.

Snowflake Card

here's how...

Punch snowflakes out of the blue paper and glue them randomly to the front of the card.

2 Using the blue stamp pad, stamp the word "Thanks" on the card and stamp small snowflakes randomly around it.

3 Use the glue marker to apply a coat of glue to the punched blue snowflakes, then sprinkle glitter over them.

4 Punch one snowflake out of the front of the card.

310

Hanukkah Card

This card doubles as a gift—there's a dreidel game inside for kids to play with their friends.

here's how...

1 Cut the paper to 5½x9 inches and fold it in half to make a 4½x5½-inch card. Referring to the photo for help, stamp the front of the card with the Hanukkah and dreidel stamps. Let the ink dry about 10 minutes.

2 Use the fine-tip markers and a ruler to draw a double border around the front of the card.

3 On the inside of the card, copy the Hebrew symbols shown *at right*, drawing one symbol on each edge of the card as shown. Also draw a border around the "game board."

4 To make the spinner, stamp the dreidel image on a scrap of watercolor paper, and cut an arrow shape around it. To find the center of the game board, measure the width and divide it in half; do the same for the length. Cut a small hole in the center and attach the spinner with the paper fastener. Attach the fastener loosely enough to allow the spinner to move when you flick it with your fingers.

nun: wins nothing

gimmel: wins everything in the "pot"

hay: wins half the "pot"

shin: puts one into the "pot"

family traditions

B ecause Hanukkah is actually a relatively minor festival in Judaism, and Christmas is so central to Christianity, there really should be no comparison between the two; but because they occur so close together and because of the marketing hype surrounding Christmas, children can sometimes feel left out. To counter this in our home, we play Hanukkah music tapes in the car while running errands and we put up colorful streamers and stars around the house. We always try to make charity part of the Hanukkah experience, too—the children use their own money to buy toys, which we then donate to Toys for Tots.

— *Paula Rudofsky*
Mount Kisco, New York

Holiday Greetings

Send greetings from the group with this card. It's a good project for a class or youth group.

SHOPPING LIST

From a crafts store:
8×11-inch sheets of
    heavy green paper
    (such as charcoal
    paper)
rubber stamps
clear rubber stamp ink
Winter Wonderland
    opaque embossing
    powder
electric embossing tool
glue sticks
envelopes to fit card (about
    4¾×5¾ inches)
pencil, ruler, and scissors
adhesive tape
color photocopies
    of photos

Make as many photocopies of the collage of faces as you have children in your group and have each child decorate and assemble a card. Deliver the cards to nursing home residents or children in the hospital over the holidays, or send cards to speakers or visitors who have led field trips or enrichment classes for the group during the year.

here's how...

1 For each card, fold a sheet of paper into thirds across the 11-inch width. Trim the card height to 5½ inches.

2 Open out the card and draw a simple tree shape in the center of the middle section. Cut out the tree.

311

3 Turn the card over and use rubber stamps to add a greeting below the tree and a star to the top. To make embossed images, press the rubber stamp onto a rubber-stamp pad inked with clear ink. Press the stamp firmly on the paper, then sprinkle embossing powder over the image.

4 Shake off the excess powder. If you work with children under age 10, melt the powder for them, using an electric embossing tool. Older children can do this themselves, with supervision.

5 To make the collage of faces, first make color copies of the children's faces. Tape as many photos as will fit onto an 8½×11-inch piece of paper and make a copy, then cut out the faces and arrange them to fit inside the tree shape. Copy as many as you need for cards made from this collage.

6 Position the color copy behind the tree cutout and secure it with adhesive tape. With the back of the collage facing you, fold the left section of the card over to cover the back of the collage and glue it in place. Add a message on the right section (the inside of the card) from the class.

Cookie "Tostadas"

with about 1 tablespoon pudding mixture. Sprinkle tinted coconut (yellow to resemble cheese and green to resemble lettuce), chocolate pieces, and cherries on top to resemble "tostadas." Makes 14 to 16 cookies.

*Note: To make yellow- and green-tinted coconut, combine half of the coconut and a few drops of yellow food coloring in a small bowl. Mix until all coconut is colored. Repeat with remaining coconut and green food coloring.

Nutrition facts per cookie: 113 cal., 5 g total fat (2 g sat. fat), 3 mg chol., 85 mg sodium, 16 g carbo., 0 g fiber, 1 g pro. **Daily values:** 0% vit. A, 0% vit. C, 1% calcium, 2% iron

Cookie "Tostadas"

½ of an 18-ounce roll refrigerated sugar cookie dough
1 3.5-ounce container refrigerated chocolate pudding
¼ of an 8-ounce container frozen whipped dessert topping, thawed
¼ cup yellow- and green-tinted coconut*
 Miniature semisweet chocolate pieces and chopped red maraschino or candied red cherries

Wrap and freeze the half-roll of cookie dough for 30 minutes or until firm (refrigerate remaining half-roll for another use). Using a serrated knife, cut frozen dough into ¼-inch-thick slices. Place on ungreased cookie sheets.

Bake in a 350° oven for 8 to 10 minutes or until set around the edges. Cool on cookie sheet for 1 minute. Remove cookies and cool completely on a wire rack.

Just before serving, fold together the pudding and whipped topping in a small mixing bowl. Top each cookie

Christmas Tree Cookie Treats

Peanut-flavored cookies in the shape of Christmas trees are especially fun to decorate with assorted candies and colored frosting.

½ cup peanut butter
¼ cup shortening
¼ cup butter, softened
½ cup granulated sugar
½ cup packed brown sugar
½ teaspoon baking powder

½ teaspoon baking soda
1 egg
1 teaspoon vanilla
1⅓ cups all-purpose flour
 Flat wooden sticks
 Purchased frosting and small candy pieces (optional)

Grease tree-shape aluminum cookie treat pans. Set aside.

Beat peanut butter, shortening, and butter in a large mixing bowl with an electric mixer on medium to high speed for 30 seconds. Add granulated sugar, brown sugar, baking powder, and baking soda; beat until combined. Beat in egg and vanilla until combined. Beat in as much of the flour as you can with the mixer. Stir in any remaining flour with a wooden spoon. If necessary, cover and chill dough until easy to handle.

Pat 1 rounded tablespoon of dough into each tree shape in prepared pan. Place a flat wooden stick about 1 inch into each tree shape on top of dough. Pat 1 rounded tablespoon of dough on top of stick.

Bake in a 350° oven for 12 minutes or until edges are lightly browned. Let cool for 10 minutes in pan on a wire rack. Remove cookies from pan; cool completely on rack. Decorate with frosting and small colored candies, if desired. Makes 15 cookies.

Nutrition facts per cookie: 198 cal., 11 g total fat (4 g sat. fat), 22 mg chol., 132 mg sodium, 22 g carbo., 1 g fiber, 4 g pro. **Daily values:** 3% vit. A, 0% vit. C, 1% calcium, 5% iron

312

Christmas Tree Cookie Treats

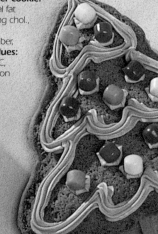

Polka-Dotted Cookies

kids *in the* kitchen

Polka-Dotted Cookies

Buttery sugar cookies studded with colorful candy-coated pieces are a playful version of the classic Mexican Wedding Cake or Sandies cookie recipes.

  1 cup butter, softened
  ⅓ cup granulated sugar
  1 tablespoon milk
  1 teaspoon vanilla
  2¼ cups all-purpose flour
  ½ cup miniature candy-coated
      semisweet or milk
      chocolate pieces
      Red- and/or green-colored
      sugar (optional)
  1 cup sifted chocolate-flavored
      powdered sugar

Beat butter in a large mixing bowl with an electric mixer on medium to high speed for 30 seconds. Add granulated sugar; beat until combined, scraping sides of bowl occasionally. Beat in milk and vanilla until combined. Beat in as much of the flour as you can with the mixer. Stir in any remaining flour and the miniature chocolate pieces with a wooden spoon.

Shape dough into 1-inch balls. Place the balls about 1 inch apart on an ungreased cookie sheet. (If desired, dip tops of cookies in red- or green-colored sugar before baking.)

Bake in a 325° oven for 18 to 20 minutes or until bottoms are lightly browned. Transfer cookies to a wire rack and let cool. For cookies not dipped in colored sugar, gently shake cooled cookies in a plastic bag with the chocolate powdered sugar. Makes 48 cookies.

Nutrition facts per cookie: 75 cal., 4 g total fat (2 g sat. fat), 10 mg chol., 39 mg sodium, 9 g carbo., 0 g fiber, 1 g pro. **Daily values:** 3% vit. A, 0% vit. C, 0% calcium, 1% iron

No-Measure Bars

These rich, chunky bar cookies are quick to make and simple enough for young children to help assemble.

  ½ stick butter or margarine
      (¼ cup)
 15 to 18 graham cracker squares
  1 12-ounce package semisweet
      chocolate pieces
  1 3½-ounce can flaked coconut
  1 2-ounce package chopped
      walnuts (½ cup)
  1 14-ounce can sweetened
      condensed milk

Line a 13×9×2-inch baking pan with foil, extending foil over edges of pan. Place butter in pan. With adult help, heat in a 350° oven about 1 minute or until butter melts.

Place graham cracker squares in butter in pan, breaking them, if necessary, to cover bottom of pan. Layer, in order, the chocolate pieces, coconut, and walnuts. Pour sweetened condensed milk evenly over all.

Bake in a 350° oven for 25 to 30 minutes. Cool. Lift foil and cookies from baking pan. Cut into squares or bars. Makes 24 to 36 cookies.

Nutrition facts per cookie: 194 cal., 11 g total fat (2 g sat. fat), 11 mg chol., 77 mg sodium, 24 g carbo., 0 g fiber, 3 g pro. **Daily values:** 3% vit. A, 0% vit. C, 4% calcium, 4% iron

No-Measure Bars

Candy and Caramel Corn

314

Visions of Sugar Plums

Kids will have fun helping make these treats for snacking and gift giving.

Candy and Caramel Corn

6 cups popped popcorn
   (about ¼ cup unpopped)
3 tablespoons butter
¼ cup light-colored corn syrup
1 tablespoon molasses
1 cup dry roasted peanuts
1 cup red and green candy-
   coated milk chocolate pieces

Place the popped popcorn in a 15×10×1-inch baking pan. Melt butter in a small saucepan. Remove from heat. **Stir corn syrup** and molasses into

melted butter. Slowly drizzle the corn syrup mixture over popcorn in baking pan. Using a wooden spoon, toss the popcorn and coat it as evenly as possible with corn syrup mixture.
Bake in a 325° oven for 15 minutes, stirring with a wooden spoon every 5 minutes. Pour caramel corn into a large, nonplastic serving bowl. Stir in peanuts. Let caramel corn cool.
Stir candy-coated pieces into cooled caramel corn. Store in a tightly covered container at room temperature. Makes 6 cups.

Nutrition facts per ½-cup serving: 202 cal., 12 g total fat (3 g sat. fat), 8 mg chol., 133 mg sodium, 21 g carbo., 1 g fiber, 4 g pro. **Daily values:** 2% vit. A, 0% vit. C, 1% calcium, 4% iron

Marbleized Mint Bark
✻

Kid's Job: Swirl melted chocolate into the peppermint-dotted candy coating mixture.

⅓ cup mint-flavored semisweet
   chocolate pieces or
   semisweet chocolate pieces
1 pound vanilla-flavored candy
   coating, cut up
¾ cup finely crushed candy cane
   or finely crushed striped
   round peppermint candies

Line a baking sheet with foil; set aside. Heat chocolate pieces in a small saucepan over low heat, stirring constantly, until melted and smooth. Remove pan from heat. Heat the candy coating in a 2-quart saucepan over low heat, stirring constantly, until melted and smooth. Remove pan from heat. Stir in crushed candies. Pour the melted coating mixture onto the prepared baking sheet.
Spread the coating mixture about ⅜ inch thick; drizzle with the melted chocolate. Gently zigzag a narrow metal spatula through the chocolate and peppermint layers to create a swirled effect in the candy.
Let candy stand at room temperature for several hours or until firm. (Or, chill about 30 minutes or until firm.) Use foil to lift candy from the baking sheet and carefully break candy into pieces. Store, tightly covered, for up to 2 weeks. Makes 1¼ pounds.

Nutrition facts per ounce: 159 cal., 8 g total fat (4 g sat. fat), 1 mg chol., 22 mg sodium, 22 g carbo., 0 g fiber, 2 g pro. **Daily values:** 0% vit. A, 0% vit. C, 4% calcium, 1% iron

Christmas Tree Brownies

Start with a brownie mix and create festive trees that kids can decorate and offer proudly as gifts for teachers and friends.

1 21½-ounce package fudge brownie mix
1 beaten egg
¼ cup cooking oil
¼ cup milk
¼ cup water
¾ cup miniature semisweet chocolate pieces or finely chopped nuts
   Decorator icing (optional)
   Miniature candy-coated semisweet chocolate pieces (optional)

Combine brownie mix, egg, oil, milk, and water in a large mixing bowl. Stir in chocolate pieces or nuts just until combined. Spread in a greased 13×9×2-inch baking pan. (If desired, to remove the baked brownies easily from the pan, line the pan with foil, extending the foil over the edges of the pan slightly; grease the foil. Spread batter in pan, bake, and cool. After cooling, lift the baked bars out of the pan and cut into shapes.)

Bake in a 350° oven for 30 minutes. Cool completely in pan on a wire rack.

Cut into triangle shapes. Decorate with decorator icing and miniature candy-coated semisweet chocolate pieces, if desired. Makes 30 trees.

Nutrition facts per brownie: 130 cal., 5 g total fat (1 g sat. fat), 7 mg chol., 80 mg sodium, 21 g carbo., 0 g fiber, 1 g pro. Daily values: **0% vit. A, 0% vit. C, 0% calcium,** *4% iron*

Rudolph's Peanut Butter Cookies

315

Rudolph's Peanut Butter Cookies

½ cup butter
½ cup peanut butter
½ cup sugar
½ teaspoon baking soda
½ teaspoon baking powder
¼ cup honey
1 egg
½ teaspoon vanilla
1¼ cups all-purpose flour
¾ cup chopped peanuts
80 small pretzels
40 small red gumdrops
   Semisweet chocolate pieces

Beat butter and peanut butter in a large mixing bowl with an electric mixer on medium to high speed for 30 seconds. Add sugar, baking soda, and baking powder and beat until combined. Beat in honey, egg, and vanilla until combined. Beat in as much of the flour as you can with the mixer. Stir in peanuts and any remaining flour with a wooden spoon. Divide dough in half. Wrap in plastic wrap. Chill dough for 1 hour or until easy to handle.

Work with half the dough at a time, keeping the rest refrigerated. Using 1 tablespoon dough for each cookie, shape into a triangle about 2½ inches long and 2 inches wide on an ungreased cookie sheet. Lightly press pretzel antlers into side at wide end of triangles. Add gumdrop noses and chocolate pieces for eyes.

Bake in a 375° oven for 7 to 8 minutes or until bottoms are lightly browned. Cool 2 minutes on cookie sheet. Carefully transfer to a wire rack and cool. Makes 40 cookies.

Nutrition facts per cookie: 103 cal., 5 g total fat (2 g sat. fat), 11 mg chol., 114 mg sodium, 12 g carbo., 1 g fiber, 2 g pro. **Daily values:** *2% vit. A, 0% vit. C, 0% calcium, 2% iron*

index

recipes

index *continued*

319

metric

Metric Cooking Hints

By making a few conversions, cooks in Australia, Canada, and the United Kingdom can use the recipes in this book with confidence. The charts on this page provide a guide for converting measurements from the U.S. customary system, which is used throughout this book, to the imperial and metric systems. There also is a conversion table for oven temperatures to accommodate the differences in oven calibrations.

PRODUCT DIFFERENCES: Most of the ingredients called for in the recipes in this book are available in English-speaking countries. However, some are known by different names. Here are some common U.S. American ingredients and their possible counterparts:
• Sugar is granulated or castor sugar.
• Powdered sugar is icing sugar.
• All-purpose flour is plain household flour or white flour. When self-rising flour is used in place of all-purpose flour in a recipe that calls for leavening, omit the leavening agent (baking soda or baking powder) and salt.
• Light-colored corn syrup is golden syrup.
• Cornstarch is cornflour.
• Baking soda is bicarbonate of soda.
• Vanilla is vanilla essence.
• Green, red, or yellow sweet peppers are capsicums.
• Golden raisins are sultanas.

VOLUME AND WEIGHT: U.S. Americans traditionally use cup measures for liquid and solid ingredients. The chart, below, shows the approximate imperial and metric equivalents. If you are accustomed to weighing solid ingredients, the following approximate equivalents will help.
• 1 cup butter, castor sugar, or rice = 8 ounces = about 230 grams
• 1 cup flour = 4 ounces = about 115 grams
• 1 cup icing sugar = 5 ounces = about 140 grams

Spoon measures are used for smaller amounts of ingredients. Although the size of the tablespoon varies slightly in different countries, for practical purposes and for recipes in this book, a straight substitution is all that's necessary.

Measurements made using cups or spoons always should be level unless stated otherwise.

320

EQUIVALENTS: U.S. = AUSTRALIA/U.K.

⅕ teaspoon = 1 ml
¼ teaspoon = 1.25 ml
½ teaspoon = 2.5 ml
1 teaspoon = 5 ml
1 tablespoon = 15 ml
1 fluid ounce = 30 ml
¼ cup = 60 ml
⅓ cup = 80 ml
½ cup = 120 ml
⅔ cup = 160 ml
¾ cup = 180 ml
1 cup = 240 ml
2 cups = 475 ml
1 quart = 1 liter
½ inch = 1.25 cm
1 inch = 2.5 cm

BAKING PAN SIZES

U.S.	Metric
8×1½-inch round baking pan	20×4-cm cake tin
9×1½-inch round baking pan	23×4-cm cake tin
11×7×1½-inch baking pan	28×18×4-cm baking tin
13×9×2-inch baking pan	32×23×5-cm baking tin
2-quart rectangular baking dish	28×18×4-cm baking tin
15×10×1-inch baking pan	38×25.5×2.5-cm baking tin (Swiss roll tin)
9-inch pie plate	22×4- or 23×4-cm pie plate
7- or 8-inch springform pan	18- or 20-cm springform or loose-bottom cake tin
9×5×3-inch loaf pan	23×13×8-cm or 2-pound narrow loaf tin or pâté tin
1½-quart casserole	1.5-liter casserole
2-quart casserole	2-liter casserole

OVEN TEMPERATURE EQUIVALENTS

Fahrenheit Setting	Celsius Setting*	Gas Setting
300°F	150°C	Gas mark 2 (very low)
325°F	170°C	Gas mark 3 (low)
350°F	180°C	Gas mark 4 (moderate)
375°F	190°C	Gas mark 5 (moderately hot)
400°F	200°C	Gas mark 6 (hot)
425°F	220°C	Gas mark 7 (hot)
450°F	230°C	Gas mark 8 (very hot)
475°F	240°C	Gas mark 9 (very hot)
Broil		Grill

*Electric and gas ovens may be calibrated using Celsius. However, for an electric oven, increase the Celsius setting 10 to 20 degrees when cooking above 160°C. For convection or forced-air ovens (gas or electric), lower the temperature setting 10°C when cooking at all heat levels.